A House Through Time

A House Through Time

DAVID OLUSOGA &
MELANIE BACKE-HANSEN

PICADOR

First published 2020 by Picador
an imprint of Pan Macmillan
The Smithson, 6 Briset Street, London EC1M 5NR
Associated companies throughout the world
www.panmacmillan.com

ISBN 978-1-5290-3724-1

1 3 5 7 9 8 6 4 2

A CIP catalogue record for this book is available from the British Library.

The photo credits on p. vi constitute an extension of this copyright page.

Typeset by Perfect Bound Ltd
Printed and bound by CPI Group (UK) Ltd, Croydon, CR0 4YY

MIX
Paper from
responsible sources
FSC
www.fsc.org   FSC® C116313

CONTENTS

List of Illustrations

PLATE SECTION

1 Charles Booth's poverty map: Lisson Grove, Paddington, 1902. *Antiqua Print Gallery/Alamy Stock Photo.*

2 Borough of Liverpool Mortality Map of Typhus, 1865. *Wellcome Collection. Attribution 4.0 International (CC BY 4.0).*

3 Bristol Bomb Plot Map, 1940–44. *Bristol Archives: 33779/8.*

4 Nicholas Barbon. *The History Collection/Alamy Stock Photo.*

5 Cruck House, Stowe, Lichfield. *Wikimedia Commons, CC BY-SA 3.0.*

6 Portrait of Inigo Jones, circa 1757–1758. *Public domain, via Wikimedia Commons.*

7 Sir John Kerle Haberfield, 1845 or 1846 (oil on canvas). *Parkman, Henry Spurrier (1814–64) / Bristol Museum and Art Gallery, UK / Lent by the Diocese of Bristol, circa 1973/Bridgeman Images.*

8 Covent Garden piazza and market in 1737, looking west towards St Paul's Church, by Balthazar Nebot. *Public domain, via Wikimedia Commons.*

9 Royal York Crescent, Clifton, Bristol. *Sue Martin/Shutterstock.com.*

10 Georgian home with bricked-up window in Ampthill, Bedfordshire. *Reproduced by permission of Fiona and Andrew Challacombe.*

TEXT ILLUSTRATIONS

INTRODUCTION

The Changing Idea of the Home

When we move into a new house we instantly set about stamping our tastes and our identities on to it. We redecorate, we arrange our furniture and our books, the collected volumes that we hope say something about us and our lives. This, and the frenzy of cleaning and scrubbing that precedes it, is about much more than domestic hygiene and personal taste. It is also an attempt to exorcize the lingering presence of past residents from our new private space.

In our frantic urge to turn an old house into a new home we attempt to conceal an unavoidable fact – that until recently it was the home of other people, and before them yet more people; a line of strangers stretching back decades and often centuries. But the truth is that no matter how many layers of paint we slap on or alterations we make, we can never succeed in wiping away the traces of the lives that have been lived there before us. If walls could talk it would be ordinary homes, not grand public buildings or the mansions of the rich, that would have all the best stories. This is because it is at home, behind closed doors and drawn curtains, that we live out our inner lives and family lives. Only there, in the domestic space, in living rooms, kitchens and bedrooms, either alone or in the company of our partners, parents and children, are we genuinely ourselves.

There is a simple but harsh truth about houses – they live longer than we do. Their ages are counted in centuries rather than decades and some have multiple lives. Houses are malleable in ways that we are not.

They can change function and status, they can be restored and brought back from the dead. Houses can adapt to changing times, they can survive economic downturns by slipping into states of almost suspended animation, living on long enough to be rediscovered and restored. Millions of British homes bear the marks and scars of such restorations and transformations: patches of new stonework or brickwork amidst the old and the ghostly outlines of doorways and windows that were long ago filled in. Our fleeting lives become single chapters in their longer stories. We might leave our marks, but they are overlain by those of later generations who will undo what we have done and make our spaces their own. For millions of people these stark realities are invigorating rather than disheartening. Rather than lament their ephemeral place in the stories of our homes they are enthralled by the possibilities these realities open up. They accept that our homes, the most intimate spaces in our lives, and the most expensive purchases we ever make, come to us second-hand, with a history of their own already written. Instead of being unsettled by these realities they are drawn to the twin prospects of becoming a small part of a bigger history and of uncovering the previous hidden chapters.

Our homes are acutely familiar and yet their histories are concealed from us. The urge to know more, to discover something of lives lived in the same space in earlier times, is seemingly innate. Most people who are given a map of their home town from a previous century instinctively look for their own house and street. If we are lucky enough to discover a picture of our home from the past most of us find the experience both profound and unsettling. The effect is more profound if the faces of past occupants stare back out at us. To see them standing in our doorways, tending our gardens, smiling out into the street from our front windows is mesmerizing and at the same time disconcerting. In recent years thousands of people have surrendered to the urge to know more about the past lives of their homes. House histories have become the new frontier of popular, participatory history. Many of those who set out to discover the secrets contained within their own four walls are those who have already uncovered their ancestors in the archives. Enthralled by those discoveries they set out to become the curators of another history within which they are the inheritors.

* * *

Many books about the history of the British home focus largely on one thing – architecture. The history of domestic architecture, along with the history of design and home organization, will be part of this book. How could it not be? However, the true significance of the material histories of our homes is that the lifeless things that estate agents love to call 'original features' enable us to commune with past residents, members of the generations for whom our homes were originally built. The features and decoration that they so valued offer us a glimpse into their lives and a better understanding of the societies they knew and the times they lived in. Innately we care about flesh and blood more than bricks and mortar, and material history only matters because it mattered to them.

What inspires twenty-first-century homeowners to head off to the archives and wade through trade directories, deeds, land-registry documents, electoral registers, wills, birth and death certificates, parish registers, maps, census returns, local newspapers and other sources is not the thought of discovering lost plans or architectural drawings, but the hope of linking those original features or later modifications to the people who lived in our personal spaces. People to whom we are connected by shared space and separated only by the single dimension of time.

At its most fundamental and visceral, history is about people. No new discovery, no original theory or ground-breaking revelation from the archives, really matters unless it can tell us something about the lives of human creatures, just like ourselves, who lived and died before our birth. This is the essence of what the historian G. M. Trevelyan called the 'poetry of history . . . the quasi-miraculous fact that once, on this earth, once on this familiar spot of ground, walked other men and women, as actual as we are today, thinking their own thoughts, swayed by their own passions, but now all gone, one generation vanishing into another, gone as utterly as we ourselves shall shortly be gone, like ghosts at cockcrow.' No 'spot of ground' is more familiar and important to us than our own homes, and therefore perhaps no connection with those vanished generations – other than the genealogical bonds of kinship and blood – is stronger than the connection to shared private space.

Those who set out to discover the histories of their homes report experiencing profound feelings of empathy for the people who came before them. But their encounters in the archives with people who long ago left this world are enormously amplified upon returning home with the thought that their hands gripped the same wooden banisters and pushed open the same doors, that they sat by the same fireplaces and looked out of the same windows – although to see radically different views. Such close encounters are thrilling and ghostly and also – it would seem – addictive.

To learn of the lives of the people who once walked through the rooms and corridors of our homes, to read their letters, to come across their signatures on yellowed documents, to hold in our hands copies of papers that shaped their fortunes; all of that is powerful enough. But to do so and then return home to the rooms from which those letters were written and in which those documents were first read is almost to commune with the dead. It is to have intimate encounters with people we could never have known and could never have met but with whom we have a powerful connection. Those connections are stronger still if we come across an old photograph that brings us face-to-face with them. What are the questions we would ask them? What did our home mean to them? Did it make them happy and what role did it play in the story of their lives? Who came and who departed in the years when our homes belonged to them? What were the key scenes played out in the rooms we now occupy?

Amateur house historians are often deeply moved to discover that many of the people they meet on the pages of documents suffered terrible tragedies within the shared domestic space. Perhaps we should not be surprised; after all, we don't have to go very far back into the past to arrive at an age in which births and deaths took place at home, rather than in hospitals. How many lives began in the rooms in which we now sleep? How many lives drew to an end within the walls of our homes? History, at its most visceral, is about these sorts of shiver-down-the-spine moments.

It is not just the oldest of homes that have such stories to tell: even relatively modern houses harbour such dark secrets. We need only journey backwards seventy years to encounter an age in which Britain's homes were more than dwelling places. During the Blitz a quarter of a million homes were destroyed. Another two million – an incredible figure – were damaged, and today thousands still bear the scars of bomb damage. Within what are today our personal spaces recent generations cowered inside Morrison shelters, steel survival spaces disguised as dining-room tables. In what are now our gardens they nightly lived a troglodyte existence, half-buried in Anderson shelters. Shrapnel marks, black scars from fires, and patches of repaired brickwork – all have stories to tell. This most tantalizing of questions, who lived in my house during the war, can be one of the easiest to answer as in 1939 the government carried out a national register of every home in England and Wales. It preceded the issuing of identity cards and ration books, but seven decades later this special, one-off census provides us with a snapshot of Britain at the start of the war. As such it carries names of most of the forty-six thousand people who were killed in the Blitz, and it lists most of the quarter of a million addresses that would not appear on the first post-war census. The comparatively easy online exercise of looking up who was living in our homes in 1939 can be the gateway drug that leads people to deeper research and a deeper sense of connection.

Just as the history of any house is more than its architectural history, the story of any single dwelling is something that spills out into the surrounding streets. The history of every home and the lives and the circumstances of the people who lived within its walls is intimately wrapped up in the history of the neighbourhood in which it stands. Then, as now, it is 'location, location, location' that matters. The story of Britain's towns and cities is one characterized by great shifts in the fortunes of each district and neighbourhood. Their rises and falls are critical to understanding the histories of the individual homes within them. This is where the little histories contained within our homes intersect with bigger histories, both national and international.

The many stories uncovered from within the walls of the three houses explored in the three series of *A House Through Time*, 62 Falkner Street in Liverpool, 5 Ravensworth Terrace in Newcastle-upon-Tyne, and 10 Guinea Street in Bristol, reveal how the big themes of the past can be reduced to granular detail by focusing on a single address. The ups and downs of the economic cycle, the coming of the railways, the arrival of new industries and the decline of old ones, slavery and its abolition, endemic and epidemic disease, the two world wars, the loss of empire, and feminism all influenced the lives of the residents who lived in those three homes over the decades. To an extent those forces determined who those residents were and from where in society they were drawn.

The history of a house can be shaped by what happens elsewhere within its city. The fortunes of each of our houses in *A House Through Time* were undermined by the emergence of fashionable new suburbs whose creation condemned the once desirable inner-city districts in which all three of our houses stand to precipitous decline. Today they find themselves in districts that are once again regarded as desirable. They are the beneficiaries of waves of regeneration and, more latterly and controversially, gentrification. Yet for decades each of those streets and the other streets surrounding them sank down the social spectrum and became urban twilight zones. Falkner Street sank the furthest and by the 1950s was regarded as a slum. Each of our three houses – all of them large, designed for wealthy families – was at various points in its story subdivided, turned into a lodging house or tenement.

What was true for those three homes was also the case for many hundreds of thousands of others. The pattern of decline, subdivision and eventual decay was so common that foreign visitors to Victorian and Edwardian Britain noted with surprise that the poor lived, packed sardine-like, in elegant homes originally designed for the rich. And it didn't take much for a once desirable residence in a formerly fashionable area to become a cheap lodging house. A new railway line cutting across a Victorian city, for example, could condemn the streets on one side to decay and decline. Literally on the wrong side of the tracks, such areas cascaded ever downwards, and this was just one of the mechanisms by which houses built for the rich became the homes of the poor. In the case of 10 Guinea Street, the rise of Bristol's glamorous district of Clifton was key to its decline, as the rich who might have once lived in its wood-panelled rooms preferred the Georgian elegance and panoramic views from the new homes and apartments built on the cliffs. Many of Britain's grand Georgian town houses, more modest terraces and beautiful Victorian villas have humbler chapters in their pasts. For the house historian, this means the range of occupations, life experiences and social status of past residents is often remarkably broad. A home built for the wealthy and perhaps today once again valuable and highly desirable may, in earlier ages, have been the resting places of the semi-destitute and the desperate, home to those on the fringes of society who sought out single rooms or shared rooms in what were then decaying houses in downbeat districts.

**

This book is the work of two authors, David Olusoga and Melanie Backe-Hansen. Melanie is a highly respected house historian who has worked as a consultant on *A House Through Time*. Her previous books have uncovered the hidden pasts of individual houses and set their stories within the wider historical context. Drawing on her experience, eye for the practical details, and extensive knowledge of the archives, this book aims to offer tips and advice to budding house historians and to provide a modest work of social history. In her chapters, and in her notes on resources, Melanie will help readers learn how to read the clues contained in the physical fabric of their homes and direct them towards the documents and resources they will need in order to uncover the unique stories of their homes (chapters one, two, eight and nine). Both Melanie's and my own chapters are peppered with stories of homes and their past residents that have emerged from previous explorations as well as the three houses featured in *A House Through Time*. We have both benefited from the knowledge and advice of social historian Gavin Weightman, whose help has been invaluable as we completed this book.

Together our chapters plot developments in the history of the British home and explore the changing social idea of the home – something which has never remained static or settled. As the history of every urban home is shaped by the history of the city in which it was built, there will also be chapters on the development of the British city. These passages reveal how the urbanization of the country changed how homes were built and lived in, and their patterns of ownership. Elsewhere we explore the ever-changing functions that past generations allotted to the rooms of the homes we have inherited.

Always, however, we are drawn to the people who lived before us, and it is their stories that echo through the corridors of our homes. If you live in an old house then you share it with the ghosts of the people who lived there before you, because your space was once their space.

David Olusoga, 2020

CHAPTER ONE

WHERE TO START?

Deeds, Documents, and Archives

Every house has a story: a unique history all of its own. The nuances and details of the people that have called it home and the events that have unfolded within its walls make the history of every home different. The three houses in Liverpool, Newcastle-upon-Tyne, and Bristol that feature in *A House Through Time* were built in a bygone age. But much of England's surviving housing is older than we might imagine. Of the twenty-three million or so inhabited houses standing today around a fifth were built before the outbreak of the Great War in 1914.

Architectural styles change but the great majority of homes, the grand terraces, suburban villas, and humble back-to-back streets, were put up by speculative builders who did not own the land they built on but who hoped to turn a profit by satisfying changing tastes as fashion dictated. In time the brand-new terrace might become run-down and multi-occupied or turned into a hostel or some other kind of institution. Then, if it survived demolition, it might have a new lease of life as a newly fashionable 'gentrified' town house cherished by its new owners. It is a familiar pattern repeated through the centuries.

If walls could talk, all of these pre-1914 houses would have extraordinary stories to tell. Much of the drama that has been played out in them might be difficult to retrieve, but a great deal can be unearthed with some detective work and persistence. It can be exciting, and to learn about the history of your house inevitably leads to a fascination with past lives and the discovery of the rich social history of the home. *A House*

Through Time is not so much about the buildings as about the lives of former residents who once thought of them as homes.

Some of the detective work which went into the revelations of the television series can be a guide for anyone fascinated by the lives of those who shared the four walls of their home in history. This book is both an introduction to the many sources of information that can be found in documents held in archives, and a social history of housing from Roman times until the present day.

The older the house, the richer the history is likely to be. But there is still a great deal to discover about the past life of your home if it's one of the semi-detached suburban houses built between the world wars. Just under four million survive today and they represent a clear break with the past in a great many ways. As in the Victorian era, the majority were put up by speculative builders who created huge new estates. But, from 1918, for the first time in the country's history, the government provided the funds to build council-house estates: what we now call 'social housing'. In fact between the wars there was fierce competition for land between councils and private builders as the major cities spread over the countryside.

Whatever the age of your house, if you want to delve into the history of the area in which you live, or perhaps where you lived when you were younger, you have to start somewhere. If you wonder when the house was built then its appearance, its architecture, is the first clue. Getting it exactly right might be difficult, but broadly speaking with a little knowledge, you can tell if a house is Victorian or built between the two world wars. With a little bit more knowledge you might judge the house is Georgian, built during the reigns of the Hanoverian kings from 1714 to 1830.

There are many different approaches to researching the history of a house and its former residents. You can go to any of the archives now available: the national censuses (for the years 1841 to 1911), the electoral registers, the street directories, the Land Registry, and the title deeds, to name just a few. However, before jumping into the documents and and perhaps finding youself a little muddled, a key tip for researching the history of a house is to work backwards in time. Start with what you know, such as the names of more recent occupants, and this will provide clues about which sources to research and how best to use them

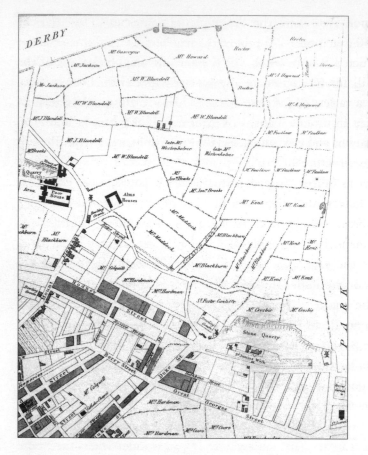

A map from 1796 shows the area of Falkner Street, Liverpool, prior to major development. A number of fields are owned by 'Mr Faulkner'.

as you search further back in time. Street names and house numbers often change, sometimes several times, so this will also help to ensure you are researching the right house and people.

Perhaps the most instantly rewarding and enjoyable starting point is to go to the great variety of maps which can offer a vivid picture of the changing setting and fortunes of our homes. Only a few specialized maps will tell you about the people living in the area (some are described later on), but you can check on the era in which your street was built. It might not exist on an 1860s map but appear on one drawn ten years later. You can also find, if the map is large-scale, roads which have been renamed since a map was drawn.

In local archives there will be maps of your area or town, such as those that form part of landowner surveys, municipal maps for the building of new roads, or maps of industrial sites or in preparation for new developments. One such map of the 'Town and County of

Newcastle-upon-Tyne and the Borough of Gateshead' by Thomas Oliver in 1830 (see page 128) provided a wonderful visual image of the newly constructed Ravensworth Terrace and the neighbouring gardens of Summerhill for series two of *A House Through Time*. Other maps, produced for a variety of purposes, can also be revealing. These include the Goad Fire Insurance maps, of Charles E. Goad Ltd, which were produced in towns and cities to assess fire risk. They provide fascinating details of the structure of buildings and often record how they were used, whether as offices, homes, institutions, or hotels, or as shops for hairdressers, tailors, and other trades.

The outbreak of disease sometimes prompted authorities to commission maps. In Liverpool, the unique 'Mortality map of Typhus', 1865, reveals the extent of the city's typhus epidemic (see the plate section). Not only does it provide a striking visual representation of the tragedy of the epidemic, but also gives clues to the conditions of the city at that time. It provided a significant clue to the reasons behind the death of John Bowes at 62 Falkner Street in Liverpool in 1854. Although he died of cholera, the typhus map provides important evidence of the state of the poorer working-class areas of Liverpool during the mid-nineteenth century that contributed to the spread of disease.

However, there is one outstanding series of maps with a long and fascinating history with which a great many people are familiar. These are produced under the rather odd name of the Ordnance Survey. Some are on a small scale of one inch to the mile (the most recent are metric), but there are others which show much greater detail, right down to the identification of individual properties. These are used nowadays by the Land Registry to define the ownership of individual plots of land.

The history of the Ordnance Survey can be traced back to the mapping, between 1747 and 1755, of the mountains and glens of the Scottish Highlands by a young engineer called William Roy. These maps were commissioned as an aid to the 'pacification' of Scots who fought to restore the Stuart monarchy by installing Charles Stuart (the so-called Bonnie Prince Charlie) on the British throne.

No other call for accurate mapping was apparent when Roy had finished his work in Scotland, but, by chance, an astronomical problem gave him the opportunity to continue his work and improve on it. A dispute between the Observatory at Greenwich and the Paris Observatory about their exact geographical positions could only be resolved by accurate mapping. Though Britain and France were at war at the start, a collaboration using the French mapping technique of 'triangulation' solved the problem in 1790. Roy produced the British map.

The prospect of producing a series of accurate maps of the country proved to be inspirational for the Board of Ordnance, which was responsible for the forts, munitions, and equipment for the defence of Britain. The Board invested in a Ramsden theodolite, an essential instrument for the cartographer, in 1791. Some argue this was the true beginning of the Ordnance Survey maps, which were in time noted for their exceptional detail and accuracy.

From the outset these official maps were the responsibility of the military and the very first one-inch-to-the-mile map produced in 1801 with the Ramsden theodolite was of Kent at a time when there was a very real fear of invasion. Napoleon had amassed an armada on the other side of the Channel and appeared to be intent on launching a seaborne invasion.

Over the next twenty years, the mapping of southern England continued though the threat of invasion had passed with the defeat of the French and Spanish navies at the Battle of Trafalgar in 1805 and of Napoleon's army at Waterloo in 1815. There was a project to cover the whole country but it was abandoned. And there was an issue over accuracy. One of the giants of Ordnance history, the surveyor Captain Thomas Colby (1784–1852), who recorded that he had once walked 586 miles in twenty-two days in 1819, found serious inaccuracies in the early maps and he set about revising them.

It was 1844 before there was a complete set of one-inch maps for Britain below a line drawn from Preston in Lancashire to Hull in Humberside. As early as 1786 a large-scale six-inches-to-the-mile map had been drawn of the important naval town of Plymouth and the area around, but although there were some other large-scale maps made of military installations, the six-inch map was not widely produced until the mapping of Ireland in the 1830s. These maps really had nothing to do with Ordnance: they were mapping for taxation. From this time on the Ordnance Survey was employed chiefly to provide the kind of detailed information required by government, local authorities, and developers, as Victorian industrial towns grew at tremendous speed.

Maps at several different scales were published by the Ordnance office, covering the whole of Britain. This makes the hunt for the maps relevant to your own house and street especially exciting, though occasionally quite frustrating. During the mid- to late-nineteenth century, the Ordnance Survey produced maps of twenty-five inches to the mile, while some urban areas had maps of five feet to one mile (and later ten feet to one mile). These revealed extraordinary detail of streets and houses, including the specific parameters of a house, as well as the layout of gardens, and the location of wells, pumps, and post boxes. The strengths of the Ordnance Survey maps were not only their level of detail, but the fact that they were updated every twenty to thirty years, so it is possible to track the development of your house and street through subsequent maps.

If you are out looking for Ordnance Survey maps of various scales you will find most of these in your local authority archives. However, the best place to look is still the British Library map room, which has a comprehensive collection of just about everything ever produced.

A very useful online map finder is provided by the Charles Close Society, which was founded in 1980 by a group of Ordnance Survey enthusiasts. They named their society after Colonel Sir Charles Arden-Close, the Director-General from 1911 to 1922, who was influential in making Ordnance Survey maps more widely available. Their free website has a great deal about the history of the Ordnance Survey with advice on how to find maps (see the resources section). Especially useful is their online index. If you enter an address on a street in any town, it will list all the Ordnance Survey maps of different scales that cover the area. For example if you enter the address of 62 Falkner Street, Liverpool, featured in the first series of *A House Through Time*, there are more than twenty maps listed, going back to 1864 which was surveyed in the 1840s. There are similar lists for Ravensworth Terrace in Newcastle-upon-Tyne and Guinea Street in Bristol.

In addition, the National Library of Scotland has an easy map search for Ordnance Survey maps and these cover all of the United Kingdom. There are also a growing number of digital map sites, including Know Your Place: West of England, and Layers of London, which shows a variety of map 'layers' from the Romans to today. (For further details on websites and map sources, see the resources section.)

Ordnance Survey maps do not record year by year the changes to the countryside or the towns, as they were commissioned and surveyed at intervals of several years, and they lack any details of ownership of property or the social standing of the people who lived in the streets and houses. Fortunately for those researching the history of their house and its occupants there is a great variety of maps that can fill in the details.

Most local archives or county record offices will have some historic maps of towns and rural districts dating back to periods earlier than the Ordnance maps, though they are unlikely to be very detailed. However, in the National Archives there are several series of maps which were commissioned for a special purpose that can be rich in detail. Of these perhaps the most intriguing, especially for those whose houses were built in the second half of the nineteenth century, are the tithe maps.

'Tithing' was a tax in which farmers were obliged to donate each year one tenth of their produce, whether it were eggs or wool, to the local church and its incumbent clergy. Like all taxes it was resented, but it at least had some justification when the country was predominantly rural and its wealth rooted in agriculture. It originated in the ninth century and was not entirely abolished until 1977. Yet by the early nineteenth century it was patently out of date both for the beneficiaries and those paying the tithe. Paying rent in the form of sides of pork, chickens, eggs, and corn had become ridiculous and was a tax on farmers at a time when industrialists paid no tax at all.

Sir Frank Markham, in his *History of Milton Keynes and District*, which was once a very rural part of Buckinghamshire, provides a fine example of the absurdity of the tithe system. At the end of the eighteenth century every farmer in Bletchley, Water Eaton and Fenny Stratford had to deliver to the Rector of Bletchley every year, in addition to the 'tenth sheaf of corn', the following:

> Underwood, Lambs, Wool, Pigs and Fruit, they are or should
> be paid in kind, for Milk twopence is paid for a milch Cow and
> Heifer, Eggs are paid for the Wednesday before Easter of the
> rate of two eggs for one Hen, and three eggs for a Cock, one
> halfpenny for a Garden Honey and calves pay at the rate of the
> tenth penny they are sold for and if a calf be eaten by the owner
> and his family there is only one halfpenny due for it but the 7th

calf may be demanded by the Rector paying back to the owner 3½d for each calf weaned and every odd lamb and every odd Fleece there is due one halfpenny. For every sheep sold before Candlemas there is due one penny, for every sheep sold after Candlemas the whole tythe is due.

Parliament, after the Great Reform Act of 1832 which extended the right to vote to owners and tenants of properties worth over £10, recognized the problem and brought in a new law which sought to rid the country of the tithing custom. In some regions, especially those in which the enclosure of land had been widespread, tithes had already been abolished and replaced by some form of rent or monetary equivalent. The process of converting tithes into a money rent was called 'commutation'. When Parliament decided to act to get rid of tithes, the law passed in 1836 was entitled the Tithe Commutation Act.

Commissioners set about making a record of existing tithes known as 'the apportionments' and these were recorded on maps, paid for by landowners who protested that they did not need expensive surveyors for the purpose. An Act in 1837 allowed all kinds of maps to be drawn up by a variety of people. From then on there were two categories: maps regarded as accurate by the Tithe Commissioners, which were designated 'First Class' (1,900 maps making up 16 per cent of the total), and the rest, rated 'Second Class'.

Accordingly, the quality of tithe maps was variable but they are, by and large, a wonderful record of the lie of the land in England and Wales. Between 1836 and 1852 the Tithe Commissioners redistributed the tithe apportionments in over eleven thousand districts in England and Wales and in every case there is a map to accompany their deliberations. Most of the maps had been drawn up by 1850, but in some places the haggling over who should get what went on for thirty years or more. You can find even on the outskirts of the largest towns, including London, tithe maps which illustrate the rustic nature of whole areas which were soon covered in bricks and mortar. There is a detailed guide to what you can find in tithe maps in the National Archives publication *Maps for Family and Local History* by Geraldine Beech and Rose Mitchell.

Where there are gaps in the tithe map coverage it is generally because the transformation from tithe to money rent, or 'rentcharge' as it was called, had already begun where landlords had enclosed fields. Enclosure has a history going back to the sixteenth century. The term applied to the conversion of fields in which individuals farmed narrow strips into larger units, the cultivation of wastelands and heaths, and the expropriation of what had been communally owned land in a village by a new owner. Anyone with a legal right to land would be compensated. Thousands who believed they had rights based on custom lost out.

A new Act of Parliament was needed before each enclosure could go ahead. Between 1761 and 1801 about two thousand such Acts were passed and another two thousand between 1802 and 1844. It is estimated that these latter-day parliamentary enclosures affected six million acres in England, about a quarter of all cultivatable land. It is a matter of chance whether or not your house is in a former agricultural area that was enclosed, but it is now fairly easy to find out as a comprehensive guide to all enclosures between 1595 and 1918 has been compiled after extensive research at Exeter and Portsmouth Universities, funded by the Social and Economic Research Council and the Leverhulme Trust. A book by Roger Kain and others describing all the enclosure maps that can be consulted is published by Cambridge University Press. The authors state in the preface: 'At scales of 1:10,000 and larger, they provide a record of parish and township boundaries before major changes took place, of enclosed and open fields, of farms and settlement forms, and of rural land ownership and use.'

A more recent set of maps covering the countryside was produced between 1941 and 1943. It might at first sight appear unlikely that an eighty-year-old survey of farms would be of more than passing interest to the house history hunter. However, for those who live on estates built after the Second World War, there is the potential for some fascinating discoveries. More than 13.5 million homes have been built in England and Wales since 1945, many of them on what had been farmland, and the possibility of discovering the rustic antecedents of your suburban back garden is enticing. You might be able to find the name of the farmer and what he had in the way of livestock and crops, as well as a map showing the pattern of the fields.

When war broke out in September 1939 the threat of food shortages became real and acute. The German U-boats attacked the merchant vessels that unloaded millions of tons of imported meat and grain and fruit, and there was an urgent need for Britain to feed itself as far as possible. To the slogan of 'Dig for Victory' parkland was ploughed up, pigs were herded on derelict sites in towns, and thousands of pockets of land were turned into miniature market gardens. In the countryside, County War Agricultural Executive Committees were set up with potentially draconian powers: they could tell farmers what to grow; to plough up pasture if they thought it would be more beneficial as arable land; to direct labourers where to work; and even, though this was rarely used, to forcibly take possession of land. Between June 1940 and early 1941 a rapid survey was undertaken of all but the smallest farms in England and Wales.

When this first emergency measure had been taken it was decided that a wartime Domesday Book should be compiled, providing an inventory of farms, which would form a sound basis for planning when the war was over. Between the spring of 1941 and 1943, farms of five acres or more in England and Wales were surveyed in detail – three hundred and twenty thousand in all. The tenants and owners filled in a fairly lengthy questionnaire on the livestock they had, the crops they grew, and the staff they employed. Later an assessment was made of the farm by a surveyor and each was put into a category, A for the best, B for the average, and C for the worst.

The maps compiled for the farm survey were based either on those of the Ordnance Survey of 25 inches to the mile, reduced to a scale of 12.5 inches, or the old 6 inches to the mile maps. A unique code was devised for each farm and its extent marked in most cases with a colour wash. To track down the area you are interested in involves a series of stages a bit like peeling back the skin of an onion. There are key sheets to the maps and on the maps themselves the code numbers for individual farms. Along with the farmer's questionnaire and the surveyor's comments (not always complimentary!) you might well find that you have a fascinating portrait of the site of your house at the time of the Second World War. If you live in a village which has not been substantially built over in the past seventy years or so the maps will also be of great interest. You might even find who lived in your cottage. For further reading there is a comprehensive study of the survey in Brian Short et al., *The National Farm Survey 1941–43: State Surveillance and the Countryside in England and Wales in the Second World War* (see the resources section).

Of all the maps you might scan in your quest to understand how the world was ordered in the past, none could ever have quite the impact as those hand painted to accompany the monumental *Life and Labour of the People in London*. The author was Charles Booth (not to be confused with William Booth, founder of the Salvation Army), a businessman who had made his fortune in trade with South America and who chose to spend a considerable amount of it on gauging the extent of poverty in London.

Charles Booth had a pious upbringing in Liverpool, where his father was a corn merchant and member of the Unitarian Church. He left school at the age of sixteen to take up an apprenticeship with a shipping company. When his father died, Charles and his older brother Alfred were left with a considerable inheritance. They decided to form their own company trading in skins and leather across the Atlantic, with offices in New York and Liverpool. In time the company prospered with the development of pneumatic tyres, shipping raw rubber from Brazil. Charles built the port of Manaus for the rubber trade.

All this time, he lived in Liverpool. In 1871 he married Mary Macaulay, a niece of the famous historian Thomas Babington Macaulay. They moved to London in 1875, and Charles was introduced to some of the leading reformist figures of the day. There was a dispute amongst philanthropists and others about the extent of poverty in the capital. Booth set out with Mary's help to map the whole of London, street by street, giving each a colour code indicating his estimation of its wealth and social class.

He recruited a motley crew of investigators. School Board inspectors, whose job it was to walk the streets looking for children who were not in school, were joined by police constables, all of them noting the social conditions from the grand houses with footmen at the door to the dark enclaves of abject poverty. He liked to order things, to classify them and define them, and he applied this methodical approach, which he had developed as a trader, to the social fabric of London. He decided on a fivefold classification of the social classes from the wealthiest to the poorest. It was not without a certain moral censure, though there was nothing sanctimonious about his view of the poor. He had lost his religious faith long before and liked to say that what he believed in was 'purpose'.

The painstaking observations of every street across a very large part

Charles Booth, social reformer and creator of the renowned London poverty maps.

of London in 1889, and a second survey a few years later, were used to create social-class maps which at a glance gave a picture of the wealth and poverty in each district. These maps (the original hand-painted sheets are kept in the Museum of London) provide in colour a mosaic of social classes in every street and courtyard: see the plate section.

The very wealthiest London streets are coloured yellow. Going down the social scale the streets occupied chiefly by the middle classes, many of them shopkeepers, are marked in a bold red. Then there are the roads marked pink, which were judged to be chiefly lived in by people who were 'fairly comfortable with good ordinary earnings'. Streets marked purple were judged to have a mix of comfortably off and poor people. Then there were those streets marked in light blue in which the average family weekly income was 18–21 shillings, barely enough to get by.

The streets of the very poor, relying on casual employment, are marked dark blue, but they were not at the lowest level of his classification. Here was a touch of moral judgement: the streets and enclaves painted black were in the lowest class, categorized as 'occasional labourers, street sellers, loafers, criminals and semi-criminals'. All of these maps are available online and the London School of Economics has digitized many of the notebooks of the investigators (see the resources section). A book, entitled *Charles Booth's London Poverty Maps*, has also been produced by the London School of Economics.

In the late 1920s and early 1930s *The New Survey of London Life and Labour* with maps that covered what was then the county of London was published and can be used to illustrate the changes since the last of the Booth surveys at the end of the nineteenth century.

A decade after the last of the Booth maps was published, an attempt to map wealth rather than poverty was made by the then Chancellor of the Exchequer, David Lloyd George. He was out to tax the rich, or 'the unemployed' as he sometimes liked to call the landed aristocracy, whose wealth increased with the rising value of land and property despite the fact that they contributed nothing themselves by way of improvements. In order for his scheme to work Lloyd George first needed to have an estimate of what an estate was worth at a fixed point in time, so that when it was sold the difference could be calculated and taxed. There was an element of the modern-day inheritance-tax principle in it and it was about as popular with the well-to-do.

As you might imagine, there was huge opposition to Lloyd George's valuation survey but the law to implement it was finally passed as the Finance Act (1909–10). Between 1910 and 1915 an inventory was drawn up to identify the property owners with more than fifty acres of land worth £75 an acre or more. They would have to pay a duty of 20 per cent on the increase in the value of their property between the baseline set at 30 April 1909 and when it was sold, or leased for more than fourteen years, or on the death of the owner. Although the owners of less valuable property did not face the 'incremental tax', it was decided to include them in the survey anyway as it was thought the information might be useful when the rating system was reformed or property was compulsorily purchased by the government.

At the time this new Domesday survey was commissioned the

Valuation Office had been established only a short while and had just 61 employees. To carry out the survey the permanent staff was increased to 600 and 4,500 temporary employees were taken on. Using maps of various scales drawn up by the Ordnance Survey, they set off to make detailed notes on all the property in England and Wales. For the purposes of the survey – and this is worth knowing if you are hunting for your property on a map – England and Wales were divided into 14 Valuation Divisions and within these there were 188 Valuation Districts. At the outset, landowners were sent a form to fill in giving an account of their property and faced a stiff fine if they refused: £50, equivalent to £5,000 in 2018. A number of landowners challenged the validity of the survey in the courts and delayed its completion, but of 10.5 million forms sent out, 9 million were returned completed within the first year.

Evaluators with Ordnance Survey maps then reviewed the properties and wrote descriptions in field books. The quality of these varies a great deal, but many demonstrate a real dedication to duty. You might find a description of your house that lists the number of rooms and their use, the condition of the exterior, the name of the owner and of the occupier (if it was rented, as most properties were), the date it was built, and information on when it was sold in the past and for what price. Unfortunately, the whole project was slowed by the outbreak of war in August 1914, when many valuation staff went off to fight in France.

As a method of taxation, the scheme was a failure. It cost about £2 million to set up and when the Act was repealed in 1920 had raised hardly any tax at all. But the maps and the field books hoarded away in the National Archives have proved to be one of the most exciting sources for the house history hunter. You can begin your search online with a new device provided by the National Archives (see the resources section). Some valuation books and survey records have also been retained in local archives or record offices.

Unfortunately there are areas of the country where it is not worth looking:

Basildon, Essex: many records destroyed in a fire
Birkenhead and the Wirral: most records lost in bomb damage
during the Second World War

Chelmsford: lost, possibly in the Basildon Valuation Office fire
Chichester: destroyed by a Second World War bomb
Coventry: lost in the Second World War
Liverpool: lost in the Second World War, possibly bombing
Portsmouth: lost in Second World War bomb damage
Southampton: lost in Second World War bomb damage
Winchester: destroyed in enemy action.

The aerial bombardment that destroyed a number of the Lloyd George Domesday maps brought death and destruction to London and some of the more important port and industrial cities in the country. The capital took the brunt, hit with seventy-one raids that killed an estimated thirty thousand people. Liverpool, Birmingham, Glasgow, Plymouth, Bristol, Exeter, Coventry, Portsmouth, Southampton, Hull, and Manchester all suffered some bomb damage and loss of life. The national death toll is estimated at forty-one thousand.

In the first two weeks of the Blitz in 1940 around two hundred thousand houses in London were damaged, many of them in the poorest districts of the East End. As the bombs rained down, first from the continuous night-time waves of the Luftwaffe and later in the war from V1 and V2 rockets, the damage done to buildings was logged meticulously by the London County Council. Judgements were made about which homes had been so badly damaged they could not be saved, and those that might be shored up. If a building had historic value every effort was made to save it. This was the origin of the listing of buildings we are familiar with today. Rubble from the early raids was loaded onto freight trains – 1,700 of them – and used as hard core for Bomber Command runways in East Anglia.

Surveyors from the London County Council who inspected the damage marked the details on large-scale Ordnance Survey maps which, with some updating, had been completed at the outbreak of war in 1914. They were colour-coded to indicate the severity of damage in every street. Astonishingly every single bomb and rocket was logged with the position it fell and exploded along with a note on its impact. At the end of the war the maps were preserved in the archives of the London Metropolitan Authority and can now be viewed at the London Metropolitan Archives. A book was also published by Thames and Hudson (Laurence Ward,

St John's Lane in Bedminster, Bristol, suffered extensive bomb damage.

2015). The Layers of London website additionally shows bomb damage maps for the entire length of the war in London. Another website provided by the Bomb Sight project offers an easily searchable series of maps for each London borough with notes on the bombs dropped between 7 October 1940 and 6 June 1941. With a zoom you can easily find your address if you live in the area covered. (See the resources section for websites.)

Ouside of London, county and city record offices hold various records for the war years, ranging from bomb damage maps and photographs to diaries and oral testimonies from those who lived through the war. In the National Archives there are also a series of maps which mark where bombs and rockets fell in different parts of the country. These are the bomb census maps which were put together by regional officers of the Ministry of Home Security Bomb Census Organisation, collating information provided by Civil Defence workers and the police. These maps give no indication of whether a building was destroyed or not but they nevertheless make for fascinating, if ghoulish, reading.

As an important dockyard on the south coast of England, home of the Supermarine factory and birthplace of the Spitfire, Southampton, was a prime target. During the nights of 23/24 November and 30 November and 1 December 1940, the Southampton Blitz reached its climax as the city came under sustained attack. Hundreds of tonnes of bombs were dropped during the two nights, whilst on 30 November alone some 634 individual properties were left ablaze. A report by the Ministry of Food describes how the resulting destruction 'equalled anything so far in aerial attack on this country', but even so, it is very hard now to comprehend the scale of the damage, let alone the impact it had on the people who lived through it.

The Ordnance Survey with the help of the National Archives and Southampton City Council created a map based on records from the time that pinpoints where 712 of the bombs fell. The bomb sites are overlaid on modern mapping to show the scale of the damage (see the resources section).

All local archives will have collections of photographs which often vividly illustrate the effects of bombing. In *A House Through Time* the photographic collection held by Historic England had pictures showing the destruction around Guinea Street in Bristol. Long after the war photographic records revealed the destruction of housing around Falkner Street in Liverpool during the great slum clearance programmes before the tower blocks arose from the rubble. And the fate of 5 Ravensworth Terrace in Newcastle when it ceased for years to be a home was brought to life with a wonderful collection of photographs taken when it was a Salvation Army Goodwill Centre. Even a study of old postcards can be rewarding. Many images can now be tracked down online from a variety of collections such as Historic England's (see the resources section). Record offices and archives across the country will also have their own collections.

There is a great deal you can discover from maps and photographs but when you're researching the history of a house and its past inhabitants, you need more detail and something more comprehensive in its coverage. For this you will inevitably turn to the national censuses that have been held every ten years since 1801, with just one omission in 1941 (the 1931 census was destroyed in the war).

When it was first introduced in England, Wales and Scotland in 1801 there was little indication that the Census of Population was ever going to be much fun. For much of the eighteenth century there had been fierce arguments about whether or not the number of people was rising or falling. In the absence of a government-sponsored headcount there was no resolving the issue, though some very ingenious methods were devised for estimating numbers. The debate was given a new urgency by the publication in 1798 of *An Essay on the Principle of Population* by the Revd Thomas Malthus, who foresaw a terrible future unless birth rates were held back by what he called 'moral restraint', i.e. less sex. It seemed inevitable to Malthus that population increase would outstrip the ability of the land to provide food for the greater numbers and that the country – and much of Europe – was heading for war, disease, or famine, or all three.

Malthus was quite right in his belief that population was rising rapidly at the end of the eighteenth century and that it would go on rising in the nineteenth at an unprecedented rate. There were, from time to time, wars, diseases and famines, but never on a scale that threatened the growth in numbers. And the more intensive use of farmland as well as imports of food kept the millions fed. But if it was his gloomy predictions that finally got the census commissioned then we owe him a great debt. Now accessible online, the censuses are hugely popular among genealogists, family historians and house history hunters (see the resources section).

It should be pointed out, however, that census returns can sometimes be limited in the detail they provide. The most recent information obtainable is from the 1911 census: the last hundred years is a blank for the good reason that publication of returns remains confidential until a century is up. (From 2022, however, you should be able to view the 1921 census.) In addition, the earliest census which has information of any real value is that of 1841: the previous four decennial censuses were just headcounts. The census also records the inhabitants of a property on one day of the year. If, at the time, most of the family is away then the place will seem empty. Names are spelled wrongly on occasion, or they are undecipherable, and road names change. The search criteria are not always consistent between censuses. For example, with the 1901 census you can search by road name and district.

Despite their fallibilities, common to all sources of raw data, census returns can, nonetheless, provide a wealth of information about people who lived in your home, listing not just the head of the household but other residents, including children, servants, lodgers and visitors. They also reveal key personal details: ages, occupations, places of birth and the marital status of former occupants. The 1911 census was an important source when retelling the stories for all three houses in *A House Through Time*. It revealed that 5 Ravensworth Terrace in Newcastle-upon-Tyne was a boarding house run by Grace Eagle, who lived there with her daughter, nineteen-year-old Leonora, who was a shop assistant, and her son, fourteen-year-old Henry, who was at school. Meanwhile, there were five boarders, including a 'merchant's agent', plus an actor and three 'music-hall artists', which brought to life the story of the music-hall theatre in Edwardian Newcastle.

Searching the census returns can also be richly rewarding. The Office of National Statistics has had a bit of fun with it by unearthing the entries of famous historical figures. At Buckingham Palace, Her Majesty Queen Victoria lists her occupation in the 1851 census as 'The Queen' and awarded her husband, the beloved Albert, the title 'Head of the Household'. In 1841 she gives her name simply as 'The Queen, aged 20' with just a tick in the 'Occupation' box. In the 1881 census, the cricketer W. G. Grace, then aged thirty-two, gives his profession as surgeon: he was a qualified medical practitioner, though he made his fortune out of cricket. In the 1861 census Florence Nightingale is down as 'Formerly Hospital Nurse', when she was aged forty and very ill staying in the Burlington Hotel in London, which she used as an office. When he was living in Dean Street, Soho, in 1841, Karl Marx is down as Charles Marx; his occupation is given as doctor, and in brackets, 'philosophical author', birthplace, Prussia. With his wife Jenny he has three daughters and a son and they employ a domestic servant and a nurse. The ageing William Wordsworth at seventy-one was in London at the time of the 1841 census, staying in Upper Grosvenor Street with his wife Mary. He describes himself as 'Distributor of Stamps', an office he was given in Westmorland to provide him with an income he could never have earned as a poet.

At the outbreak of the Second World War the General Register Office conducted an instant census carried out along the same lines as

Grace Eagle and her children Leonora and Henry lived at 5 Ravensworth Terrace, Newcastle, during the early 1900s.

the regular decennial censuses to record the whereabouts of the civilian population. It was needed to keep track of the population when rationing and the evacuation of those vulnerable to bombing was planned. It was also a record of those liable to conscription in the armed services. There was to have been a full census in 1941 and the preparations for that were put into practice. The 1931 census was compiled and stored but it was destroyed by fire during the war and as no census was possible in 1941, the 1939 register is an invaluable resource for family and house historians.

It is available on several family history sites and is entertaining to use. For example on the census day, 29 September 1939, we find the playwright Noël Coward at his enormous manor house Goldenhurst in Kent with a party of nine others, actresses, a theatrical manager,

ADDRESS.	SCHEDULE.		SURNAMES AND OTHER NAMES.	O. V. S. P. or I.	M. or F.	BIRTH-		S. M. W. or D.	PERSONAL OCCUPATION.
	No.	Sub. No.				Day.	Year.		
1	2	3	4	5	6	7	8	9	10
9 Guinea Street	169	1	Corbett Henry A.	-	M	26th July	85	M	Haulage Contractor
		2	Corbett Ellen	-	F	27th Jan	84	M	unpaid domestic duties
		3	Corbett Jonathan	-	M	15 Feb	14	S	market Gardener (agricultural worker)
	170	1	Rickard Thomas H.	-	M	27th apl	06	M	General Labourer
		2	Rickard Daisy E.	-	F	5th mch	05	M	unpaid domestic duties
11		3	Rickard Hazel B.	-	F	3rd Feb	36	S	under School age
		4	Hutchon Arthur T.	-	M	19th June	28	S	at School
10 ditto	171	1	Wallington Frederick A.	-	M	8th June	61	W	Painter & Decorator. (Retired
		2	Wallington Hilda	-	F	7th nov	84	S	unpaid domestic duties
		3	Wallington W.	-	F	15th Dec	93	S	unpaid domestic duties
		4	Delaney, Henrietta	F		17th aug	99	M	unpaid domestic duties
		5	Delaney B.	-	M	19th July	36	S	under School age
		6	Fill A. A. H.	-	F	13th mch	29	S	at School
		7	Wallington N.	-	M	11th Sep	86	S	Painter & Decorator
	172	1	Gale Albert	-	M	18th Oct	88	M	General Labourer (Warehouse man)
		2	Gale Albert J.	-	M	3rd Jan	18	S	Grocers Assistant
		3	Gale Vera	-	F	1st Jan	94	M	unpaid domestic duties
	173	1	Hale Samuel	-	M	10th mch	48	W	(Seaman) Cargo Hand
	174	1	Priscott Sarah A.	-	F	27th Dec	62	W	unpaid domestic duties
11 ditto	175	1	Read Edward	-	M	6th July	70	M	Coach Body maker (moto)
		2	Read Annie May	-	F	13th Dec	82	M	unpaid domestic duties

labourers, a dairyman and a Winifred Ellis who had 'unpaid domestic duties' (a common term for the lady of the house as opposed to a paid domestic). Goldenhurst was requisitioned by the army during the war and Coward did not return there until 1951. The expense of running it and the attention of the Inland Revenue drove him into exile. John Gielgud, under his full name Arthur J., was staying at 26 Park Road, Blackpool. Gracie Fields was in the home she shared with her parents, The Haven, Telscombe Cliffs Way in Sussex. The register contains the names, occupations, marital statuses and ages of around forty million people, recorded in more than sixty-five thousand volumes.

The 1939 Register lists who was living at 10 Guinea Street on 29 September 1939.

Electoral registers and poll books offer another avenue for research into the occupants of a house. In most cases, it is the electoral registers from the late nineteenth century and through the twentieth century, a time when those eligible to vote increased substantially, that will be of most use for the house historian. The earlier records, known as poll books, are literally a 'poll' of voters, who they voted for, and the location of the property that gave them the eligibility. From 1696 to 1832 the eligibility to vote in county constituencies was based on ownership of freehold land valued at forty shillings or over, although from 1763 this was extended to those who received annuities or rent charges on freehold land.

Until 1832, most names were taken from the land tax, but after the passing of the Reform Act in 1832, the right to vote in parliamentary elections was extended to both owner and tenants of a property with an annual rental value of at least £10. From this time electoral registers were compiled for each area. Further extensions of the electorate were introduced in 1867 and 1884, which meant that by the final years of the nineteenth century, two out of three men were able to vote. However, women were still disenfranchised in parliamentary elections (although some property-owning women were eligible to vote in local elections). In 1918, the property requirement for men to vote was removed, enfranchising all men over twenty-one, and the vote was finally extended to women over thirty who met minimal property qualifications. It wasn't until 1928 that women over the age of twenty-one were granted full suffrage, regardless of property ownership.

The early poll books and electoral registers only recorded certain members of the community. The electoral registers for the late nineteenth century began to record far more information, and along with people's names, their eligibility to vote or otherwise was noted, providing a clue to their social status. This included lodgers (sometimes recording the name of the landlord, how many rooms were occupied, whether the room was furnished, and how much rent was being paid). Registers may also record the details of an owner and their eligible property, along with the address where they live.

As a result, electoral registers, particularly if used alongside directories and census returns, can help to build up a good picture of former residents. However, it is worth noting that electoral registers only provide a list of names and not details of family relationships, so it can be difficult to distinguish between parents and children, as well as who might have been a servant or lodger. In addition, electoral registers were not compiled during the First and Second World Wars, and many non-British residents were not eligible to vote.

The registers are organized by the polling districts and wards within each parish. While some will have street indexes, others may not, so you need to identify the parish and ward for your house back through the years (and these sometimes change). Guidelines for this can usually be found at the record office where the electoral register is held. Also, early electoral registers (even up until the 1970s) might list names rather than addresses.

The British Library holds a complete collection of electoral registers from 1947, while an increasing number of electoral registers and poll books are becoming available online through genealogical websites, although again the options for searching by address can be limited. Alternatively, you can search the collections for your area held in the county or city record office, or local studies or reference library.

When you first get your hands on a historic local directory, which were published in various forms from the seventeenth to the twentieth century, there is often a frisson of excitement. They might list your road and the occupants of every house, often giving their names, professions and trades. There it is, just as you hoped: Acacia Avenue. You run your finger down to the number of your house . . . and it is not there. Why? Was the house knocked down? Is everything you had learned about when it was built in some way inaccurate? It is worth trying another year, the next perhaps, in the hope that your house has reappeared. It might well have done. Or maybe you have to jump two years to find it. You then have the name of the occupant, or the one whose name was listed. But there is no description of the household as there is in the census. The advantage of street and trade directories, especially those published in the nineteenth century and later, is that they give an annual check on at least one name at a property and they provide information later than the last available census.

There are some very early directories, such as that published by a Samuel Lee in 1677 with the title *A collection of the names of the merchants living in and about the City of London; very useful and necessary. Carefully collected for the benefit of all dealers that shall have occasion with any of them; directing them at the first sight of their name, to the place of their abode.* This defines pretty well what the early trade directories that appeared in many towns in the eighteen century were for. Birmingham's first was probably that published by James Sketchley in 1763, and Elizabeth Raffald, who had a confectioner's shop and kept the Bull's Head Inn, produced Manchester's first in 1772. Gore's Directory, first published by John Gore in 1766, revealed many details about the occupants of Falkner Street in Liverpool for the first series of *A House Through Time*.

If you have a house built in the eighteenth century it is worth looking at the older trade directories, some of which are likely to be held in the local county archives. In the past many more people 'lived over the shop' than is the case today and artisans would most likely have their workshop on the same premises as their home. However, it is not until the expansion of postal services in the nineteenth century that directories appear which cast their net wider than merchants and tradesmen and begin to include professionals of various kinds and, eventually, just anybody living in a particular street.

London's first Post Office directory was published in 1800. A Post Office employee, Frederic Kelly, got the copyright in 1837 and began to publish the directories, which became the best known and are still of tremendous value to anyone exploring the history of families and cities. In time Kelly's directories included more and more information on local services, transport, and the like, greatly increasing their value to the local historian.

Directories can be found on several genealogy sites, but they often have varying dates and locations. While searching by address is not an option for most, it is possible to search by county and then town in order to locate the right area. Collections of directories, both original books and on microfilm, can be viewed at county or city record offices or local studies libraries. They do come with a bit of warning, however, as directories sometimes included out-of-date information, and mistakes were repeated across various editions. The slum districts were generally left out and when directories became more widespread some people refused to be listed in them. It is not surprising therefore that the reach of directories can be quite limited. A study in Liverpool found that only 65 per cent of households recorded in the 1851 census were listed in the town's directories. The situation in London was far worse: the Post Office directory for 1851 listed only 6 per cent of households recorded in the census of that year. Despite this, directories can still be a useful tool for house historians and provided some key information across all three series of *A House Through Time*.

* * *

In your search for accounts of the local history of the area in which you live you might come across volumes of the Victoria County History, which are so weighty that you would imagine they are the product of some kind of officially commissioned, government-backed project to document the nation's past. In fact these essential volumes for the local historian are the work of a private enterprise which has struggled to survive over the years and is still at work. (It is now available online: see the resources section.)

Why the 'Victoria' County Histories? Sir Laurence Gomme, an antiquarian and folklorist, and first clerk to the London County Council, is generally believed to have come up with the idea in commemoration of Queen Victoria's Diamond Jubilee in 1897. He discussed the possibility with the publisher Herbert Doubleday, who was a partner with Archibald Constable & Co. According to legend Doubleday was so enthused by the proposal he imagined it as a much more lavish project than Gomme had originally conceived. In 1899 the two of them drew up a prospectus for the histories and appointed themselves joint editors. The first volume came out in 1900 and covered Hampshire, with Doubleday as editor. Shortly afterwards Gomme ceased to be involved, leaving Doubleday to promote the project as best he could.

Doubleday was very keen to get the blessing of Queen Victoria to attach her name to the volumes. He did get approval from Her Majesty with the help of the librarian at Windsor and the royal library became the first subscriber. But Victoria refused to lend her patronage. This was naturally a disappointment for Doubleday's enterprise, whose success was dependent on the sale of the volumes as they appeared.

A number of leading academics of the day did lend the histories some gravitas, by sitting on an Advisory Committee or the Records Committee which, in theory at least, made recommendations on the direction the volumes should take. It was decided that there should be a set number of volumes per county with Yorkshire topping the lists at eight and little Rutland at the bottom with two. London was included in Middlesex. At the outset the various volumes were to cover natural history (including geology), prehistoric, Roman and Anglo-Saxon remains, ethnography, architecture, ecclesiastical, political, maritime, economic and social history, the industries, arts and manufactures, the feudal baronage, sport, persons eminent in art, literature and science, and bibliographies. There would also be a new Domesday listing all owners of estates of five acres or more, as well as topographical accounts of all parishes and manors.

That was all very well as an ambition. But how was all this historical evidence going to be gathered, edited, and prepared for publication? Doubleday went cap in hand striking deals. An agreement with the Public Record Office to lend copies of documents to contributors working a long way from London was made in return for a gift of Victoria History volumes. A variety of research arrangements was tried, some more successful than others. Early on a company of 'record agents', Messrs. Hardy and Page, became involved in the project as suppliers of material to one of the contributors. William Page was persuaded to become a co-editor with Doubleday and a team was put together to sift through thousands of indexes in the Public Record Office. The workforce for these first volumes of the Victoria County History was, to quote the official history, 'a team of university women, who had qualified in history or classics'. They were 'trained' by Page in the practicalities of research in the official records.

The whole enterprise was in the hands of a private limited company called the County History Syndicate. It was decided that, to make a profit, work had to start on all the counties simultaneously, beginning with the general volumes which could be produced relatively quickly. There were seven of these by 1902, and twenty-seven were produced between 1905 and 1907. Making ends meet, however, was difficult. In 1908, when twelve volumes were printed, the price was raised, but in the following year everything ground to a halt. An attempt was made to get some kind of endorsement from Edward VII, but to no avail. All he would hint at was that anyone who put money into the Victoria County Histories might be rewarded with a baronetcy.

Somehow the project survived, though it is not clear where the money came from. A variety of benefactors helped it along over the years and the volumes continued to appear. Notable among them was Frederick Smith, who, with his father and grandfather – both named W. H. Smith – built up the prominent newsagent's business which is still familiar today. In 1920, when the syndicate financing the volumes went into receivership, Frederick bought it so that it could continue and volumes continued to appear, though only with the greatest difficulty. William Page, who had been editing through these difficult years, moved home from Hampstead to Middleton near Bognor Regis, taking with him fourteen tons of research materials which he kept in a hut in his cottage garden.

Some volumes needed local benefactors to see them through to publication and the Histories remained a shoestring operation. In 1928 when Frederick Smith died his son continued to fund the enterprise but had to withdraw during the economic crisis of 1931. Page was given ownership of all the volumes which somehow had continued to appear under his editorship. Eventually, in 1933, Page handed over the Victoria County History (VCH) project to the Institute of Historical Research which had been founded in 1921 as part of London University. It remains there to this day.

After the Second World War there was a great surge of interest in family and local history which ought to have brought the Victoria County Histories centre stage as the long surviving chronicler of parish records. However, it did not quite turn out like that. The criticism was made that the compilers of the VCH volumes, known as 'Red Books' from their familiar covers, were far too interested in the history of the 'manor' and often gave the impression that the only inhabitants of a parish were the squire and his relatives. Meanwhile there grew up a network of county and borough record offices which provided a range of original documents for local historians. Before the war there had been only seven local authorities with local record offices. Between 1946 and 1950 a further fifteen were added and new legislation gave official backing to the creation of local as opposed to national records relating to the history of different parts of the country. By 1974 every county except West Yorkshire provided an archive service. At the same time local history gained in academic respectability with new chairs in the subject and the creation of the British Association for Local History in 1982.

Although the Victoria County Histories remained rather aloof during this period it continued to publish county volumes. Finally the decision was made in the 1990s to join the great local history bandwagon and to apply for a grant from the National Lottery Heritage Fund. This has transformed the VCH and provided ample justification for its survival over the years when it was often in danger of disappearing. With the Lottery money more than a hundred volumes of the histories have been made available on-line. Some volumes have been published in cheaper paperback versions and, most significant of all, the VCH has taken a much greater interest in wider social history.

The problems of funding the remaining volumes continue. There are some counties which have not yet been covered and the continuing involvement with the project nationally is patchy. A very useful summary of the work that has been completed and where work is still to be done can be found on the VCH website.

The journey you embark on when researching the history of a house and its occupants can be thrilling and rewarding, but it is not an easy task. You will be able to find names from street directories or a perusal of the electoral register and, if your house is old enough to have featured in the last available census, perhaps something about the household a hundred or more years ago. But there will be gaps, and even when you have a name and occupation it might not mean much.

If your house was built in the period between 1841 and 1911, when details of the occupants are likely to be given for your address, that is a head start. Otherwise there are street directories or the electoral roll. The Land Registry may be able to provide valuable clues to the transfer of ownership and former residents of your property. Historic deeds, the legal documents relating to a house, including leases, mortgages, as well as historic forms of property transfer, can all provide detail on the history of your home. From the nineteenth century, deeds also began to reveal more about houses and may record the layout, materials used and a brief descriptions of internal fireplaces and doors. Deeds are well worth investigating and can be found in record offices or may still be held by your mortgage provider.

But what you need from whatever record you choose to look at first is a name. Once you are able to search for an individual you can go to the historic parish registers of baptisms, marriages and burials, and from 1837 the registry of births, marriages, and deaths. With luck you might soon begin to build up a picture of an individual and be able to trace them through time.

Tucked away in local archives and record archives you may unearth other useful documents, such as building and drainage plans that reveal names of past owners as well as clues to renovations and changes made to your house. Sales particulars and auction catalogues can also provide

1879.	Marriage solemnized at Counterslip Baptist Chapel in the District of Bristol in the County of Bristol							
No.	When Married.	Name and Surname.	Age.	Condition.	Rank or Profession.	Residence at the time of Marriage.	Father's Name and Surname.	Rank or Profession of Father.
70	Nineteenth November 1879	Owen William Pow	23 years	Bachelor	Porter	Victoria Street Temple Bristol	Owen Stancel Pow (deceased)	House Decorator
		Mary Louisa Hillier	20 years	Spinster	—	Victoria Street Bristol	Alfred Charles Hillier	Mason and Builder

Married in the Counterslip Baptist Chapel according to the Rites and Ceremonies of the Baptists by Certificate by me, Samuel B. Wearing

This Marriage was solemnized between us, { Owen W. Pow / M. L. Hillier } In the Presence of us, { George Key / Emma Jane Hillier } Robert Olive Registrar

423	Twenty fifth October 1880 10 Guinea Street	Emma Louisa	Girl	Owen William Pow	Louisa Pow formerly Hillier	Porter at China Shop	Louisa Pow Mother 10 Guinea Street Bristol	Twenty ninth November 1880	Henry George Carey Registrar

4	Fourteenth January 1881 10 Guinea Street W.S.D.	Emma Louisa Pow	Female	10 weeks	Daughter of Owen William Pow Labourer	Tubercular Meningitis 7 days Certified by F. B. Logan L.R.C.P.	Mary A. Pow Mother Present at the death 10 Guinea Street Bristol	Eighteenth January 1881	Henry George Carey Registrar

further detail, as can house insurance policies.

Long before council tax came into our lives, early forms of local tax were introduced and the surviving records can also fill in the gaps as to who was living in your home through different generations. Often known as parish rates, occupants paying the rates (some of which contributed to poor relief in each parish) were detailed, particularly from the eighteenth century through to the twentieth century. In 1750, the 'Lampe and Scavenging Rates' in Bristol were a key source in uncovering details about the doctor and politcal satirist John Shebear (or Shebbeare), living at 10 Guinea Street in Bristol. The link revealed his extraordinary story and the unearthing of his series of essays, 'Letters to the People of England', which led to his arrest, conviction for treason and eventual pillorying at Charing Cross in London.

Wills and probate can also provide important clues about former occupants of your home, sometimes even shedding light on relationships or tensions within families. Strained relations were apparent in the will of Jonas Glenton, the father of Richard Glenton of Falkner Street in Liverpool, which revealed that Richard had been disinherited by his father and within a few months was forced to sell up and move away from the area (see p. 87).

Marriage, birth, and death certificates show that 10 Guinea Street resident Owen Pow married Mary Hillier in 1879. Their daughter Emma Louisa arrived in 1880, but sadly died ten weeks later.

* * *

Newspapers have always been a gold-mine for historians but until recently they were not very accessible, stored in local record offices and libraries and the British Newspaper Library in North London. Now, miraculously, they are at your fingertips. Thousands of pages have been digitized and are available on several of the family history websites. Put in a name or an address and specify a time frame and the chances are you will come up with some information. It could be a room to let, a court case, an advertisement for services, or just something for sale. Newspapers used to carry a huge number of small ads and personal advertisements. You might find your house advertised as brand new or to let. It is worth remembering that very few homes were owned outright until the 1930s.

Newspapers were invaluable for the research into the lives of the former residents of the homes featured in *A House Through Time*. In Newcastle, there was the tragic story of a glass maker, Frederick Todd, who tried to kill a solicitor (and then himself) in 1858, and then his wife Mary who died in 1867 when she caught fire while drunk. In Liverpool, the story of a Danish broker, Edward Lublin, and his wife Esther, was told with marriage announcements in *The Times*, along with Edward's letters regarding the electric telegraph. After their separation, notices in the *Jewish Chronicle* also revealed Esther's commitment to the education of her daughters. And in the third series, newspapers revealed the story of Joseph Holbrook, slave owner, who put a notice in *Felix Farley's Journal* in 1759 offering a reward for the capture of his servant, a 'negro man named Thomas'. All their stories appeared in the local press.

Reports of court cases also filled column inches of newspapers and a name might bring to light a crime in which the person you are looking for was a defendant or a witness. Court records are held both in local archives and the National Archives. All those cases heard at the Old Bailey, London's Central Criminal Court from the seventeenth century up to 1913, can be searched online (see the resources section).

Court records were important for the history of 5 Ravensworth Terrace when it was revealed that the first occupant, William Stoker, was robbed of two umbrellas by two boys, Richard Ferguson and Edward Stewart. A combination of newspaper reports, court and convict records revealed that the two boys, who were just fourteen and from poor circumstances, were found guilty and transported to Australia for seven years. Later in the story of the house, court records, along with newspapers and divorce records, revealed former occupant Florence Smyth had been married to a John Thomas Clark, who committed bigamy – and was sentenced to four months in prison.

There really is no end to the sources for the house historian. Along with the documentary sources, there are also many active local history societies and knowledgeable archivists and librarians. (See the resources section for details and links.)

What once involved weeks of travel in search of different sources is now available instantly online, and more and more archival material is being made available every year, so that a house historian is able to find out a great deal in a short space of time. It does not mean, however, that the old method of 'asking about' is no longer relevant. There might just be someone living down the road who has the original deeds for their house which was built at the same time as yours by the same builder. Or you might have neighbours who have lived next door for fifty years and can give you some of the history you are looking for.

Something of the possible excitement as well as the frustrations of embarking on researching the history of your house through time is described in great detail by the novelist Julie Myerson in her book *Home*, published in 2004. Not nearly so much was available online then, but with persistence she managed to discover some touching stories. She had had no intention of writing about her house when she came across the 1881 census in her research for a work of fiction.

She lived in a Victorian house in Clapham, South London, which had been built in 1872. It is often the case that when you start to look at historical records you get sidetracked and begin to follow leads that are nothing to do with your original quest. In Myerson's case she thought she would see who lived in her house in 1881. When she discovered the head of the household had been a writer with three children the same age as her own her imagination was fired. Redecoration of her house revealed some Victorian wallpaper under layers of paint, and that was it.

As with so many houses from that period, Myerson's home had been multi-occupied for years. She tracked down a woman who had lived there just after the Second World War. She had not been there long,

Florence Smyth, who, with her second husband John Walter, ran 5 Ravensworth Terrace in Newcastle as a boarding house.

renting just one room. In a room below, she recalled, was a lady who worked as a cook in Joe Lyons' Corner House. When she got married to an American serviceman she held her reception in that one room and invited the woman and her husband from upstairs down for a drink. This had become the bedroom for Myerson and her husband.

To uncover that charming episode in the history of her house took Myerson months of hard labour, assisted by her husband and, occasionally her children. The directories and a whole variety of printed sources were valuable but not enough for what she wanted. The Myersons sent out hundreds of letters in their determination to follow the footprints of those who had at some time in their lives occupied one or more of the rooms in their house.

She adopted a two-pronged approach, researching the census returns and other official documents for the earliest occupants, and working backwards for those who had lived in her house more recently and might still be alive. Fortunately for her, the people from whom she and her husband bought the house were easy to find and only too pleased to recall their days in their Clapham home. But that was only a start.

Though she went way beyond what most of us would attempt – she was writing a book about her research after all – Julie Myerson made use of every available archive which she could find fifteen years ago. Her task would have been much easier today.

In a way what the history of houses through time illustrates is the fact that a home and a house are not quite the same. Mulling over the history of the rectory he bought in the Norfolk countryside, the writer Bill Bryson concluded: 'Houses are really quite odd things. They have almost no universally defining qualities; they can be of practically any shape, incorporate virtually any material, be of almost any size. Yet wherever we go in the world we know houses and recognize domesticity the moment we see them.'

CHAPTER TWO

BRITAIN'S EARLY HOMES

Towns and Villages Before the Georgian Age

There is nothing like a major road improvement scheme to illustrate the layer upon layer of settlements that led over centuries to the building of today's towns and villages. Take, for example, work begun in 2016 to widen the A14 road between Cambridge and Huntingdon, making it three lanes each way at a cost of £1.5 billion. On either side of the road for twenty-three miles quiet countryside was excavated, with quarries dug to provide hard core and sand for cement. An agreement between an international team of two hundred and fifty archaeologists and the road builders turned the A14 into a monumental 'dig'.

Working just ahead of the bulldozers, these 'rescue archaeology' teams identified a lost world of villages that must at one time have hummed with life. Patterns were revealed of wooden post pits, which would have provided the structure for simple thatched homes, some dating to the ninth century. A later village appears to have been deserted when the woodland it needed to survive was annexed by a Norman king. There are no Roman buildings on the A14 route but this had been a Roman road and there were many artefacts as reminders of their four centuries as imperial rulers of this country. Motorway- and road-building schemes, ripping open pages to the past, are always likely to reveal more buried homes than those they bulldoze to improve the flow of traffic.

There is such a rich history in the stories of the villages, towns, and

— { 41 } —

cities that were lived in before the Georgian and Victorian eras when the three terraced houses featured in *A House Through Time* were built that a social and architectural history of what preceded them can be no more than a sketch. The end of Roman England is taken here as the starting point, for this was a cataclysmic event. No town or church or road anything like as well built and maintained as those the Romans left behind appeared in the English landscape for centuries.

The Romans built to last. Wherever they became established as their empire spread they found and quarried stone. This had not been done before in England. Nor had there been any brick-making. The Romans built brick kilns wherever they went. They established reliable water supplies with aqueducts which fed through lead pipes into individual properties. They constructed sewerage systems. Fumes from their fires and under-floor heating were drawn out through clay chimney pots. When Christianity became accepted in the empire, they built stone churches. Roads were paved. Stone walls protected towns.

When their empire began to collapse, the Romans withdrew from England, abandoning their forts and fine stone villas and public buildings. Invaders from tribes in western Europe began to colonize the country, establishing their own kingdoms. They spoke different languages from the Britons and brought with them different cultures, most significantly an entirely different approach to house-building and domesticity. The occupying peoples who became known as the Anglo-Saxons had no interest in Roman towns. Even the finest of them like London and Winchester were left empty, their stone walls protecting nothing except a few grazing cattle. The archaeological evidence is unequivocal: no sign of life for maybe two or more centuries.

In the early Anglo-Saxon period nothing was built with stone or brick: everything was made of wood. There was nothing resembling a Roman villa. The village excavated during the A14 archaeological dig had evidence of forty-seven dwellings built in an apparently random fashion. Often these villages had huts with sunken floors, suggesting they might have had wooden floorboards with straw beneath for insulation. The timber structure would have been clad in either a wicker framework, which would be plastered with mud or clay, or wooden boards. The roof would have been thatched. But there would have been no chimney: the interior would have been very smoky and blackened over time from a central fire on which meat was cooked and which provided warmth in winter. Water would have been drawn from a well or a river or collected in rain tubs.

The structure of these post-Roman homesteads varied according to the traditions of the invaders. In the north where the Vikings invaded they were more likely to be 'longhouses', with people at one end and animals at the other. Most in the Midlands and the south were 'cruck structures', with twin bows of timber fixed at the apex and tied in with crossbeams. But it is fair to say they were all primitive, perhaps similar to the basic huts Britons lived in before the Roman occupation.

The fabric of the Roman towns was left to fall into ruin, but the towns themselves did not disappear. A fairly recent excavation provided the solution to a puzzle about what happened to London when the Romans retreated. Archaeological investigation beneath the modern offices of the square mile of the City found few traces of human occupation between AD 407 and 886. Roman London, a thriving trading port on the Thames, had clearly been abandoned for about four centuries. Yet the Venerable Bede writing in 731 in his *Ecclesiastical History of the English People* referred to a place called Lundenvic which was a vibrant centre of trade. Evidently a new London had been established but there was no record of where. The puzzle was not solved until the 1980s when excavations in Covent Garden revealed a Saxon settlement to the west of the Roman town. There was no doubt this was Bede's Lundenvic, a little up river. It was not until the Saxon King Alfred the Great moved back into the old Roman ruins of London using it as a fortress against Viking invaders that the modern history of the capital began. The abandoned Saxon London was later referred to as Aldwych.

There was a similar pattern in the history of the other Roman towns: abandoned by the new settlers for several centuries they were recolonized in the later Anglo-Saxon period. The tribe of Britons occupying the area of Winchester in Hampshire were the Belgae, who appear to have put up little resistance to the Roman legions who built a market town they called Venta Belgarum. It had streets laid out in a grid pattern and in the third century a wooden stockade was replaced by stone walls. When the Romans left, this vibrant town fell silent. It was not reoccupied at all until the seventh century when Christianity had been adopted by the Anglo-Saxon settlers who built a church in the Roman ruins.

As the Christian faith spread to the Anglo-Saxon kingdoms of Kent, East Anglia, Sussex (south Saxons), Middlesex (middle Saxons) and Wessex (West Saxons), churches and abbeys were built, mostly with stone pillaged from Roman ruins. It is likely that some royal houses were built with Roman bricks and stone. In his history of Alfred the Great, who became King of Wessex in 871, Bishop Asser wrote: 'What shall I say of the cities and towns he restored, and of others which he built where none had been before? Of the buildings marvellously wrought with gold and silver under his direction? Of the royal halls and chambers, wonderfully built of stone and of wood at his command? Of royal vills [villas] made of masonry removed from the old sites and most admirably rebuilt in more suitable places by the king's order?'

Alfred, crowned when he was just twenty-one years old, became a modernizer, reoccupying Roman Winchester (the Saxons called it Venta Ceaster which was later corrupted to the modern name), reinforcing its defences and eventually taking his resistance to the Viking invaders in London. After an incursion of a few years with the Dane King Cnut the Great, the long era of Anglo-Saxon rule came to an end with the defeat of the last king, Harold, at the Battle of Hastings in 1066.

William the Conqueror imposed his own Norman administration on that already in place: the shires and boroughs that in the later Anglo-Saxon period had marked out the regions of the country. Faced with a hostile population the Normans were ruthless in suppressing dissent and set about building castles wherever they came across an Anglo-Saxon settlement. Many of these were made of timber at first and rebuilt in stone. After twenty years of occupation they set about making an inventory of their newly acquired territory. Their findings were recorded in two volumes which became known, with a touch of satire, as the Domesday Book.

It is not complete in its description of England in this early Norman period as there are odd omissions. No mention of London, for example. But the Domesday Book is fascinating in its detail nonetheless. The basic unit is the manor, an administrative unit introduced by the Normans, which might have as its overlord a bishop or a monastery or a wealthy landowner. Some manors were no more than a couple of farms, others extended over large areas. All land was owned ultimately by the king, who farmed it out in allocations to tenants-in-chief who were obliged in turn to equip knights or make cash payments for the defence of the realm. Nobles who held land had the same obligation as tenants-in-chief.

Although the Normans superimposed their baronial political system on Anglo-Saxon England, the Domesday Book is essentially a record of what the country looked like in terms of wealth and social structure when they first invaded. A surprising number of 'towns' are recorded in a landscape that is still predominantly rural. Alfred the Great had encouraged the building of fortified settlements with ramparts and sometimes stone walls with material taken from Roman ruins. These were called burhs, later boroughs, around which markets developed. In the Domesday Book there are a hundred and twelve burhs recorded, their size roughly gauged by the number of burgesses, who were the tradespeople with a status above that of peasants and often had some responsibilities for the administration of their towns.

It has been argued that these towns recorded in the Domesday Book represented the true beginnings of urban life in post-Roman England. They became important centres for trades and industry; some reached a significant size with populations of four to five thousand. Specialist guilds were being formed by weavers and leatherworkers and other trades. Burgesses could buy and sell property once it had been held without any conflict for a year and a day. They lived in houses built along the high street, sometimes with gardens. These might be a little larger than peasant houses at the time and would generally be built of timber, but they would lack chimneys and glass windows – these improvements were some way away.

The burhs were set in a landscape which was extensively cultivated and farmed. Timber was important for building and for fuel, but by the time of the Domesday Book there was practically no wildwood left in England. The leading historian of woodlands, the late Oliver Rackham, thought half the wildwood had gone by 500 BC. Clearance, chiefly to turn woods into farmland, had been going on since the Iron Age. By the time of the Domesday Book every copse or stretch of forest was owned by someone. England was intensively farmed with 35 per cent of the land arable, 25 per cent pasture and meadow, and 15 per cent woodland, which was valuable not only for fuel but also for building materials and for the hunting of game. The remaining 25 per cent was non-agricultural land: wild heaths and mountains, and villages and small towns. Small oaks were felled for peasant houses, but some timber for larger buildings had to be imported from Europe.

Woodland cover continued to shrink with a rising population. Then in 1348 there was an abrupt halt and it was centuries before tree-felling resumed on any scale. This year brought a great hiatus in medieval history: the outbreak of bubonic plague, which devastated the population and wiped out hundreds of villages. The calamity which killed untold thousands nevertheless brought prosperity for the survivors.

Before plague struck it is thought fifteen acres was enough land to feed a family, and that few holdings exceeded that in the first half of the fourteenth century. After what became known as the Black Death peasant landholdings doubled in size, radically altering the rural economy. With more land there might be a surplus to sell at the market. A shortage of labour meant that peasants could demand cash for their labour. With a better standard of living the peasant population – a catch-all term for several different classes of rural farmers and workmen – were able to embark on what might be called home improvements.

The received wisdom until recently was that the only houses that would have survived this period after the years of plague were those of the wealthiest. Architectural historians referred to what they called the 'vernacular threshold', the point in time when the most modest peasant houses were built to last, which they assumed would be some time in the seventeenth century. But a recent study of a hundred and twenty medieval houses in the Midlands and southern England found that there were so many that they could not all have been lived in by wealthy people. Timbers from eighty-three of the houses showed they were built between 1260 and the 1550s.

The houses examined in this study funded by the Leverhulme Trust were of the cruck design but with three bays, making them much roomier than earlier 'cottages'. There were no chimneys and they were all single-storey. A great deal of timber went into the building of these superior peasant houses. It was calculated that a hundred and eleven trees were used to build one of them at Mapledurham in Oxfordshire. Six were from large branching trees, thirty from medium-sized woodland trees, and seventy-five from young trees with a girth of six inches. Not all the timber was sourced locally: some was bought in the market. The construction was probably a joint effort of the peasant whose family was to occupy it, digging foundations and preparing the site, and specialist craftsmen such as carpenters.

The era following the Black Death saw rebuilding of houses, although a great many were abandoned as plague swept across the country. Unless carefully maintained these wooden structures quickly rotted. It is thought that about half a million houses became ruins between 1350 and 1500. Peasants could be fined for not keeping their houses in good repair or for knocking buildings down. Many went into rent arrears. So it was a mixed picture of dereliction and improvement.

In the early days of Norman rule the manor houses were not necessarily very grand, as some were to become much later. Many were fortified and surrounded by a moat, but the lord of the manor had to get the king's permission to put up one of these castellated buildings as they could represent a challenge to his authority. As well as a display of conspicuous consumption the manor house had an administrative function. In its great hall rents would be collected and manorial courts held. The poor might be fed at the door but the clergy, lawyers and pilgrims would be received at the invitation of the lord.

An innovation which was to transform the nature of housing up to the present century was pioneered in the great houses of the Middle Ages: the fireplace with a chimney to expel the smoke and fumes. Royalty were the first to discover the great convenience of the chimney. In 1229 Henry III had a new chimney installed in the great chamber at Havering Palace, in Essex. At about the same time there were chimneys in Winchester; Windsor had a chimney in 1237 which required repair. At Oxford University in 1305 lectures were given in a building named Chimney Hall. London taverns were installing chimneys as early as the 1300s and some shops too adopted the new and revolutionary form of heating. The provision of fireplace and chimney became an act of benevolence when they were introduced to almshouses and infirmaries. A chimney was constructed in a hospital in Newcastle-upon-Tyne in 1380.

The social consequences of the adoption of chimneys cannot be over-estimated. As the technology was refined it enabled the development of small rooms away from the great hall which could be heated. This gave rise to a privacy which had been impossible with the single great hall. It enabled the building of upper storeys which were not shrouded in suffocating smoke. As can be imagined, the possibility of a fire to

Gathering around a medieval fireplace, complete with a stork's nest on top of the chimney, c. 1338–1344.

warm the bedroom transformed the pleasure of going to bed in winter. Bedrooms became cherished rooms. In time there might be a multiplicity of rooms each with its own fireplace: offices, workshops, studies. Monks who had to give up writing in the winter could, with the introduction of a fireplace with chimney, continue working in the coldest weather.

Naturally the lords of the manor had to have chimneys, which began to change the relationship between them and those they had mingled with in the great hall. They could now dine alone in a private chamber and many chose to do so. In his poem *Piers Plowman*, written at the end of the fourteenth century, William Langland captured the sense of resentment this spurning of communal living caused those excluded:

> Woe is in the hall in all times and seasons
> When there neither lord nor lady likes to linger
> Now each rich man has a rule to eat in secret
> In a private parlour, for poor folks' comfort
> In a chamber with a chimney, perhaps and leave the chief assembly
> Which was made for men to have meat and meals in

The chimney became a status symbol when it was still relatively rare, with early examples built up like little turrets rising well above the roof.

The place of the chimney was sometimes at one or both ends of a building and sometimes arranged centrally. Over time a great many houses and later cottages which had been built without chimneys had them added on to the outside.

In his *Description of Elizabethan England* the clergyman William Harrison wrote:

> There are old men yet dwelling in the village where I remain which have noted three things to be marvellously altered in England within their sound remembrance. One is the multitude of chimneys lately erected, whereas in their young days there were not above two or three, if so many, in most uplandish towns of the realm (the religious houses and manor places of their lords always excepted, and peradventure some great parsonages), but each one made his fire against a reredos [a screen] in the hall, where he dined and dressed [cooked] his meat.

When the fuel for the fire was wood the fireplace was usually quite large. Kitchen fires could be cavernous with a grate for burning large logs, sometimes called an inglenook fireplace, framed by a heavy oak beam ('ingle' was the Old English for fire, and 'nook' a corner). In time the fireplace became a popular feature of the fashionable house and the design of chimneys more sophisticated.

Although fires with chimneys were probably less likely to set fire to a thatched roof than those set in the centre of a room, if the chimneys were fashioned from wood or plaster they were certainly a hazard. The first cottage chimneys were very crude, as brick was a very rare and expensive commodity. The art of brick-making had been lost when the Romans left and was not reintroduced until the fourteenth century. Long, thin bricks salvaged from Roman ruins were the first used in the revival of brick buildings. But the art spread from Italy to Germany and finally to eastern England. By the start of the reign of the Tudors in 1485 brick-making had become skilful, though indigenous English bricks tended at first to be uneven. As the industry became established brickwork became more than a practical alternative to timber and wattle-and-daub or stone: it had a decorative quality and it was a mark of status.

The classic and much imitated 'Tudor' style of building was 'half-timbered', that is to say with the main beams of the structure showing with an infill of bricks. By over-baking some bricks a variety of colours could be produced that were used to create attractive patterns. Many buildings which appeared to be brick-built were just wattle and daub structures with brick-like tiles pinned on as a kind of cladding.

If windows had had any covering before the Tudor period it was not glass but thin-cut animal horn, which let in some light while keeping out wind and rain. In the seventeenth century glass windows were still a luxury but the better class of house had some luxuries: fireplaces, separate rooms for eating, sleeping and cooking, brick walls or a brick facade, and glass windows. These were certainly regarded as luxuries for they were all taxed at one time or another. A Hearth Tax introduced in 1662 (repealed in 1689) charged two shillings a year for each fireplace in houses valued at twenty shillings rental. There was a Window Tax introduced in 1696 which was levied on houses with more than ten windows. It is said that this tax, which was very unpopular, gave rise to the phrase 'daylight robbery'. Much later, in 1784, a tax was levied on bricks at the rate of two shillings and sixpence per thousand. In response the manufacturers made larger bricks, the government countering with an act determining the allowable size of bricks.

By the fifteenth century there were a great many restrictions in London and other towns on the materials that could be used for building, most of them relating to the danger of fire in the towns. As early as 1212 thatched roofs were banned in London after a disastrous fire which killed about a thousand people, a large part of the population. Owners of houses with roofs of reeds and rushes were given eight days to plaster them over or their homes would be demolished. Thatch was plentiful and cheap so many refused to abide by the law and repeated attempts were made to persuade householders to replace straw with tiles. Thatched roofs were banned in Salisbury in 1431 and thatch and timber chimneys were banned in Worcester in 1467.

After the years of plague in the fourteenth century, the population was rising and towns were growing. From the days of the arrival of Christianity, the Church, especially the monasteries, had played an important part in the lives of all social classes. Every town and the countryside around was familiar with monks and friars and nuns who in their monasteries and friaries and nunneries provided hospitality for travellers, charity for the poor, education, and patronage of music. Some monasteries were major landowners. There were an estimated 900 'religious houses' in England when Henry VIII, in dispute with the Catholic Church, began to close them down. Between 1536 and 1541 the land and buildings they owned were confiscated and sold off to those who could afford it, creating, some historians say, a whole new class of 'gentry', which included Oliver Cromwell's father. In contrast to the new landed wealth was a huge increase in landless vagrants who had relied on the monasteries for food and sometimes lodging.

There is no agreement amongst historians about the wider repercussions of this massive transfer in land ownership on house-building and the growth of towns. What is not disputed is the fact that the poorest lost the charity and succour of the monasteries, friaries, and nunneries. Along country roads from villages and towns there were vagrants with nowhere to seek help. Sometimes they were regarded as a threat, a disinherited body of people who might at any time become violent. One by one parishes and towns began to open up what they called workhouses to accommodate the destitute. The earliest have been recorded from the 1630s, prompted by an Act of the Relief of the Poor in 1601 which made parishes responsible for looking after their own destitute men and women. A poor rate was levied, the precursor of council tax. At first most of the grants of money, food, and fuel were made as what was called 'out-relief', which allowed people to stay in their own homes, such as they were, and live as paupers. But the workhouse gradually evolved as a cheaper alternative for the parish which also provided some cheap labour.

The workhouses of the sixteenth and early seventeenth centuries were not purpose-built for the most part but buildings adopted and adapted. Not all were regarded with fear and loathing by the indigenous poor, certainly not in the way the first workhouses of the Victorian New Poor Law of 1834 were. But in both villages and urban parishes the workhouse became a feature and a reminder that it was not only decorative architecture which was worthy of attention.

What then were the repercussions of the abolition of the religious houses for those who were moneyed? Did it make estate management more efficient and hasten the oncoming of a new industrial society? It must have increased that class of gentry who could afford to buy land and develop it at a time when speculative house-building was growing in importance. Speculative builders constructed homes not for a client, but in the hope that they could find a buyer or a tenant once the home had been completed. The lure of profits from house-building was summed up neatly in a Victorian jingle published in the *Handbook of House and Property*:

> The richest crop for any field
> Is a crop of bricks for it to yield
> The richest crop that it can grow
> Is a crop of houses in a row.

There was nothing entirely new about making money out of the promotion of housing developments. Landowners in the thirteenth century attempted to promote the growth of towns by making available plots of land on the market square for buildings to rent. In order to get as many properties on such a limited site, houses, and in some cases shops, were confined to narrow plots, their gable ends facing the street and extending a long way back. It was an arrangement known as burgage, promoted by the landowner to increase his wealth. Stepping through the door of a late medieval or Tudor town house, you might first come across a shop or workshop. Behind would be a hall, often the full height of the house, with a central fire and smoke escaping through the roof. Later in the Tudor period, chimneys, floors, and separate spaces were added, along with the distinctive feature of jetties or upper storeys that extended beyond the dimensions of the floor below.

A very different and more haphazard form of speculation arose in the sixteenth century when rising population put pressure on the land available on the fringes of towns. The subsequent century saw what has been described as an 'urban renaissance' as provincial towns grew in wealth and stature and developed a sense of urban pride. There was a kind of league table of the largest and wealthiest towns, excepting of course London, which was unassailable in size and importance. The demographer Anthony Wrigley has set out the ups and downs in the urban league at intervals between 1520 and 1801. In that period England was becoming less rural and more urban, the proportion of the

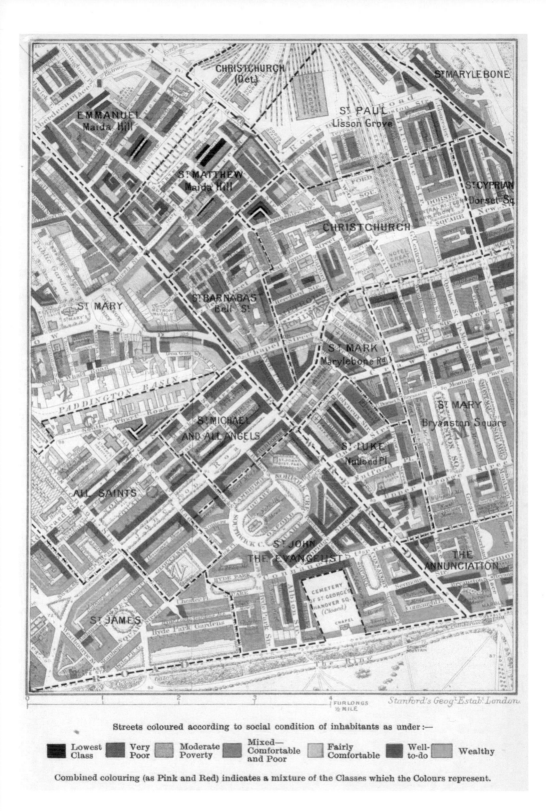

Streets coloured according to social condition of inhabitants as under :—

Lowest Class | Very Poor | Moderate Poverty | Mixed—Comfortable and Poor | Fairly Comfortable | Well-to-do | Wealthy

Combined colouring (as Pink and Red) indicates a mixture of the Classes which the Colours represent.

The colour-coded maps produced by Charles Booth in the 1880s and 1890s show where the rich and poor lived in London's streets, here in the area of Paddington and Marylebone.

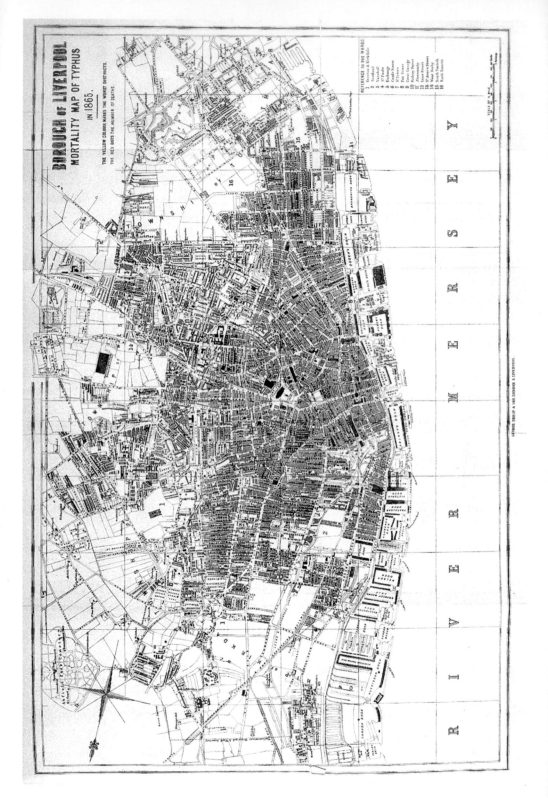

The 1865 Mortality Map of Typhus reveals the extent of the typhus epidemic in Liverpool, a year before cholera killed one of 62 Falkner Street's residents.

Top: A Bristol bomb plot map shows the extent of bombing during the Second World War.

Above: Nicholas Barbon, the ruthless property speculator and builder of terraced houses in London.

Above: A rare survival of a cruck-framed house in Lichfield, Staffordshire. The building dates back to the late fifteenth century and was originally two cottages before it was restored in 1971.

Above: Inigo Jones, the famed seventeenth-century architect of Covent Garden.

Right: John Kerle Haberfield, Mayor of Bristol and resident of 10 Guinea Street.

Below: Grand terraces surround the newly-designed piazza of Covent Garden, London, 1737.

Above: Royal York Crescent in Clifton, Bristol was the suburban home of John Kerle Haberfield in the 1850s.

Right: Georgian homes of all types featured sturdy railings to deter burglars. Note the bricked-up window designed to avoid the Window Tax, which was eventually repealed in 1851.

Above: Laird's new shipyard in Liverpool, 1857. By the nineteenth century, Liverpool had become a major shipping manufacturer and port.

Left: Traditional terraced brick houses in Dublin, Ireland.

Below: An outside privy situated in the courtyard of one of the reconstructed back-to-back houses in Birmingham.

Left: *Devil's Acre in Westminster* by Gustave Doré. The area near Westminster Abbey in London was one of the capital's worst slums.

Below: Saltaire near Bradford in West Yorkshire. Built from the 1850s onwards, the model village encompassed textile mills, public buildings, and houses for workers.

The Peabody Wild Street estate in Drury Lane, London in the early 1900s (above) and in 2014 (below). The estate was opened in 1882 as part of Peabody's efforts to clear London's slums.

population living in towns rising from just over 5 per cent to 27 per cent. The leading towns grew at different speeds according to the source of their wealth.

According to Wrigley, in 1520 the top six (excluding London) were Norwich, Bristol, York, Salisbury, Exeter, and Colchester. In 1600 promotion and relegation had Norwich still top, followed by York, Bristol, Newcastle, Exeter, and Plymouth. It was the coal Newcastle sent to London that was the basis of its wealth in this period. In 1670 Norwich remained top, followed by Bristol, York, Newcastle, Colchester, and Exeter. In 1700 Bristol and Newcastle were second and third, but Liverpool was still way down the league. By 1750 Bristol was the second largest city in England, Newcastle third, and Liverpool fifth and by 1801 Manchester, Liverpool, Birmingham and Bristol took the first four places. Newcastle had slipped to eighth.

It was not just a growth in population that put these towns on the map. They were developing an urban culture increasingly based on leisure and enjoyment. Catering for the tastes of an emerging middle class were a growing number of craftsmen: jewellers, watch- and clock-makers, gunsmiths, and wrought-iron workers. The towns were smartened up with better paving and more brick-built houses. From the 1690s, more were getting their first piped water supplies. The Parliamentary Act creating the Bristol Waterworks Company was passed in 1696 with supplies fed from a reservoir at Barton Hill through hollow elm-tree pipes into the town. Newcastle-upon-Tyne had a limited water supply in 1698 taken directly from the Tyne and available just one day a week to a limited number of homes. Liverpool had to wait longer, relying on deliveries by cart from a single well in the seventeenth century.

The emerging urban culture in the eighteenth century encouraged the development of a distinct kind of urban architecture, emphasizing the street as an entity lined with houses, built increasingly in brick with little ornamentation. Landowners sought to increase their fortunes by leasing land for building houses 'all in a row' with a kind of planned uniformity. The standard of building could vary a good deal according to the skills of the craftsmen who put up the housing, all of it as a speculative investment. But who were the speculators?

According the historian William C. Baer, while historians have carefully monitored the rise in population of towns in the eighteenth century and later they have not asked how all these townsfolk were housed. His study of London suggests that the city builders were a motley crew of craftsmen some of whom were able to make a fortune. Baer writes: 'In this regard, London did not just spontaneously "grow" to meet all this housing need; it expanded after forethought and deliberate action by a great many men and women acting as speculators and building projectors.'

There was no guild of builder-developers, just companies of carpenters, bricklayers, joiners, paint-stainers, tilers, glazers, and so on. Detective work was required to discover who the speculators might be. Some publications giving advice to builders appeared in the last decades of the sixteenth century. And there are records of builders from court cases and in particular the prosecution of those who tried to build illegally, which was more often than not the case, for in Elizabethan and Stuart London edicts forbade unauthorized housing developments.

It was not all about new building. The rickety state of much of London's housing meant that it needed constant repair, and many an ancient property was patched up and extended. James I complained of builders putting in staircases, chimneys, brick walls and dormers, 'knitting and fastening together the sayd new Additions unto the old . . . whereby old deformities is only continued but is increased.' A lot of houses became, according to another commentator, the dwellings of 'rascality' before disintegrating entirely into a heap of overgrown rubble.

There was no shortage of work for builders shoring up London's housing. But who were the speculators building for? Most of those arriving in London from the countryside and creating the rising demand for housing were young men and women with little money. Many found a bed in alehouses or slums but the luckiest found work where a master gave them a roof over their heads. They could in time save the money to look for their own place. The speculator might be anyone who was brave enough to gamble their money.

One of the most spectacularly successful builders in London was an illiterate tailor from Taunton in Somerset called Robert Baker. Born in 1578 or 1579 Baker had little or no schooling when he began work apprenticed to a tailor. As a young man he decided to make his way to London to see if he could set up shop in a favourable area. He took to making the fashionable pleated collars that men wore called piccadills and as business boomed he employed journeyman tailors, many from his home county. He married a woman who appears to have had an interest in his business and they prospered together.

In time Baker sold a cottage he had owned in Taunton and built himself a house more or less where Great Windmill Street is in London's Soho today. It was nicknamed Piccadilly Hall. He then acquired more land and began to put up houses for rent. As his wealth increased he no longer described himself as a tailor: he had become a gentleman. He appears to have avoided prosecution for building on the edge of built-up London despite the edicts prohibiting development or the dividing up of properties into tenements.

London commanded the English economy in the early seventeenth century, handling the lion's share of imports and exports through its livery companies which controlled many trades. By 1660 it had become, in effect, two great centres of wealth on the north bank of the Thames: the City itself, which had a considerable degree of self-government, and Westminster, the royal and political capital. For most of the merchant class London was home. For the gentry and aristocratic Members of Parliament Westminster was a London base: their homes were on their country estates. The poorer artisans set up shop away from City regulations. By 1660 these outlying districts beyond the city boundaries were considerable, though exactly what the population was it is not possible to say. It was still the case then that the wealthiest, like the diarist Samuel Pepys, lived within the City, and the poorest outside it.

The population of London increased without pause for much of the seventeenth century. This increase was entirely due to the arrival of newcomers – immigration – as during that period, and for long afterwards, more Londoners died every year than were born. The historical demographer Anthony Wrigley has calculated that up to eight thousand newcomers would be needed each year to compensate for the shortfall of 'natural increase' (births over deaths) and account for the rising population. This pattern of population growth continued well into the eighteenth century, with death and disease ever present.

In 1665 bubonic plague returned to London and other cities in England. Buboes, painful swellings, appeared in the lymph nodes of the armpits, neck and groin, and turned black when they haemorrhaged under the skin. It is thought that up to 15 per cent of the population died, with those living in slum conditions in the suburbs – a derogatory term in Elizabethan and Stuart England – hardest hit. Those who could leave town did so until the plague had abated. It did return in 1666 but in a milder form.

The summer of 1666 was very hot and dry. Water levels in the Thames and its tributaries were low. Though there had been repeated attempts to get the City to enforce regulations on building materials, a very large number of houses and livery halls were constructed largely of timber. The streets were very narrow with overhanging upper storeys. Traffic congestion as the number of wagons increased was appalling. Packed into this highly flammable, densely populated urban mass were huge stores of combustibles: tar, spirits, hay, sugar, and so on. Fires were frequent and sometimes very destructive. Firefighting was a community responsibility: buckets, ladders, and hooks for pulling away burning timbers were to be kept by livery companies and householders.

A fire that took hold in the home of the baker Thomas Farriner (or Faryner) in Pudding Lane in the early hours of 2 September 1666 should have been controllable. The Lord Mayor, Sir Thomas Bloodworth, notoriously dismissed it as minor when called to inspect the burning building. He is reputed to have exclaimed: 'A woman could piss it out.' But a strong east wind fanned the flames and the fire began to spread with alarming speed. With no central command, the reaction of the majority of those whose houses and businesses were affected was to get their possessions out and make a run for it. As the flames spread there was an exodus from the centre of the conflagration. It was not until Pepys took the news to Charles II that a concerted effort was made to control the fire, by which time the only way to stop it was by the creation of fire breaks. Buildings had to be blown up with gunpowder or pulled down.

After five days, when the fire was finally halted, a vast area north of the Thames, from the Tower in the east to the Temple in the west, was smouldering ruins. This had been the second largest (after Paris) and wealthiest city in Europe. The Great Plague had decimated the population; now the Great Fire had razed most of the core of the City to the ground.

There were fears, in the immediate aftermath, that London was finished. Some merchants did move away for good, setting up in

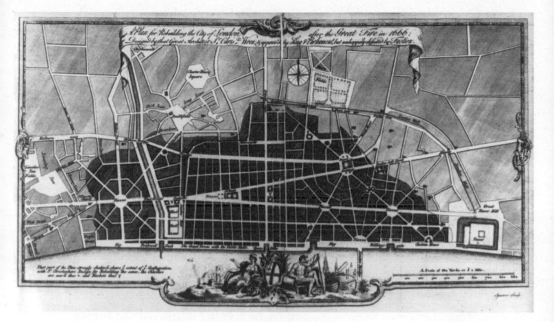

Sir Christopher Wren's proposed plan for rebuilding the City of London after the Great Fire, with broad boulevards and grand piazzas.

other ports, such as Liverpool. Refugees from the fire – estimates vary between eighty thousand and two hundred thousand made homeless – camped out in Moorfields and other parts of the rural hinterland of London. Some will have returned to their homes in the countryside, others crammed into the suburbs that escaped the fire. The king ordered temporary markets to be opened in Islington and other outlying districts. A nationwide charitable appeal was launched.

Remarkably the City carried on in the ruins, rebuilding to new and stringent rules but rejecting grandiose schemes so that much of the old road pattern stayed the same. To regulate the rebuilding of houses and to minimize the risk of fire, an Act for the Rebuilding of the City of London was passed in 1667. It ruled that buildings should be constructed in brick, and stipulated wall thicknesses and floor heights, as well as specifications for sash windows. The Act also specified that four different models or types of house should be built, each based on the number of floors and location on the street. The smallest was two storeys with cellar and garret, to be located in side streets and lanes, while the largest was for 'Mansion houses, for Citizens, or other Persons of extraordinary Quality' of four storeys and was not to be built close to the street, with the other two types in between. The internal layout of the four models was similar, only differing in the size of the rooms, and was intended to maximize the space inside the house. The 1667 Act also brought in stipulations regarding the width of streets (and the appropriate height of house that could be built on the appropriate width of street), as well as early regulations regarding drainage, street cleaning, paving, and gutters on houses. Another key element was the appointment of the first building surveyors, who would oversee and monitor construction. In effect, the 1667 Act created the design of the domestic urban house that would be adopted across London and would influence the building of terraces in other towns.

Terraces, rows of houses put up as one block, had been built in London since the fourteenth century. In the 1630s the fourth Earl of Bedford had employed the king's favoured architect Inigo Jones to build the three grand terraces that surrounded the piazza of Covent Garden, part of the earl's London estate. All building in London then required royal consent and the earl had to seek special dispensation to build at Covent Garden. The licence he obtained, at a cost of £2,000, stipulated that he construct 'houses and buildings fit for the habitations of gentlemen and men of ability'. The early residents were for the most part exactly that, but the raucous market at the centre of the piazza undermined the respectability of the area and fought against the sense of tranquil order that Inigo Jones's Italian Renaissance-style facades sought to evoke. Strictly speaking the houses at Covent Garden were not terraced homes, rather they were arranged into flats. Yet from the exterior they gave the appearance of what was to become the classic terrace.

The 1667 Act was only applicable to the City of London, but it was soon adopted elsewhere in London and then other parts of the country. When other cities suffered fire damage or were undertaking new building, the London rebuilding act was often quoted or a new act for that town was introduced, often in an attempt to follow the fashionable tastes established in London. Further building acts followed during the early eighteenth century, including in 1707 and 1709, which added more stipulations and regulations for the construction of new houses, including the use of timber and the distance of the window frame from the external brickwork. The medieval and Tudor timber-framed houses that had dominated across the country for hundreds of years were on

12 Buckingham Street, central London, constructed under the direction of Nicholas Barbon and occupied at different times by diarists Samuel Pepys and John Evelyn.

the way out: the archetypal brick terrace house would dominate for the next two centuries.

The rebuilding programme in London provided an opportunity for the most unscrupulous property speculator of the last decades of the seventeenth century, Nicholas Barbon. Born in 1637 he was the son of a London leather merchant and politician, Praisegod Barbon, who gave him the baptismal name of If-Jesus-Christ-had-not-died-for-thee-thou-hadst-been-damned. He was damned anyway by the many people he infuriated with his rampant capitalism. Barbon studied medicine at Leiden and Utrecht, the leading universities of the day, and was admitted to the College of Physicians in London in 1664. However, he recognized that there was profit to be made from the urgent need to re-build London after the Great Fire. His first venture was in 1680 when he founded the insurance office for houses, which offered fire insurance for up to five thousand properties in London and is thought to be the first such company in the world.

Barbon had seen the loss of buildings in the Great Fire and recognized the need for some kind of protection for property owners. He introduced fire marks on houses that had been insured and retained 'watermen', who wore livery and badges like prototype firefighters. He was involved in the redevelopment of the Strand, which linked the City and Westminster. He built houses in Bloomsbury, which was being laid out as an elegant square. Barbon bypassed or simply ignored the surviving legislation that had acted as a brake upon new construction. He was unconcerned about the opinion of the crown and scorned the majority of city dwellers, which led to clashes that were sometimes violent. When he tried to build on Red Lion Fields without permission from the lawyers who worked there his men were beaten off in a pitched battle.

Barbon was a flashy dresser and impervious to criticism according to his contemporaries, who called him a knave and a rogue. His speculations were often reckless and he got into debt and when he died on 6 February 1699 he had nothing to his name. But he was responsible for some fine houses which survive today, notably York Buildings between the Strand and the River Thames. For a time both Samuel Pepys and John Evelyn lived in a Barbon terraced house in Buckingham Street. The building is of course pre-Georgian but the future is clearly there in its design and the way it was put up by the arch-speculator of a previous age.

What Barbon taught future developers of town housing was that when building rows of houses shoulder to shoulder, as it were, with narrow frontages, in other words 'terraces', the greatest returns could be made by leasing each plot to a builder. It was a formula that was used to put up acre upon acre of mean houses in mining towns as well as elegant town houses like those featured in *A House Through Time*. In a sense the terrace defined the Georgian era and it remains instantly recognizable today where the eighteenth-century streets survive.

CHAPTER THREE

THE GEORGIAN HOME

The Birth of the Modern City

The hundreds of thousands of elegant brick, stone, and stucco-fronted Georgian homes that today are scattered across Britain, from Bath to Bristol, Glasgow to Liverpool, are the shared obsession of two generations who lived centuries apart. To 'them', members of the Georgian middle classes, such properties represented access to independence, maturity, and respectability. No young man could fully become a gentleman until he first became master of his own home. His wife, likewise, would remain only a wife until she was established as the mistress of their marital abode; the bearer of a jangling bundle of keys, the responsibility for domestic security set on her shoulders. The homes they left behind were, to 'them', status symbols, sanctuaries, and investments. To 'us', the Britons of the early twenty-first century, those same properties have become the focus for a strange fixation, one that sometimes bemuses foreign visitors. Modern Britain has become thoroughly enchanted by a highly seductive and pervasive 'National Trust' image of the eighteenth-century home.

The notion that within living memory many such houses, in some districts of some cities, were regarded as almost worthless, and that many thousands were demolished to make way for motorways and modern housing schemes, is today difficult to believe. We see things very differently now. The demolition and destruction has been halted and the decades of decline that preceded them are over. Our Georgian spa towns and the surviving Georgian quarters of our larger cities have become the flames to which millions of tourists are drawn. Many of the homes within them have been restored to within an inch of their life, the districts in which they stand largely gentrified – with both positive and negative consequences. Even for the most cynical the charm of these districts is difficult to wholly dismiss. But Georgian homes are more than features within our built heritage. They are also portals through which we can explore the history of the Georgian age and the lives that millions of our ancestors lived; both as wealthy residents of those homes, and as the servants who worked below stairs and slept in tiny attics. They were brought into existence by the great forces that made the British eighteenth century such a dynamic and radical age and their exterior appearance and interior features speak to other elements of that remarkable era.

The age of the Georgian kings, from 1714 to 1837, which includes the Regency period (c. 1810–30), was as much an era of radical transformation as the post-war decades of redevelopment and urban planning. The population of Britain grew from five million at the beginning of the eighteenth century to almost nine million by the century's close and to fourteen million by the 1830s. By the 1780s the population was increasing 10 per cent each decade, despite migration to the colonies. The birth rate in England between 1780 and 1820 was around 36.8 births per thousand, more than three times the current UK birth rate of 11.1 per thousand. Those birth rates fed through into the population increases of the Georgian period despite appalling levels of child mortality. The ubiquity of child mortality throughout the eighteenth and nineteenth centuries, among both rich and poor, is amply demonstrated by the many stories that involve the loss of young children among the families who lived in the houses featured in *A House Through Time*. The eighteenth-century inhabitants of 10 Guinea Street, built four years before the start of the Georgian era, were regularly forced to confront the realities of child mortality.

The increases in the nation's population were accompanied by equally profound changes in its distribution. Urbanization, the vast and unprecedented movement of huge numbers from the countryside to the towns and cities, was among the greatest transformations in this transformative age. By modern standards eighteenth-century cities were tiny, but to the eighteenth-century mind London was a megalopolis, the 'monster city', as it was called. From around 575,000 inhabitants in 1700 the capital increased to around 1 million by the end of the century, making it certainly the largest city in Europe and one of the biggest in the world – only Beijing and Edo (modern Tokyo) were comparably colossal. Paris over the same period grew only by a few tens of thousands. It continued into the nineteenth century: Manchester went from a market town with a population of around 10,000 at the end of the eighteenth century to an industrial city of around 89,000. Its population doubled between 1801 and the 1820s and then doubled again by 1851, reaching about 400,000. These population figures for the size of Britain's eighteenth- and nineteenth-century towns and cities are estimates because no calculations were made at the time. A bill to determine the size of population, through registering births, deaths, and marriages, was rejected by parliament in 1753, largely on grounds of cost and fears that a census could be used to make the collection of taxes more efficient or to organize conscription into the army. A successful census bill (the Population Act) was not passed into law until 1800; the first modern census was not taken until 1841.

Whatever their actual size it is clear that what accounted for the growth was above all migration. Both the capital and Britain's industrial cities became crowded with migrants from the British countryside but also with immigrants and emigres from across Europe and the growing empire. Daily life within the cities was profoundly dislocated and atomized when compared to the rural lives most of the migrants had left behind. Cities concentrated the poor and the rich together and imposed upon them new and impersonal modes of life. The city increased opportunity, but it also heightened competition and increased awareness of the stark inequalities of the age. As the rural dispossessed became the urban poor they were also made starkly aware of what they did not have and would never possess. While London was to some degree residentially segregated – the wealthy West End and the poorer East End – there and elsewhere the rich and poor intermingled in a way that laid bare the great scale of wealth, from aristocrat to pauper.

Behind this demographic transformation lay a revolution. At times the Victorian era is imagined as being synonymous and coterminous

with the industrial revolution. The two do partially overlap but the forces of transformation that shaped life in Queen Victoria's Britain began in the reigns of her Georgian predecessors many decades before she came to the throne. Historians struggle – with good reason – to

Built by Richard Arkwright, Cromford Mill was the first modern factory.

attach fixed dates to such a complex phenomenon. Yet many scholars consider the 1760s, when George III was king, as the decade in which the first stirrings of the industrial revolution began, although many of the great changes that we now associate with the rise of industry and the industrial city had their roots in even earlier decades, and many of the effects of industrialization were not truly felt until well into the nineteenth century. If, as well as an approximate start date, the age of the factory can be said to have a point of origin, one strong contender for that title would be Cromford in Derbyshire. There, in 1771, Richard Arkwright opened a cotton mill in which yarn was spun on his new water frame. This was a significant step towards the automation of a slow and labour-intensive industry. Cromford Mill, like many of the early factories, was built in a rural setting, near a fast-flowing river whose waters were harvested to drive the machinery. The invention and slow refinement of the steam engine, however, allowed factories to be built in cities, closer to available pools of labour. Steam power enabled the factory and the city to come together and spawned the industrial city – a wholly new phenomenon in human history. By the middle of the nineteenth century Britain was the first society in which the majority of people lived in cities. It was not until around 2008 that the world population passed the same milestone.

Urbanization was driven by pull factors, such as the availability of comparatively well-paid work in the expanding cities, but there were also profound push factors in operation. The enclosure of the countryside had begun long before the Georgian age but it accelerated in the eighteenth century, undermining traditional rights and old modes of life as common lands were amalgamated into larger and larger farms. Between 1740 and 1810 Parliament enacted a series of 'Inclosure Bills', over four thousand of them, that brought millions of acres under private control; in 1801 the Inclosure Consolidation Act streamlined and accelerated the process. Enclosure and the coming of the factory brought new concentrations of workers to the cities and generated wealth among the expanding middle classes. Both forces were reflected in how people lived and the homes that were built to house them. Urbanization in the eighteenth and early nineteenth centuries spawned both the elegance of the Georgian squares and terraces and the squalor of the slums that existed alongside them.

In each town, local politics, topography, and economic circumstance determined the pace and nature of its growth. But almost everywhere town and city land was needed to meet an enormous demand for new homes. Those who owned plots within the cities or – more significantly – large rural estates on the urban fringes found themselves well placed to expand their fortunes. Keen to maximize their profits these landowners, and the speculators with whom they worked, focused their attention on building homes for the wealthy, developments that offered the highest potential return on precious urban land. The form these new developments took was most commonly the terrace, a not entirely new innovation, as seen with Inigo Jones's grand terraces in Covent Garden, London, in the previous chapter.

The terrace offered a solution to multiple problems. It allowed for

expensive urban land to be used most efficiently and most profitably; its architectural uniformity allowed for a standardization of materials, features, and ornamentation (what little there was), which helped keep building costs down. Fashionable new districts comprised elegant terraces, with uniform and restrained decoration, offered the prospect of new ways of urban living, in new

Two types of Georgian terrace home, both designed for vertical living on multiple floors.

urban estates that were very often conveniently distant from the noise and pollution of the older parts of the cities and the pollution of the growing industries. The march of the Georgian terrace involved not just the annexation of green fields on the edges of Britain's towns but also the absorption into the urban spaces of what had previously been surrounding villages. The terrace, in its various forms, thus became one of the architectural emblems of the Georgian age, the means by which Britain's urban areas surged past their medieval boundaries into the country estates surrounding them. Terraces preponderated not just in large cities, but also in the fashionable spa towns like Bath, Cheltenham, and Buxton. Later, when the spa towns went into decline, new and often grand terraces enabled Britain's seaside towns, such as Brighton and

Scarborough and Margate, to become the new centres of middle-class recreation, tapping into the new craze for sea bathing.

Some builders and architects were hired by wealthy clients to build detached homes to order, but what the key players in the housing booms of the Georgian era discovered was that, once they had dispensed with the decorative features and the ground-floor arcading that Inigo Jones had included in Covent Garden, terraces could be built relatively cheaply, and if they retained enough grandeur and exclusivity they would still attract well-to-do buyers and tenants. The driving forces behind the new spate of home-building were the landowners and the speculators. The latter were men with big ideas and access to capital. Some were trained architects who conjured up grand schemes on a vast scale. Others were strictly small-time players who developed a small number of houses on a small number of plots and, if successful, played another spin of the dice and began the whole enterprise again. Some of the speculative builders worked directly for the landowners, surveying their land, planning the roads and the sewerage systems, dividing the estate into plots upon which houses were to be built. Others worked for themselves, leasing parcels of land from the owners and then laying it out into plots and designing the houses.

The speculative building system that created Britain's Georgian terraces and squares appears, to modern eyes, needlessly and farcically complex and convoluted. The landowners did not sell their land to the speculative builders, they leased it instead. Once this leased land had been divided into plots the speculative builders would either build the homes themselves or sublease the plots to other builders – sometimes called undertakers – who were instructed to build houses to a specified design and by an agreed date. Often the design of the homes in question was only vaguely expressed; at times the instructions given to builders amounted to little more than for them to build new houses that matched the design and layout of those already erected on nearby plots. Behind them were a small armies of artisans, tradesmen, and labourers, as well as the critically important lawyers and financiers. To complicate things further the builders might subcontract the actual building work to these hired artisans and craftsmen. While the houses were being built the speculators would pay nominal, peppercorn rents to the landowner. This arrangement usually lasted for between one and three years. After that substantial ground rents were due to the landowner.

Behind the elegance of the Georgian terrace lay many hard-nosed commercial considerations. As the cost of construction was borne by the builders, speed was of the essence, so that finished properties could be sold or let out and they could make a profit. Uniformity of architectural design permitted the use of standardized materials and methods that helped speed up the building process, although if they found themselves in the right place and at the right time some speculative builders were able to sell the houses before they were finished, the new buyers purchasing what was called the 'carcass' of the house, which they would then have completed to their own specifications and tastes. It was common for some speculative builders to sell off house carcasses if they had been unable to complete the house during the term of the peppercorn rent, to avoid paying the much higher ground rents then due.

Then as now, house-building was capital-intensive and therefore a risky endeavour. While many speculative builders read the markets well and grew rich, some were caught out by rises in the interest rate or the cycles of boom and bust or war and peace. Some ended up bankrupt or, far worse, in a debtors' prison. On occasion desperate builders held lotteries to sell off unwanted and empty houses and settle their debts: even the celebrated Adam brothers, the builders of stately homes in the Palladian style, had to resort to this ruse when their grand Adelphi scheme failed to attract necessary buyers. Others wasted their energies and depleted their resources in the courts, as the system of leases and subleases inevitably led to disputes and litigation.

Ultimately, however, the whole system of speculative building was rigged in favour of the landowners, not the builders. The land upon which the new houses were built continued to belong to the landowners, and when the lease expired the land and the houses built on it reverted to them. Leases varied in duration. Some lasted just a few decades, sometimes thirty-three years. More generous terms offered sixty-one years and gradually ninety-nine years became common, thought of as 'three lives', the span of three generations. Yet no matter how long or short the lease in the end the landowners were usually to be counted among the winners. In London the system reflected the fact that the landowners held their estates in trust for their descendants. As land had to remain within the family they were unable to sell their holdings outright. The building lease system enabled them to sidestep this problem and have their estates developed with minimum expenditure on their part, although on occasion landowners acted as their own speculative builders, and spent their own capital on construction, to maximize profits and increase their level of control and oversight.

This system was not universal. Land was sold outright as freeholds in many provincial cities, and in Scotland a wholly different system was in operation in which land was sold for substantial amounts, with additional income coming to the estate owner in the form of regular payments of fixed rent (feu). However, where it existed, the system of speculative building on plots leased for ninety-nine years or less created perverse incentives. Speculative builders, well aware that they were constructing homes that would eventually pass to the landowner's family, had little motivation to build high-quality homes that would last beyond the term of the lease. Despite the uniformity and repeatability of design, maximizing profits by cutting corners led to poor workmanship and shoddy construction. Much of this was often hidden and only became apparent many years later. It is not unknown for twenty-first-century renovators of Georgian homes to have to pay the price for substandard and slapdash building work carried out two centuries earlier. In some infamous cases the use of poor materials and a general disregard of proper building standards by unscrupulous builders resulted in houses that collapsed not long after completion. One contemporary, the Philadelphia-born engraver James Peller Malcolm, who took up residence in London in the early nineteenth century, complained of 'the practice of the London builders to erect houses at the least possible expense, because their tenures are almost exclusively leasehold'. He warned of the dangers to passers-by posed by the city's 'frail buildings' and estimated that there were 'at least 3,000 houses in a dangerous state of ruin within London and Westminster'. The French writer and traveller Pierre-Jean Grosley wrote with some bemusement about the house-building in England in *A Tour to London, Or, New Observations on England and Its Inhabitants*, published in English in 1772. First protesting that renting houses in London was 'extremely expensive', he described how the quality to which homes in London were built directly reflected the duration of the lease granted to the builders by the landowner.

> Those which are let [leased] for a shorter term have, if I may be allowed the expression, only the soul of a house . . . It is true

the outside appears to be built of brick; but the walls consist of only a single row of bricks; and those being made of the first earth that comes to hand, and only just warmed at the fire, are in strength scarce equal to those square tiles or pieces of earth, dried in the sun, which, in certain countries are used to build houses. In the new quarters of London, brick is often made upon the spot where the buildings themselves are erected; and the workmen make use of the earth which they find in digging the foundations. With this earth they mix, as a phlogiston, the ashes gathered in London by the dustman. I have even been assured that the excrements taken out of necessary-houses entered into the composition of bricks of the sort.

Landowners, of course, had a strong incentive to ensure that the new houses on the land they leased were constructed to high standards and built to last. Aware that the system virtually enticed speculative builders to cut corners, landowners often issued leases that came with stipulations attached. Thomas Wriothesley, the fourth Earl of Southampton, provided parcels of land in Bloomsbury to speculative builders on leases that lasted a mere forty-two years, but on the condition that the houses built upon each plot were to be substantial.

Given this strange, convoluted, and circuitous system, with its potential for miscommunication and error, as well as its incentives to cut corners and conceal problems, it is remarkable that so many homes were completed successfully and that so many were built to a standard high enough to weather the subsequent centuries. Remarkable too is that most Georgian squares, crescents, and terraces are as uniform as they appear; but it is hardly surprising, given the system from which they sprang, that when examined at close quarters small differences and diversions from standard designs can be found. Over the course of the nineteenth century this unwieldly and imprecise system was slowly overtaken by the rise of the architectural profession and the emergence of building contractors who oversaw more of the building process themselves, directly employing the needed craftsmen. This increased standards while the regularity of house design was improved by the adoption by builders and architects of the numerous pattern books that emerged to assist them.

One legacy of this phase of British urban expansion can be found in the names given to many streets and districts of our cities, which so often record the names and titles of the landowners on whose once rural estates they stand. This is particularly marked in London: the names Bedford, Grosvenor, Chandos, Portman, and Harley link parts of the city to the families who made fortunes over multiple generations from leasing land in the centre and to the west of the capital into which London expanded. The influence of landowners can be felt in another way: some imposed restrictive covenants on the leases they issued, which were intended to control the character of the area. There were covenants that prohibited the opening of public houses and others that banned the keeping of cattle or the running of certain types of noisy or polluting trades. Soap-making, brewing, distilling, the opening of butcher's shops or blacksmith's forges were all activities that could be ruled out. Even when land for building was sold as freehold, rather than leased, restrictive covenants could still be imposed.

In 1774 a new building act was passed to control and regulate the standards of new homes and outlaw some of the corner-cutting practices adopted by the jerry-builders. The new act updated building controls that had been laid out in previous laws of 1707 and 1709, which themselves followed on from the act of 1667, the year after the Great Fire of London. The act of 1774 built on existing rules that stipulated which materials could be used to build houses. It dictated the dimensions and thickness of exterior and party walls, seeking to remove one of the corners most commonly cut by jerry-builders, and strengthened regulations that controlled the use of external timberwork, which had been largely done away with by earlier acts, in order to reduce the risk of fire spreading across a city. Protruding window frames and door surrounds, as well as cornices and eaves, were all prohibited. Only simple door frames and shop frontages were allowed; windows were to be recessed into the brickwork. The Act was a watershed, although there is ample evidence that builders found ways around the parts of the legislation that increased their costs or most inconvenienced them. The imprecisions of the whole construction process and the possibility to conceal and camouflage shoddy workmanship provided enormous leeway for builders to get away with violations, even though district surveyors were empowered to check and certify the builders' work.

Like the society that produced it, the Building Act of 1774 was fixated with categorization and with notions of class. All new properties were to be placed in one of seven 'rated' classes, four of which applied to terraced houses. These classifications were based on the overall size, the number of storeys, and the value of the home. A 'first-rate' terraced house occupied over 900 square feet of land and was valued at more than £850 a year in ground rent. Most of these grander terraced homes had four storeys and a basement and could have a floor area of over 4,500 square feet. At the other end of the terraced scale a 'fourth-rate' property occupied less than 350 square feet and was valued at under £150 a year in ground rent. The four rated classes largely followed the same patterns and conformed to specified design proportions; a 'fourth-rate' house was thus, to some extent, merely a much smaller, cheaper, and less well-appointed version of a 'first-rate'. Houses built in each class had to follow codes that laid down building requirements and standards of construction. Fourth-rate houses were built in huge numbers to house artisans and other skilled workers. 62 Falkner Street is a third-rate house, as is Ravensworth Terrace in Newcastle. 10 Guinea Street was built in 1718 and thus predates the Building Act.

The economies of scale and the rationalization of materials and design that made the terrace attractive to the speculative builder tended to result in a relatively austere and unornamented cityscape. External decorative features could for the most part be rendered only in ironwork or stucco, rather than wood, meaning that the building acts of the eighteenth century, combined with the appearances of mass-produced cast-iron features, ironically ensured that what little decoration was permitted was rugged enough to have survived into the modern day. Yet that alone does not explain the lack of decorative features on the homes of the late Georgian era. The move away from decoration was as much about fashion as the law. The taste for a more severe neoclassicism encouraged the abandonment of decorative features and led to the monotony that later Victorian architects would so dramatically rebel against; particularly in the architectural playgrounds that were the future suburbs, as we will explore in chapter six. James Stuart, the author of a 1771 book, *Critical Observations on the Buildings and Improvements of London*, complained that while terraces that made up the new districts of the nation's cities did 'not fail on the whole to produce a grand effect,' they tended to create an impression more of 'neatness, than magnificence'. Thomas De Quincy wrote of London's 'never-ending terraces' in his *Confessions of an English Opium-Eater* in 1821, and Benjamin Disraeli, in his 1847 novel *Tancred*, complained that 'Though London is vast, it is very monotonous'. That monotony, he concluded, was largely a consequence of the 1774 Act, which had created districts of the capital that were 'tame', 'insipid', and 'uniform'.

> All the streets resemble each other, you must read the names of the squares before you venture to knock at a door . . . all those flat, dull, spiritless streets, resembling each other like a large family of plain children.

The terraces that today still huddle in the Georgian quarters of our industrial cities, and which we today so admire, appeared dramatically different at the time. While they might have changed little, they appear to the modern viewer without the filth on the streets and the smoke-choked air. Georgian cities smelled of smoke and fire – and worse. The skies above them were greyed by pollution. In his *Impressions of England 1809–1810* the Swedish writer and composer Erik Gustaf Geijer felt that the monotony of the Georgian terrace, when combined with the smoke and pollution of the city, created a bleak, almost overwhelming effect. 'One penetrates ever deeper into an atmosphere of coal smoke in whose twilight moves an unending multitude of people', he wrote. To Geijer the pollution had the effect of accentuating the dismal monotony of the uniform, unadorned terraced streets. 'One may say in general that the warehouse gives the character of the whole of London', he complained. The sandblasting of thousands of Georgian cities in the latter half of the twentieth century stripped away the physical imprimatur of the many decades during which smoke and smog loomed over them. They were, quite dramatically, returned to how they must have looked just after construction. Now it is only in old pictures, from the late nineteenth and early twentieth centuries, that we are reminded that for much of their long lives these squares and terraces that had been built where industry preponderated, or where industry later emerged, were so blackened and dirty.

There were ways, where money allowed, by which magnificence could be injected into otherwise regular streets. In 1728, the architect John Wood the Elder designed Queen Square in Bath, transforming what might have been a largely uniform terrace by the addition of a central pediment that broke up the street, creating the impression of a single vast and stately palace with wings to either side. (As in London, Liverpool, and elsewhere some of the money used to build the elegant houses of Queen Square came from men whose wealth had come from the slave trade and slavery.) A similar pattern had been designed, but not built, for London's Grosvenor Square and was later applied to Bedford Square. Wood's vision was to transform Bath into a city whose architecture paid homage to its ancient Roman heritage.

Within the wealthier districts the grid lines of the terraces were broken up by squares, little parks, that meant there were parts of the great Georgian developments that resembled urban villages. The centres of Georgian squares were envisaged as communal areas that made up, to some extent, for the fact that the homes themselves had only small gardens or yards. Summerhill Square in Newcastle, which 5 Ravensworth Terrace overlooks, was a nineteenth-century rendering of this eighteenth-century idea. There was a desire in London for the country to be brought into the city, reminding the aristocratic residents of the West End of their other existence, on their country estates. For this purpose the park at the centre of London's Cavendish Square was, in the 1770s, provided with its own flock of sheep, which were released to graze on the grass protected behind the iron railings. In his *Critical Observations on the Buildings and Improvements of London*, James Stuart lampooned the whole exercise.

> To see the poor things staring at every coach, and hurrying round their narrow bounds, required a warm imagination indeed, to convert the scene into that of flocks ranging fields, with all the concomitant ideas of innocence and a pastoral life.

Mingled among the grand terraces and the green square was a different form of street: the mews. These were narrow lanes lined with stables where coaches and horses were housed and provided accommodation for the coachmen and other attendants. The mews allowed the very wealthiest to maintain horse-drawn carriages, the ultimate symbol of wealth and status, the eighteenth century's equivalent of the Rolls Royce, magnified by dressing coachmen in liveried uniforms. Some of these coachmen were Africans, enslaved boys who had been brought to Britain by plantation owners or slave-ship captains. Even after carriages began to fall out of fashion the mews remained useful given their other functions. They also allowed for the discreet removal of rubbish and night soil. By the early twentieth century mews houses were being converted into small dwellings that made the most of their postcodes, rapidly acquiring an image of fashionable bohemianism. Mews were much more common in London than outside the capital, although some were built in Brighton. On the grandest streets of London's West End the separation of the functional mews from the luxurious terraces was emphasized by the erection of an ornamental gateway. The distinction was noted by Charles Dickens in *Little Dorrit*, written in the mid-1850s. In the novel Dickens has members of the Barnacle family living at 'four Mews Street Grosvenor'. But, as Dickens explained, 'Mews Street, Grosvenor Square, was absolutely not Grosvenor Square itself, but it was very near it. It was a hideous little street of dead wall, stables, and dunghills, with lofts over coach-houses inhabited by coachmen's families, who had a passion for drying clothes, and decorating their window-sills with miniature turnpike gates.' Yet despite this 'there were two or three small airless houses at the entrance end of Mews Street, which went at enormous rents on account of their being abject hangers-on to a fashionable situation; and whenever one of these fearful little coops was to be let . . . the house agent advertised it as a gentlemanly residence in the most aristocratic part of town inhabited solely by the elite.' The mews made it possible for the rich to have the servants and their carriages close at hand, but in turn created tiny strips of relative poverty within the grand squares and terraces that the Victorian social reformer Charles Booth would later colour gold in his colour-coded maps showing where wealth and poverty resided in the London of the 1880s and 1890s. But with the exception of the mews streets, London's West End was designed and laid out to be a citadel of wealth that insulated the rich from the poor, reinforcing a sense of division and a desire for segregation that predated them. Writing of London in 1712, on the eve of the Georgian age, Joseph Addison of the *Spectator* famously noted that the city was made up of distinct 'nations'.

When I consider this great city, in its several quarters, or
divisions, I look upon it as an aggregate of various nations,
distinguished from each other by their respective customs,
manners, and interests. The courts of two countries do not differ
so much from one another as the Court and the City of London
in their peculiar ways of life and conversation. In short, the
inhabitants of St. James's, notwithstanding they live under the
same laws, and speak the same language, are a distinct people
from those of Cheapside, by several climates and degrees, in their
ways of thinking and conversing together.

The districts occupied by the rich increasingly became marked out not
just by the grandeur of the homes or the fashionability of their names
but also by the quality of the urban environment built around them. The
streets themselves began to change. In the London of the 1760s Paving
Acts were passed. The resulting new streets had improved drainage and
in some places there was organized street cleaning. Thomas Cubitt,
the builder of grand stucco-fronted homes such as those of London's
Belgrave Square, not only provided his rich and often aristocratic clients
with luxurious homes, he saw to it that new roads were laid out and
sewerage systems integrated into the process of construction from the
outset. From the middle of the eighteenth century street lighting began
to be introduced, the darkness of some of the wealthier streets penetrated
by oil lamps which gave way to gas.

While some complained of the monotony of the Georgian terrace
by the latter decades of the eighteenth century, what others found most
concerning was the sheer pace of urban growth. In Tobias Smollett's 1771
novel *The Expedition of Humphry Clinker* the fictional Matthew Bramble
arrives in London to find the city in the midst of its seemingly endless
age of expansion, the terraces having stretched out beyond former city
boundaries, enveloping the once outlying villages.

London is literally new to me; new in its streets, houses, and
even in its situation; as the Irishman said, 'London is now gone
out of town.' What I left open fields, producing hay and corn,
I now find covered with streets and squares, and palaces, and
churches. I am credibly informed, that in the space of seven years,

eleven thousand new houses have been built in one quarter of Westminster, exclusive of what is daily added to other parts of this unwieldy metropolis. Pimlico and Knightsbridge are now almost joined to Chelsea and Kensington; and if this infatuation continues for half a century, I suppose the whole county of Middlesex will be covered with brick.

In the building booms of the eighteenth century thousands of homes from earlier ages were lost, crushed by the juggernaut advance of the Georgian terrace. As much as we today struggle to understand the mindset of the post-war planners who unleashed bulldozers and wrecking balls on exquisite Georgian homes, it is similarly sad to reflect that so many of the medieval or Tudor town houses that were discussed in the previous chapter were hastily demolished by speculative builders or well-to-do Georgian families in their clamour to build new homes in the new fashion. The architects and speculative builders of the eighteenth and nineteenth centuries could be just as destructive and just as insensitive to the historic value of the buildings from earlier ages. They too had their grand schemes, and when obstacles stood in their way they could be as ruthless as the planners who redeveloped Britain's cities in the 1960s and 1970s. The advantage offered to those earlier developers is that they were very often able to realize their plans on the green fields of the expanded cities rather than over the foundations of earlier properties.

The architectural monotony of the Georgian terraces was only skin deep. While the rules of proportion that governed the facades dictated the heights of the various floors, behind the walls of limestone and stucco the chaos of the Georgian streets was shuttered out and the exterior uniformity of the terraces gave way to a world of individual choice and personalization. Personalization went hand in hand with a growing clamour for privacy. As the idea of the family changed, becoming more centred around children, the design of the home became increasingly focused on the establishment of familial privacy. This desire for private space was, of course, compromised by the fact that the domestic spaces of the rich were shared with servants. Multiple rooms and vertical living, when combined with this urge for privacy, necessitated corridors, to make it possible to reach one room without going through another,

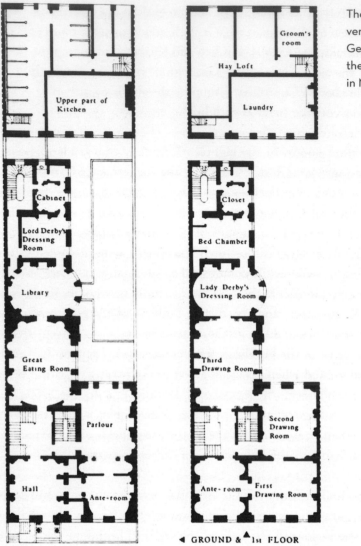

The floor plan of a very grand 'first-rate' Georgian property on the Grosvenor estate in Mayfair, London.

◀ GROUND & ▲ 1st FLOOR

separate landings and stairways, and discreet passageways from the world of high living to that of domestic service – the world upstairs and downstairs, of master and servant. Servants were cast to the very bottom and the very top of the house, as the Frenchman Louis Simond observed in his *Journal of a Tour and Residence in Great Britain, During the Years 1810 and 1811*: vertical living literally stratified Georgian society, the well-to-do tenants or owners living in the middle rooms, the servants sleeping in the attic rooms on the third or fourth floors and working in the basement kitchens and sculleries. Their working lives (and their lives consisted mainly of work) involved endless rushing up and down stairs between rooms, making the already physically demanding work of the Georgian domestic servant even more arduous.

Above the cellar was the ground floor which, confusingly, was often a little above ground level. The front door, often reached up a few steps, led to a corridor lit by a semicircular decorative glass window, the 'fanlight', despite which these corridors were and are relatively dingy, especially when painted in darker colours. The corridor opened up into the ground-floor rooms, typically a dining room and a parlour. These were not the grandest rooms but where eighteenth- and nineteenth-century residents spent much of their time. Families who owned or more often leased larger, higher-rated homes, but who fell upon hard times would often confine themselves to these rooms and rent out the grander rooms above. From the ground-floor corridor the staircase was reached, which led up to the first floor. Here the ceilings were highest and the windows the tallest. These rules can be seen at play in both 62 Falkner Street and 5 Ravensworth Terrace from *A House Through Time*, and in thousands of similar Georgian and Georgian-style houses across Britain. In more modest, lower-rated homes the main bedrooms were on the first floor but in grander houses the first floor was dominated by the dining room. Overlooking the street with high ceilings and tall sash windows – a recent and crucial invention – this was the most luxurious room in the house. The large windows were made possible by technological advances that led to a fall in the price of glass. This meant that the grandest rooms in a terraced house despite having only one wall facing the street could still be flooded with daylight. The gloomy darkness that was a feature of the corridors was notably absent in the first-floor dining room. In a status-obsessed age (although perhaps no more status-obsessed than our own) these rooms were the centre of conspicuous consumption, where guests were entertained and card games played and where relatives gathered. The performative aspects of wealth and respectability were played out in such spaces. For Richard Glenton, the first inhabitant of 5 Ravensworth Terrace, the first-floor dining room was the centre of his world. From there, as suggested by the list of furniture he was later forced to auction off when hard times came, he entertained friends and revelled in his life as a middle-class gentleman in a then thriving and desirable part of 1840s Liverpool. Behind the dining room, in the rear of the house overlooking the back yard were often situated the main bedrooms. Above these grand rooms, up another flight of stairs, were the attic rooms. This is where children slept in modest homes and where servants spent the night in more opulent houses.

Two centuries after they were built, why are these terraced homes from the Georgian era so appealing? Is it the classical mouldings, fanlights or sash windows or do the rules of classical proportion and symmetry, all underpinned by mathematics, operate upon our minds just as they were designed to do by the architects of the eighteenth century? Ideas of taste, restraint, and rationality have become deeply embedded in our culture, and inscribed into the modernism of the twentieth century. At a simple and functional level the Georgian home appeals to the twenty-first-century homeowner or house historian because it still works as a home. Endlessly adaptable, its layout permits the conversion of rooms to new functions or the adding of partitions to create new ones. This was necessitated in part by the fact that most Georgian homes lacked bathrooms. The water closet was not unknown before the 1770s but without underground drainage and a reliable supply of water such a luxury would have been impractical. It was not until the nineteenth century that it became common. Without drainage, houses instead had privies or earth closets in their yards. From these what was euphemistically called night soil was periodically collected and carted off to the market gardens that sprang up around the expanding cities, where it was used as fertilizer. As cities grew the market gardens were themselves pushed further out. Some that happened to have been established on clay soil, temporarily gave up growing vegetables and became the brick fields, firing the bricks to feed the expansion of the cities.

Vertical living in the Georgian city was necessitated by the narrow frontage of the terrace, which itself was dictated by the size of the building plots and the high cost of urban land. But the result – tall, narrow houses with multiple storeys – tended to surprise visitors from abroad. Louis Simond, more familiar with French apartments, regarded the London town house as a 'curiosity' and left a good description of how the rooms were used. 'The plan of these houses is very simple', he explained, 'two rooms on each story; one in the front with two or three windows looking on the street, the other on the yard behind, often very small; the stairs generally taken out of the breadth of the back room.'

Bemused by the narrowness of the houses he saw in London and the novelty of vertical living, he wrote:

Each family occupy a whole house, unless very poor. There are advantages and disadvantages attending this custom. Among the first, the being more independent of the noise, the dirt, the contagious disorders, or the danger of your neighbour's fires, and having a more complete home. On the other hand, a suite of apartments all on one floor, even of a few rooms only, looks much better, and is more convenient. These narrow houses, three or four stories high, – one for eating, one for sleeping, a third for company, a fourth under ground for the kitchen, the fifth perhaps at the top for the servants, – and the agility, the ease, the quickness with which the individuals of the family run up and down, and perch on the different stories, give the idea of a cage with its sticks and birds.'

Despite their malleability many Georgian houses still carry the subtle signs of original functions lost to us today. Many who live in them discover that the eighteenth-century home can be, in its own way, an eloquent guide to the turmoil and divisions that characterized Georgian society. Those who have gone in search of the histories of Georgian homes and learnt their intimate secrets have come to appreciate that they reflect not just the architectural style of the era, or fashionable modes of middle-class domestic life. In both their features and in how they appear in the records in the archives it is clear that they were also shaped by the great social panic of the age – crime.

Many Georgian homes were built to be defendable, designed and fitted out partly with the 'house-breaker' and the 'home-invader' in mind. In its interior and exterior features the middle-class Georgian home reflects the whole of eighteenth-century British society, and the social divisions and class tensions that defined it – not that the idea of social class had fully solidified in the eighteenth century. For the growing urban middle classes it was essential that their home provide them with multiple lines of defence against the dangers of the city. The desire for privacy merged into the need for defence and exclusion. The wooden shutters that so many Georgian homes have fitted in boxing on

The Georgian town house was as much a fortress as a home, its doors protected by new types of locks that emerged in the 1770s and 1780s.

either side of their lower-floor windows originally came with wrought-iron locking bars and reciprocal fitments – some homes still retain them. This ironwork was not solely intended for the purpose for which we use them today, as wooden curtains that shut out the sun; they were internal armour to fend off burglars. Likewise the breach between the street and the frontages that leads down to the basement level of many Georgian terraces was the eighteenth-century equivalent of a medieval moat, the next barrier against intruders, after the line of spiked iron railings. Larger urban villas that had their own gardens usually had or still have high walls. Behind those walls some had iron mantraps concealed in the hedges and undergrowth. This was the traditional weapon of the country landowner, developed during his long, intergenerational war against the poacher and adapted for city use. In the vaults of the Museum of London are a few horrific examples. Huge, blackened, and spring-loaded, they were powerful enough to crush bones; their serrated teeth could bite through cartilage. The other fangs that guarded the Georgian home were those of the giant mastiff hounds that patrolled kitchens and gardens. The mastiff was the favoured guard dog of the era and attacks by these giant hounds were known on occasion to be fatal, taking the lives of both would-be house-breakers and innocent passers-by.

Night fell hard on their unpoliced and largely unlit cities and the wealthy locked themselves in, bolting front doors and windows with heavy ironwork, intricate locks, and wooden shutters. The late eighteenth century was the great era of innovation and expansion for Britain's locksmiths. The 'tumbler lock' and the supposedly unpickable 'safety lock' were breakthroughs of the 1770s and 1780s respectively. Each night the servants, children, and lodgers were locked into their respective rooms, and the lowliest of maids and house boys were even instructed to sleep in the lee of the doorway, to make it impossible for an intruder to enter without waking them.

Behind these layers of defences – railings, urban moats, locks, shutters, mantraps, and attack dogs – the propertied spent their nights in candle-lit gloom, locked in and watchful. The conspicuous wealth of what were quaintly called the middling classes meant they became, to some extent, prisoners of their possessions, living in hock to their nocturnal fears. But theirs were not paranoid delusions but legitimate dread.

The middle-class Georgian home was so fortified because it was so luxurious. Our Georgian ancestors lived in an age in which there was simply more to own and therefore more to covet than there had ever been. The period between 1727 and 1820, during which Britain was ruled over by George II and George III, witnessed an explosion of what we today would call consumerism. Through much of the era Britain was getting richer and at least some of that wealth did trickle down to what Samuel Johnson, compiler of the dictionary, called the 'middling rank of men': traders, merchants, doctors, lawyers, and members of the other professions. Some of the new prosperity dripped even further down, into the hands of shopkeepers, skilled craftsmen, and tradesmen. With greater disposable incomes came opportunities (and also social pressures) to purchase new comforts and fineries. Pewter gave way to ceramic tableware. The larger, more expensive domestic items such as silverware and the new classically inspired furniture had previously been made only as one-off pieces, commissioned by the tiny aristocracy –

then just three thousand families. Suddenly market conditions and manufacturing innovations meant that these could be reproduced, in varying qualities and at a range of prices. The manufacturing boom that made this possible meant that the better-off could purchase pieces from firms that were famed as suppliers to the aristocracy, even to royalty. The more pioneering and inventive businesses produced packed – if not yet glossy – catalogues showcasing their goods. Josiah Wedgwood the potter opened showrooms in both London and fashionable Bath, and an art that we today would recognize as advertising began to emerge.

Innumerable commentators noted the improving standard of living, as large numbers of people found themselves in the unfamiliar position of being able to afford luxuries that had until recently been only available to the wealthy and the landed. Formerly exotic products – tea, coffee, chocolate, sugar – boomed in popularity. Significantly each of these new tastes demanded the purchase of yet more domestic accoutrements. Tea was brewed in urns and served in ceramic tea sets – the eighteenth-century craze for tea among the middle class and the wealthy was equal to that for gin among the poor and destitute. The sugar that sweetened the tea required domestic implements of its own. It was handled with sugar tongs and sliced with sugar cutters or sugar nips – having been delivered into the domestic realm in the form of compacted sugar loaves. Tea and coffee, as well as chocolate – then served as a drink more often than a solid – were stirred with silver spoons. Not only were all these consumer durables worth stealing, there was a healthy market in stolen and pilfered tea and sugar. The diaries of the middle classes, particularly those of women, constantly bemoaned the theft of tea by servants.

After marriage itself, setting up a household became *the* central rite of passage for young middle-class Georgian couples. Through the establishment of their marital home and the accumulation of the paraphernalia of domesticity the Georgian family did not so much purchase respectability as have it confirmed. The most personal possessions of our better-off Georgian ancestors, the contents of their trunks, jewellery boxes, chambers, parlours, and kitchens, are the same pieces that today clutter antique shops, or become the 'talking pieces' of our more minimalist modern homes. For the eighteenth-century householder, status, aspiration, respectability, and fashion were all invested in the home and in these consumer objects.

Their loss was not merely painful and costly, it held the prospect of a potential diminution of social standing; perhaps only temporary, but still distasteful. While there was nothing new in the fear of crime and the hatred of criminals, with so much invested in property and with society changing so fast the Georgians had perhaps more reason than most to fret about criminality. As in the twenty-first century the relationship between actual increases or decreases in the rate of crime and the great shifts and surges in the public perception of crime was tenuous: then as now it was perception that mattered most. In the eighteenth century an assertive and vocal press stoked fears. 'The papers are filled with robberies and breaking of houses', reported the *Gentleman's Magazine* in 1774. However, in the late eighteenth century, with no police force, there were no crime statistics, so the actual trend was impossible to know. There were court records, and statistics relating to the numbers of criminals tried, imprisoned, transported, or executed, but it was widely believed that the convicted represented a small minority of those engaged in crime – whether on a casual basis or as a full-time occupation. Various voices put forward their own estimates of the numbers of criminals at work in the nation, and in the capital in particular, but given that the populations of the cities themselves were just estimates, these were almost wholly fanciful. In this largely fact-free void, accounts of the latest criminal outrage or the latest court case were exaggerated as they were relayed from household to household.

When not attempting to estimate the size of the criminal population, eighteenth-century commentators were devising theories to explain the apparent increase in lawlessness. The writer Henry Fielding and his brother John – both of them London magistrates – claimed that the new wealth of the nation had allowed the poor to become used to luxuries and tastes which they could ill afford, and to which they had no entitlement. Others believed the poor had been enticed into luxury by unscrupulous creditors. There was also a persistent worry that the concentration of so much of the population into the cities was permitting dangerous ideas to spread like contagions. One consequence of urbanization – it was claimed – was a new current of insubordination, and a propensity for the poor to question the rights of the wealthy. The writer Daniel Defoe along with the Fielding brothers complained of a general culture of insolence. It was noted on more than one occasion that carriages and liveried servants, the ultimate outward demonstration of the wealth of those who dwelled in the grand terraces and squares of the Georgian city, attracted insults, cat-calls, and even barrages of rotten vegetables from sections of the urban poor, rather than awed respect. The belief that the poor had become restless and discontented was expressed in the regularly repeated notion that they were unwilling to accept their allotted 'station in life', a phrase and a fear that hints at the swirling, subterranean forces that were to coalesce into the concept of social class in the nineteenth century. The literal darkness of the Georgian city and the ineptitude of nightwatchmen (an ineptitude that was often wilful and pragmatic given their low pay and lack of official power) made things worse. Little wonder the idea of the home as a fortified idyll took root in these tumultuous decades, leaving behind the wooden shutters and iron railings that twenty-first-century residents lovingly restore and maintain.

We have come to know the Georgian middle class, their tastes, habits, and fears, through the art, architecture, and literature that they left behind, but also through a shared love of their homes and intimate possessions. We have much less of an opportunity to get to know the poor with whom the wealthy residents of the terraces and squares shared their cities. Ironically it is the criminal class, not the great mass of the poor, who left a clearer imprint on the historical record, through newspaper reports, court and prison records, and the exhaustive paper trails that followed those who were unfortunate enough to be transported for their crimes to the penal colonies of Australia. Georgian Britain was at once the enlightened and expanding imperial nation of neoclassical stately homes, and elegant terraces, and Hogarth's gin-sodden kingdom of street thugs, harlots, vice, poverty, and slums.

However, as the research carried out on 62 Falkner Street and 5 Ravensworth Terrace during the making of *A House Through Time* shows, Georgian terraced homes may well have been built for the wealthy but they rarely lived there alone. Even when occupied by well-to-do families such houses were also home to servants, typically young working-class women. Richard Glenton, the first tenant of 62 Falkner Street, maintained his bachelor lifestyle by relying upon the services of Catherine Smith, a fifteen-year-old who appears in the census of 1841

The will of Jonas Glenton, father of Richard Glenton, the first resident of 62 Falkner Street. Without financial support from his father, Richard had to move to cheaper accommodation.

described as 'FS', the abbreviation for Female Servant. Later residents, right up to the end of the nineteenth century, shared Falkner Street with servants. Likewise, the attic rooms of 5 Ravensworth Terrace were home to young women employed as domestic help through much of the Victorian age. The first residents, William and Priscilla Stoker, had one female servant; and in the 1840s brother and sister Joshua and Mary Alder lived in the house with two servants, Mary Hook and Elizabeth Gibson. Later resident Mary Colbeck employed the young Alice Robinson in the 1850s and 1860s.

While many of the grander types of Georgian houses saw residents share their personal space with servants, there were also expensive and luxurious houses providing homes not to one family but to multiple shared tenants, who lived in rooms or suites of rooms that were sublet to them. The census of 1801 reveals houses on Bentinck Street in Soho that only sixty years after they were built had become home to as many as six families. Families living in this manner shared hallways, landings, and stairs, as well as basement kitchens. They rented rooms as needed and, when family circumstances necessitated it and where funds were available, new doorways were cut into walls linking rooms together to create what in effect were makeshift apartments. Thousands of Georgian homes bear the scars of such modifications. Other tenants who rented single rooms in grand Georgian terraced houses were bachelors just setting out in life, or seasonal visitors to Britain's spa towns and seaside resorts. A general lack of control over the subletting of property in the eighteenth century encouraged and enabled this sort of flexibility, and then as now large properties were regarded as potential sources of income, to be drawn upon as and when needed.

Multiple occupancy and the subletting of rooms was not necessarily evidence that a house was in decline or a district unable to attract wealthy residents, although in some circumstances it could be an indicator of both of those undesirable fates. Many Georgian homes, during their difficult journeys from their eighteenth- or early nineteenth-century construction through to the modern day, passed through periods of decline and stagnation. The relentless pace of urban growth, alongside other social forces, set in train a process that saw many tumble down the social scale. The large, first-rate Georgian terraces built in the late eighteenth century increasingly came to be seen as plain and austere as fashions changed. Outdated and in need of maintenance and renovation, many of these substantial houses originally built for prosperous merchants or members of the professional classes were, by the middle of the nineteenth century, becoming more difficult to let.

Not only were the homes themselves falling out of favour, in many cases so were the districts in which they had been built. Some of the urban estates that were laid out by the speculative builders of the eighteenth century had struggled to attract well-off tenants and buyers from the outset. Others fell victim to the process of rapid urban growth of which they had once been the symbol. 5 Ravensworth Terrace and the other terraces of Newcastle's Summerhill Square, for example, were built in the 1820s on the high ground to the west of the city. The large homes looked inwards, towards the park in the centre of the square, and were insulated by orientation and distance from the noise and pollution of Newcastle's industries, which were then largely clustered along the steep banks of the River Tyne. However, by the 1870s the city and its industries had begun to climb out of the steep valley and extend along the river in both directions. Once desirable and genteel districts of the city like Summerhill, the fruit of the speculative building of the early nineteenth century, now found themselves in the midst of industrial Newcastle, rather than on its green fringes. The pollution from the new factories that developed in the Scotswood district of the city began to pass over the roofs of the Summerhill terraces and the city's poor and destitute were suddenly brought closer to the wealthy residents of the once sheltered square. In many cities the emergence of new suburban districts, a phenomenon that will be explored in chapters six and seven, offered alternative places of abode for the well-to-do middle-class tenants who otherwise might have been attracted to life in the houses of Newcastle's Summerhill Square, or to homes on Falkner Street in Liverpool or Guinea Street in Bristol.

In the face of these pressures and no longer able to attract wealthy residents, hundreds of thousands of once grand Georgian terraced homes in once fashionable districts became homes to multiple families or were run as lodging houses. By the 1890s, seventy years after its construction, 5 Ravensworth Terrace had become home to William Henry Oram, a steamship captain transporting coal to and from Newcastle, and his wife Mary Ellen, who ran a drapery shop. The Orams, despite having two incomes, rented out rooms to lodgers. By the time of the Valuation Office Survey of 1910, 5 Ravensworth Terrace had taken another step away from a family home and towards multiple occupancy and was being run as a lodging house for music-hall performers by Grace Eagle and her family. Indeed, many of the once exclusive houses on Ravensworth Terrace were recorded in the 1910 survey as having gone over to multiple occupancy. Numbers 6, 7 and 8, and 11 had all become boarding houses. Little had changed by the 1920s. The house was still a property in which rooms could be rented. The electoral register of 1920 shows it being run by Miss Rose McQueeney, who on the date the register was taken had seven male lodgers. This pattern, or variations on the theme, continued under the ownership of the Smyth family, who also rented out rooms to lodgers, through the 1940s and 1950s. It is not until 1959, when the last of the Smyths' tenants moved out, that the house once again became home to members of a single family, but only briefly as in 1964 it became a Goodwill Centre owned and run by the Salvation Army. 62 Falkner Street experienced a similar pattern of decline. Although many of Liverpool's grandest Georgian terraces, such as Rodney Street, remained respectable and prestigious addresses well into the twentieth century, Falkner Street, always regarded as being too far up the steep hills that stretched from the city centre, had slipped into multiple occupancy by some point in the 1850s, after the death of a resident to cholera left his widow in need of an income. Adverts from the time offered 'a front Sitting-room, with two or three bedrooms, or partial board for two or three young gentleman'.

From the 1790s, despite its position in the Redcliffe part of Bristol near the docks, 10 Guinea Street found itself in competition for wealthy tenants with the fashionable new suburb of Clifton, built high upon the cliffs overlooking the docks. In the first years of the nineteenth century the house was home to the wealthy Haberfield family. John Kerle Haberfield, a lawyer, became Mayor of Bristol and served six terms. Half a century later the decline had set in. The house had become a business premises, the site of a commercial school. After that it was in multiple occupancy until the 1960s when it was virtually abandoned. In the 1970s it was purchased by the first of a series of residents who would undertake the colossal (and never-ending) task of renovation and restoration and return it to being a family home.

CHAPTER FOUR

THE VICTORIAN CITY

A Tale of Two Nations

In perhaps the most famous passage of his 1845 novel *Sybil*, Benjamin Disraeli argued that Victorian Britain had become so deeply divided that it was, in effect, 'Two nations; between whom there is no intercourse and no sympathy; who are as ignorant of each other's habits, thoughts, and feelings, as if they were dwellers in different zones, or inhabitants of different planets; who are formed by a different breeding, are fed by a different food, are ordered by different manners, and are not governed by the same laws.' Those two nations, Disraeli informed his readers, were 'the rich and the poor'. The Britain that Disraeli addressed in *Sybil* was a dynamic, commercial, imperial nation of elegant terraces, sprawling suburbs, Gothic churches, and unprecedented material wealth, while at the same time it was a land of desperate poverty and rampant ill health. This same troubling duality preyed on the mind of Charles Dickens, the greatest chronicler of the age. In *Bleak House* he wrote of how 'civilization and barbarism walked this boastful island together'. In 1853, as he was completing the novel, cholera was returning to Britain for the third time in two decades. As during its earlier visitations the bulk of those whose lives were terminated by that most dreaded of diseases were poor people from the industrial districts of the inner cities. A few years earlier Henry Mayhew, the pioneering journalist who made it his mission to record and preserve the words of the Victorian underclass, wrote a vivid description

of the capital city that lay at the heart of the wealthiest nation the world
had ever known.

> By the last [census] return the metropolis covered an extent of
> nearly 45,000 acres, and contained upwards of two hundred and
> sixty thousand houses, occupied by one million eight hundred
> and twenty thousand souls, constituting not only the densest,
> but the busiest hive, the most wondrous workshop, and the
> richest bank in the world. The mere name of London awakens
> a thousand trains of varied reflections. Perhaps the first thought
> that it excites in the mind, paints it as the focus of modern
> civilization, of the hottest, the most restless activity of the social
> elements. Some, turning to the west, see it as a city of palaces,
> adorned with parks, ennobled with triumphal arches, grand
> statues, and stately monuments; others, looking at the east, see
> only narrow lanes and musty counting-houses, with tall chimneys
> vomiting black clouds, and huge masses of warehouses with doors
> and cranes ranged one above another. Yet all think of it as a vast
> bricken multitude, a strange incongruous chaos of wealth and
> want – of ambition and despair – of the brightest charity and the
> darkest crime, where there are more houses and more houseless,
> where there is more feasting and more starvation, than on any
> other spot on earth . . .

Of the two nations that Disraeli identified, only one, that of the middle
classes and the better-off sections of the skilled working class, remains
readily accessible to us. There are multiple ways by which we can connect
to that lost Britain. One is through the domestic realm, as we have
come to know the Victorians through our love and appreciation of their
homes. The secrets, comforts, and defects of their houses are well known
to the millions of us who today live in them, spending our time and our
money adapting them to our modern lives. The middle-class townhouses
of the early Victorian era, the suburban semi-detached homes of the
later nineteenth century, and the millions of simple but sturdy terraced
homes built for the more fortunate of the industrial workers are perhaps
the greatest of the many inheritances bequeathed to us by our Victorian
ancestors. Those homes are physical bridges that link many of our

personal and family lives to those of earlier residents. No such physical bridges link us to the lives of the Victorian poor; the desperate masses with whom the wealthy shared their cities.

While the families of skilled artisans who had regular work might have been lucky enough to have lived in a 'fourth-rate' terraced home or a 'through terrace', with a backyard and proper ventilation, their poorer cousins of the urban underclass lived in tiny back-to-back hovels, towering and overcrowded tenements, or dank cellars – freezing in winter, airless and foul in the heat of summer. Most such dwellings were long ago 'cleared'; the urban planner's euphemism for bulldozed.

The history of the houses that were occupied by the industrial workers of the nineteenth century is a very different history to that of the middle-class home. It is not one focused on architectural styles or changing tastes. The heroes of this story are social reformers, sanitary inspectors, and medical officers, rather than architects. It is, in essence, the history of how the domestic home became the focus of an epic political and moral struggle as reformers attempted to control the runaway forces of urbanization and industrialization.

One of the most transformative effects of the industrial revolution was that it profoundly (if temporarily) transformed British economic geography. It was in the north and Midlands of England and the central belt of Scotland, rather than the English south, that the new and enormously profitable industries concentrated. Industry was at first drawn there by fast-flowing rivers that were harnessed to drive the water-wheels which in turn powered whole floors of machines within the first modern factories. Later industry was fixed in the north and Midlands because there, beneath the earth, lay some of the richest seams of coal ever discovered. While London, itself a centre of industry, remained by far the largest city, its population exceeding two and a half million by the middle of the nineteenth century, the rate of growth in some of the new industrial cities was even higher. Liverpool began the century with a population of eighty thousand. The census of 1841 revealed the city's population to be around two hundred and eighty thousand. Back in 1773 Manchester had been a Lancashire market town of twenty-seven thousand souls. By 1801 its population had reached ninety-five thousand. It had expanded to more than three

hundred thousand by 1851. In a single extraordinary decade, between 1821 and 1831, the populations of Manchester and Salford grew by 47 per cent. Bradford in the same period grew by an even more astonishing 78 per cent. Glasgow expanded from around seventy-seven thousand in 1801 to two hundred and sixty thousand by 1841. Within these giant cities, and in the other rapidly industrializing towns, huge numbers of new houses were needed to accommodate the ever-expanding industrial workforce. Demand became even more acute in the 1840s following a vast influx of migrants from Ireland in the wake of the famine.

The desperately poor Pipewellgate district of Gateshead, with Robert Stephenson's High Level Bridge in the background.

To house these new multitudes landlords subdivided existing properties. Large houses that had been originally built for the middle classes were converted into lodging houses or tenements. Elsewhere speculative builders filled in gaps in the street plan with hastily built houses often arranged around courtyards. Yet these piecemeal developments and opportunistic conversions were nowhere near enough to meet the growing demand for accommodation in the cities. What was needed were new, purpose-built homes for the industrial workers. Part of the solution was the Victorian 'through terrace'. These were small, compact houses with two rooms on the ground floor and two rooms above. They were designed to house individual families and they were built in terraces, with back lanes separating each line of homes. They also had back yards, sometimes communal but more often private and enclosed. In these yards were located outdoor privies and sometimes coal sheds. As they had doors and windows at both the front and the back, air could pass through and they were thus easy to ventilate. Small, cheap, regular, and easy to reproduce, thousands were built and thousands survive into the twenty-first century, mainly in the former industrial centres: Newcastle, Manchester, Liverpool, Birmingham, Cardiff, Halifax. The relative comfort of the through terrace reflects the fact that there were sections of the working classes who were able to enjoy the fruits of secure employment and were able to afford regular rent payments. Many were skilled artisans whose trades had not been overtaken by mechanization. The story of how the industrial working classes were housed in the nineteenth century is thus not one solely of squalor and poverty. However, those of our ancestors who occupied 'through terraces' and who could afford basic domestic comforts were the fortunate ones. For others life in the cities was a constant and often a losing struggle to find and maintain decent accommodation.

Many of those who visited the north and the Midlands in the first decades of the nineteenth century were shocked by the conditions they encountered in the homes of the poorer industrial workers. We know about such homes because a huge body of literature was written about them and their inhabitants by social reformers, sanitary investigators, and journalists. In 1832 Dr James Kay wrote a powerful study of the conditions endured by the multitudes who worked in the towering cotton mills that were then mushrooming within and around Manchester. In 1833 Peter Gaskell published his study *The Manufacturing Population of England*. Friedrich Engels, sent to Manchester by his father to learn the ways of the textiles industry, instead spent his time investigating *The Condition of the Working Class in England in 1844*, the title he gave his classic book. We can glean further details from the work of Edwin Chadwick, the Manchester lawyer who became the foremost campaigner for sanitary and housing reform, who drafted the landmark *Report on the Sanitary Conditions of the Labouring Population of Great Britain* in 1842, while the reports and journal papers written by the civil engineer Robert Rawlinson abound with the many solutions he put forward to address the Victorian housing problem. They ventured into the cellars, courts, and terraces in which the industrial workers sought shelter. All were appalled by the conditions they encountered there. They and others were also at times shocked by the sights and sounds of industry itself, unleashed and untrammelled in Britain as nowhere else. Commentators of the age sometimes wrote of Britain's industrial cities as if they were encampments on a new type of frontier.

Hippolyte Taine, the French philosopher who toured the English north-west, considered Manchester to be a Babel of bricks, its towering factories likened to workhouses in a penal colony. Almost a century later J. B. Priestley felt Gateshead was still 'a frontier camp of bricks and mortar'. On that new frontier, the wild north of the industrial revolution, there were few restrictions or controls to determine the dimension or standards of the homes that were built for the millions of industrial workers, men and women drawn to the cities by the availability of work, or pushed out of the countryside by the enclosure of land. They had no choice but to live wherever the economics of rents, wages, and distance from employment dictated. While the skilled and the fortunate found refuge in the small, functional through terraces, many of the poorest gravitated to another form of housing that emerged in the industrial cities of the early nineteenth century.

Today, in many British towns, the Victorian back-to-back house is an extinct species, having been almost completely expunged from the urban landscape by the slum clearances of the late twentieth century. Only in Leeds, where they were built right up to 1909, and in the late nineteenth century to a higher quality than elsewhere, do they still exist in large numbers. Many have been modernized and made comfortable. Elsewhere only a handful are still standing, and for good reason. Back-to-back houses were brick terraces, usually two storeys and one room deep, that were built in double rows along a central spine. This meant that each individual house shared party walls not just with the two houses on either side of it, but also with the house built directly behind it. Only the front of the house had windows and a door, and was open to ventilation. Unlike the through terrace, the back-to-back was enclosed on three sides, which meant there was no possibility of air moving through the house. Although back-to-backs were built in various styles and arranged according to local conditions and topography they were most typically built around a communal courtyard. The houses on the outside faced the street, those on the inner side faced one another across the courtyard, within which were communal earth privies at one end and a water pump at the other. Edwin Chadwick in his report on the condition of the labouring classes described back-to-backs built around courtyards with a single pump and privy that was 'common to the occupants of about twenty houses'. The courts themselves were often only around ten to fifteen feet wide. Peter Gaskell wrote of back-to-backs in Manchester 'fronting one way into a narrow court, across which the inmates of the opposite houses may shake hands without stepping out of their own doors'. Access to these courtyards and the houses surrounding them was gained through narrow brick tunnels.

The layouts of the individual houses varied somewhat between different cities but typically the ground floor was made up of a single living room around fifteen feet square, sometimes even smaller. A narrow, spiral, almost vertical staircase led up to a second room of identical dimensions. In some back-to-backs there was a third attic floor. Cooking was carried out in the living room on an iron range, meaning there was no way of separating domestic functions. Water for both cooking and washing was gathered from the communal pump in the inner courtyard and washing was done in communal washhouses – where they were provided. With nowhere to dry clothes, washing was hung on lines across the courtyards and across the streets, as can be seen in photographs from the mid-twentieth century before the great waves of post-war slum clearance. Some back-to-back houses had cellars, which were sometimes rented out as separate dwellings; this was particularly common in Liverpool.

The conditions within a back-to-back house were no worse, and in some cases better, than those found within the sorts of rural cottages that so many of the new urban migrants had left behind; indeed they represented the further refinement and development of styles of back-to-back housing that had existed long before the industrial revolution. What was different however was the population density. Edwin Chadwick complained that they were 'without ventilation or drainage; and, like

a honeycomb, every particle of space is occupied'. Such houses, he reported, were 'erected with a rapidity that astonishes persons who are unacquainted with their flimsy structure'. In Manchester, Robert Southey reported that the poor workers were 'crowded together' in tiny houses built 'in narrow street and lanes, blocked up from light and air . . . because every inch of land is of such value, that room for light and air cannot be afforded them'. Examinations of the back-to-backs in Gateshead led Robert Rawlinson to conclude that 'the spaces between the fronts of these back-to-back rows of houses are so narrow as to render it almost impossible for either sun or wind to get at them, and to render them habitually dark and unwholesome'.

Stanley Terrace, one of the many streets of back-to-back houses in Leeds. Each block consists of eight homes with internal yards between.

However, back-to-backs found favour with speculative builders. They maximized the number of homes that could be placed on each acre of valuable urban land and the shared walls reduced the costs of construction. Great, sweeping fields of these tiny, dark, insanitary houses were built around the mills and factories in Manchester, Leeds, Leicester, Liverpool, Hull, Birmingham, and elsewhere. In Nottingham,

The tiny front parlour of one of the preserved back-to-back houses in Birmingham, this one decorated in the style of the 1870s.

where rights to common land restricted the city's capacity to grow, back-to-backs became predominant. Engels wrote in the early 1840s that 'In Nottingham there are in all 11,000 houses, of which between 7,000 and 8,000 are built back to back with a rear parti-wall so that no through ventilation is possible, while a single privy usually serves for several houses. During an investigation made a short time since, many rows of houses were found to have been built over shallow drains covered only by the boards of the ground floor.' In Sheffield by the middle of the century sixteen thousand back-to-backs had been built. By the same time there were twenty to thirty thousand in Liverpool and a similar number in Manchester. In Birmingham, by the 1870s, there were around forty thousand; in Leeds they made up 71 per cent of the housing by 1886. Yet in some towns the back-to-back never found favour. Very few were built in London or Bristol.

From the outset back-to-backs were the focus of controversy. Robert Rawlinson concluded that the back-to-back houses of Manchester were not just unhealthy by design but 'of faulty construction' as they had 'no back doors nor windows, no yard nor privy, no sinkstone [stone basin], nor internal water supply; many sleeping rooms have no flue, nor adequate means of ventilation; privies have to be used in common, and, of course, are not what the name implies; they are frequently ruinous, and sickeningly dirty.' Edwin Chadwick complained that the back-to-backs he visited in Manchester had walls that were 'only half a brick thick. . . . and that the whole of the materials are slight and unfit for purpose'. Rawlinson came across 'Back-to-back Cottages' with 'divisional walls half a brick thick; joists and rafters of three-quarter-inch boards, which a cat walking over will shake'. The weight of opinion among sanitary and housing reformers became so heavily against back-to-back houses that attempts to ban their construction began as early as the 1840s. Under the Public Health Act of 1875 local councils were given the power to prohibit the building of new back-to-backs.

Back-to-backs were synonymous with the unhealthy courts at their centre but in this feature they were not unique. The Victorians built their new industrial towns and cities over street plans inherited from earlier ages. In pre-industrial times the wealthy and the poor had lived in the same districts. The rich built themselves large homes on the main streets behind which were gardens, yards, orchards, and the homes of the poor, arranged around courts or yards. Narrow passageways linked the main thoroughfares to these smaller houses. The entrance to one court in London, Frying-Pan Alley in Field Lane, was just two feet six inches wide. As industry drew more and more people to the cities and the pressure for additional housing increased, these court houses often became overcrowded. Ever more homes were built wherever there were patches of land behind the main streets. Clusters of housing appeared in the yards and gardens of larger houses. As they were off the main streets they were hidden from general view. Robert Rawlinson wrote that near streets on which could be found rotting tenements were 'covered passages' that led 'into still narrower, dirtier, and more crowded courts' in which lay 'houses more ruinous and more crowded than those fronting the streets'. In Liverpool, eighty-six thousand people lived in court houses by 1840. In Birmingham there were more than two thousand courts that were home to fifty thousand inhabitants by 1845. A report on the 'Homes of the Bristol Poor' published in the *Bristol Mercury* in 1884 described how 'whole families' were forced to find shelter in houses that were 'hemmed in and blocked from the light'. Within one 'dark, gloomy room, without vestige of furniture or the semblance of occupation by human beings' the reporter from the *Mercury* 'found the half-naked children dreary and joyless, huddled together over a cinder fire, keeping house where both parents, were out all day'. It was within a similar court that Charles Dickens set Fagin's den, to which Oliver Twist is taken.

> A dirtier or more wretched place he had never seen. The street was very narrow and muddy, and the air was impregnated with filthy odours. There were a good many small shops; but the only stock in trade appeared to be heaps of children, who, even at that time of night, were crawling in and out at the doors, or screaming from the inside. The sole places that seemed to prosper amid the general blight of the place, were the public-houses; and in them, the lowest orders of Irish were wrangling with might and main. Covered ways and yards, which here and there diverged from the main street, disclosed little knots of houses, where drunken men and women were positively wallowing in filth . . .

In the 1840s Friedrich Engels reported that there were 2,270 courts in Liverpool, describing them as 'small spaces built up on all four sides and having but one entrance, a narrow, covered passage-way, the whole ordinarily very dirty and inhabited exclusively by proletarians'. A decade later Hugh Shimmin, a celebrated Liverpool journalist, ventured into the worst of the city's courts to report on the lives of their residents. In an article in 1850 he explained how the various rooms within the courts were rented out.

> The court houses are frequently four stories high, 'straight up and down', and contain four apartments – a cellar, a living room and two bedrooms; and often in these houses two and sometimes three families reside. At the top of the court stand the open cesspool and privy. The houses adjoining these are sometimes let at a lower rent: thus poor creatures have a premium offered them for the loss of their health and the possibility of cutting short their days. The rents vary from 2s. 9d. to 4s. 6d., according to locality.

Court housing in Liverpool in the early twentieth century. Lacking ventilation and sanitation, they were frequently the loci of epidemics of cholera and other diseases.

By 1864 the number of courts in Liverpool had risen to 3,073, constituting some 7,825 houses in which an estimated one hundred and ten thousand people lived. That same year the building of courts was banned nationally. Yet there were still around a thousand courts in Liverpool in 1903. The last were not demolished until the slum clearances of the 1960s, the clearances during which much of Falkner Street was also torn down. Liverpool City Council, in the 1860s, aware of the city's reputation for insanitary court housing and chronic overcrowding, became the first council in the country to build social housing.

Within both the older court houses and some of the back-to-backs were also found cellars. While some were used for storage or as sculleries, others were dwellings. Cellar dwellings were often slightly larger than the rooms above but this was their only advantage. Most consisted of a single room, and as they were below ground level they were dark, with light coming from a small window just above street level. Most accounts from the period concluded that cellar dwellings represented the lowest abyss of insanitary housing. As their walls were pressed against the naked earth they were damp. Heavy rains caused ground water levels to rise, flooding many of them. Mixed in with this water was the sewage from the local cesspits. A survey of Manchester conducted in 1835 concluded that within the city there were 3,500 cellar dwellings in which fifteen thousand people, around 12 per cent of the city's population, had found shelter. That same year the French diplomat and traveller Alexis de Tocqueville described how the industrial poor of the city lived, huddled in 'one-story houses whose ill-fitting planks and broken windows show them up, even from a distance, as the last refuge a man might find between poverty and death. None-the-less the wretched people reduced to living in them can still inspire jealousy of their fellow beings. Below some of their miserable dwellings is a row of cellars to which a sunken corridor leads. Twelve to fifteen human beings are crowded pell-mell into each of these damp, repulsive holes.'

Such conditions made it effectively impossible for those living in cellars to keep their homes clean and sanitary. Friedrich Engels wrote of a Manchester cellar in which 'the water constantly wells up through a hole stopped with clay, the cellar lying below the river level, so that its occupant, a hand-loom weaver, had to bail out the water from his dwelling every morning and pour it into the street.' The damp, when combined with the general lack of ventilation, meant they became widely recognized as the most unhealthy of all forms of dwelling, associated with sickness and disease. Drawing an early link between insanitary housing and ill health, the poet Robert Southey, who visited Manchester in 1807, reported that 'a great proportion of the poor lodge in cellars, damp and dark, where every kind of filth is suffered to accumulate, because no exertions of domestic care can ever make such homes decent. These places are so many hot-beds of infection; and the poor in large towns are rarely or never without an infectious fever among them, a plague of their own.'

In her 1848 novel *Mary Barton: A Tale of Manchester Life*, Elizabeth Gaskell had two of her characters, John Barton and George Wilson, venture into the cellar dwellings of Berry Street where they witnessed the conditions in which the poor were forced to live.

> It was unpaved; and down the middle a gutter forced its way, every now and then forming pools in the holes with which the street abounded . . . As they passed, women from their doors tossed household slops of *every* description into the gutter; they ran into the next pool, which overflowed and stagnated . . . You went down one step even from the foul area into the cellar in which a family of human beings lived. It was very dark inside. The window-panes were, many of them, broken and stuffed with rags, which was reason enough for the dusky light that pervaded the place even at mid-day. After the account I have given of the state of the street, no one can be surprised that on going into the cellar inhabited by Davenport, the smell was so fœtid as almost to knock the two men down. Quickly recovering themselves, as those inured to such things do, they began to penetrate the thick darkness of the place, and to see three or four little children rolling on the damp, nay wet, brick floor, through which the stagnant, filthy moisture of the street oozed up; the fire-place was empty and black; the wife sat on her husband's lair, and cried in the dank loneliness.

Conditions in the cellar dwellings of nearby Liverpool in the middle of the century were just as bad. There the poorest of the poor lived in the city centre at extraordinarily high densities. When Friedrich Engels visited in the 1840s he decried the fact that 'Liverpool, with all its commerce, wealth, and grandeur treats its workers with the same barbarity. A full fifth of the population, more than 45,000 human beings, live in narrow, dark, damp, badly-ventilated cellar dwellings, of which there are 7,862 in the city.'

The enormous and unrelenting demand for accommodation that encouraged nineteenth-century landlords to convert cellars into dwellings led others to subdivide large houses into separate rentable rooms. Some became what the Victorians called lodging houses, otherwise known as flophouses. What they offered was cheap, basic accommodation, for short-term tenants who rented beds in shared rooms by the night and for just a few pence. Lodging houses ranged from small terraced houses in which a few rooms had been opened up for lodgers to large establishments in substantial but decaying houses that could offer a hundred beds or more. Some were better and cleaner than others but in the worst lodging houses as many beds as possible were crammed into each room to maximize profits. They existed, in theory at least, for migratory workers, men who moved from town to town and district to district in search of work. However, in many lodging houses families who had fallen upon hard times and were unable to afford any other form of lodgings took refuge. In some cases life in the grimmest of the common lodging houses was only one step above life on the streets.

Like many Victorian social reformers Peter Gaskell believed that the worst of lodging houses were 'foci for crime', and that by jumbling together criminals with people who were merely destitute (especially the young) they brought 'into existence vices which might have lain dormant, if not roused into vitality by their unnatural stimulus'. Families with children took up 'abode in these haunts of crime; where, if not already debased by other causes, they are speedily reduced to the very lowest ebb of moral depravity'. In his account of a Manchester lodging house in the 1830s he revealed himself just as appalled by the supposed immorality and criminality of the tenants as he was by the conditions in which they slept.

> The extraordinary sights presented by these lodging houses during the night, are deplorable in the extreme, and must fill the heart of any man, open to the feelings of humanity, with pain and unutterable disgust. Five, six, seven beds – according to the capacity of the rooms – are arranged on the floor – there being in the generality of cases, no bedsteads, or any substitutes for them; these are covered with clothing of the most scanty and filthy description. They are occupied indiscriminately by persons of both sexes, strangers perhaps to each other, except a few of the regular occupants. Young men and young women; men, wives, and their children – all lying in a noisome atmosphere, swarming with vermin, and often intoxicated. But a veil must be drawn over the atrocities which are committed: suffice it to say, that villany,

debauchery and licentiousness, are here portrayed in their darkest character.

All three of the houses that appeared in *A House Through Time* became boarding houses or lodging houses, but all appear to have been of the more respectable varieties. For much of their time in shared occupancy most remained, to varying extents, family homes, with rooms being let out to boarders who were also provided with some of their meals – board and lodging. Other houses just as grand or even grander than 62 Falkner Street, 5 Ravensworth Terrace, or 10 Guinea Street were less fortunate and became lodging houses of the more infamous variety. Some older properties in polluted industrial city centres became tenements, properties that were subdivided like lodging houses but were intended for longer-term tenants. Many tenements were large houses that had been abandoned by the middle classes who increasingly flocked to the growing suburbs. As the districts in which they had been built declined, landlords attempted to maintain an income for their properties by subdividing them. Often the result was incongruous: the poorest strata of the Victorian urban working class living at addresses that only decades earlier had been regarded as exclusive. Thomas Beames, author of the 1852 book *The Rookeries of London*, noted that while many of the houses in which the poor found shelter were jerry-built, slap-dash structures of recent construction, made of 'mere lath and plaster', the larger of the tenements tended to be 'very ancient houses, deserted by those to whose ancestors they once belonged. The tide of fashion – the rage for novelty – the changes of the times, have also changed the character of the population who now tenant these buildings.' He wrote:

> In the dingiest streets of the metropolis are found houses,
> the rooms of which are lofty, the walls panelled, the ceilings
> beautifully ornamented . . . the chimney-pieces models for the
> sculptor. In many rooms there still remain the grotesque carvings
> for which a former age was so celebrated. You have the heavy
> balustrades, the wide staircase, with its massive rails . . . you have
> the strong doorway, with its carvings, the large unwieldy door,
> and those well-known features of the olden time, in keeping
> with the quaint and dust-stained engravings which seem to

have descended as heirlooms from one poor family to another. The names of the courts remind you of decayed glory – Villiers, Dorset, Buckingham, Norfolk, telling of the stately edifices which once stood where you now breathe the impure atmosphere of a thickly-peopled court . . .

Robert Rawlinson's description of decaying inner-city tenements was even more poignant. In 1842 he wrote of how houses

in our great sea-ports and inland manufacturing towns . . . originally erected for 'the merchant princes' are now in ruins. From having been the abodes of those possessing wealth, they are now the abodes of the improvident, of the vagrant, of the vicious [addicted to vice], and of the unfortunate. The quaint carving on the stone-work looks out of place, the walls are half in ruins, the gables are shattered, and foul weather-stains of damp blotch the surface. Within, matters are even worse: the rooms are now divided and sub-divided on every floor; the staircase is darkened, its massive hand-rail and carved balusters are crippled and broken; the once firm stairs are now ricketty and dangerous; the stucco-finished plastering is blackened and in holes, the dusty and rotten laths being in many places bare; the landing-windows, when the space is open, have neither frame nor glass, so that the rain drives in right and left; make-shift doors lead into small spaces let off as separate tenements.

Most tenements were, as Beames and Rawlinson stated, older houses that had once been owned by the rich. A few, according to Rawlinson, were centuries old, 'erected in Queen Elizabeth's reign'. In London's Cloth Fair, near Smithfield, were houses so ancient they were survivors of the Great Fire of 1666. However, on occasions speculative builders misread the winds and misjudged the market and they found themselves unable to find suitably moneyed tenants for newly completed middle-class homes. In such circumstances they often had little choice but to subdivide a brand-new house if they were to recoup some of their losses. George Godwin, editor of the *Builder*, an often insightful London architecture journal, noted in 1859 that 'vast numbers of houses are rising up every month in this metropolis built with a view to their occupation by single families which, even from the time they are finished are let in tenements to two or three.'

As tenement houses had been designed for single families they lacked the basic amenities, and what facilities there were – water pumps and privies – were shared and poorly maintained. Life in them was worse than in the back-to-back, as they offered even less privacy. As the descriptions by Thomas Beames and Robert Rawlinson demonstrate, the corridors and staircases of tenements, despite their elaborate decor, were often dirty and decaying. With so many people packed into the subdivided space there were also constant complaints about noise, fumes, and drunken behaviour. Robert Rawlinson in his 1850 *Report to the General Board of Health* described the Gateshead districts of Pipewellgate and Hillgate, across the River Tyne from Ravensworth Terrace and the grand homes clustered around Summerhill Square.

> Neither plan nor written description can adequately convey to the mind the true state and condition of the room-tenements and of the inhabitants occupying them. The subsoil on the sloping side of the hill is damp and most foul; the brickwork of the buildings is ruinous, the timber rotten, and an appearance of general decay pervades the whole district. The buildings, originally erected as residences of a superior description, have single rooms let off as tenements, which are crowded with men, women, and children; the walls are discoloured with age, damp, and rot; the windows are broken; old rags, straw, and boards, occupy the place of glass, so that means of light and ventilation are alike absent. There are no sewers nor drains, neither is there any proper (privy) accommodation; solid filth encumbers the surface; liquid refuse saturates the subsoil, and is drawn by capillary attraction through the porous bricks up into the walls; personal cleanliness or a healthy atmosphere is impossible.

But this decay to the fabric of the buildings was not just what had rendered the tenements of the Tyne so insanitary and their residents so prone to disease; the other critical factor was overcrowding. 'The poorer classes of Gateshead', Rawlinson concluded, were 'not only exceedingly ill-lodged, but also much overcrowded in their lodgings; that it is an habitual thing for an entire family to live, sleep, cook, eat, wash, &c., in a single room; the corners of single rooms thus occupied being occasionally further sub-let to other families or lodgers.' In the 1850s a single house in Hillgate was home to seventy-one people who collectively made up sixteen families.

The way large urban houses were rented out frequently led to lodging houses and tenements becoming even more overcrowded as it encouraged the subletting of rooms. Absent owners, many of whom had escaped to the suburbs, used middlemen to manage properties that they rarely visited. Short leases provided little incentive for owners to maintain or improve houses, while the constant demand for cheap accommodation from the poor meant even the most dilapidated houses could still be profitable. The preponderance of tenements and the levels of overcrowding reported in them was a reflection of the suffocating poverty that blighted a whole stratum of the urban working class. It may well have been the case that the majority of the poor of nineteenth-century London were only able to afford to rent rooms rather than whole houses. For many having the means to rent a whole room for their family alone, rather than having to share that space with others, was a luxury beyond their reach, yet to afford to rent two rooms, and thereby have a separate space for sleeping, or have the option of having children and adults sleep in different rooms, was regarded as the minimum required to maintain any pretence of respectability.

Even in good times when their wages comfortably covered their rent, poor people were often unwilling to seek out better accommodation. They feared losing their rooms if their work dried up and their income was reduced, and such fears were entirely justified. Falling sick, suffering an industrial injury, the theft of money or food, any number of misfortunes could upset the delicate balance and cast a poor family into penury. While they were able to tolerate dire insanitary living conditions, most would sacrifice anything to avoid the ultimate indignity of submitting to the less than tender care of the workhouse. In the Bethnal Green of the 1840s Hector Gavin, author of a house-to-house investigation of that district's working-class houses, encountered a man named Johnston who was living with his wife and four children in a single room in a house on Collingwood Place.

His wife was dangerously ill of typhoid erysipelas on the miserable bed, on which the whole family usually slept. The rest of the family therefore had to sleep on the bare boards, in the same room with the sufferer, thus further defiling the impure atmosphere of this dark and damp abode of helpless poverty. 1s. 6d. a week was the rent; yet the husband's peculiar trade failing him, he had, for a considerable time, been unable to earn more than 1s. a week; they were, therefore, all starving. Nevertheless, in the belief that he would get work next week, he would not consent to place himself and his four children in the workhouse.

The fundamental economic fact that determined where and how a vast swathe of the urban poor lived was that wages were low relative to the cost of rents. The Victorian poor paid a far higher proportion of their income in rent than the middle classes, and as they needed to live near where they worked they were unable to relocate to cheaper districts on the edge of the cities. They were consequently trapped in the central districts, which in many cases meant being trapped in a life that revolved around a succession of grim rented rooms.

Whether in a cellar or a tenement, what made overcrowding so catastrophic was the lack of basic sanitation – functioning sewers, properly serviced privies, and provisions for washing. In the back-to-backs, cellar dwellings, and court housing the privies were communal, located outside and shared by multiple households. Human waste from them was deposited in cesspools that were emptied a few times a year, although sometimes they were left for years. At other times the sheer weight of demand meant privies overflowed. In 1832 Dr James Kay reported that in Manchester's Parliament Street 'there is only one privy for three hundred and eighty inhabitants, which is placed in a narrow passage, whence its effluvia infest the adjacent houses, and must prove a most fertile source of disease. In this street also, cesspools with open grids have been made close to the doors of the houses, in which disgusting refuse accumulates, and whence its noxious effluvia constantly exhale. In Parliament-passage about thirty houses have been erected, merely separated by an extremely narrow passage (a yard and a half wide) from the wall and back door of other houses. These thirty houses have one privy.' Thomas Southwood

Smith, a doctor from Bethnal Green, gave evidence on conditions he found in the bucolically named Lamb's Fields, an area of east London into which flowed the waste from the 'privies of all the houses of a street called North Street . . . Nothing can be conceived more disgusting than the appearance of this ditch for an extent of from 300 to 400 feet, and the odour of the effluvia from it is at this moment most offensive'. Sure that poor sanitation contributed to ill health, he asserted that 'Lamb's Fields is the fruitful source of fever to the houses which immediately surround it, and to the small streets which branch off from it. Particular houses were pointed out to me from which entire families have been swept away, and from several of the streets fever is never absent'. Tenements, having been designed for single families, were equally ill-suited to the needs of multiple families. Robert Rawlinson reported that in the worst of the inner-city tenements, 'One privy serves for a whole court, and this is usually filthy; the cesspool full, overflowing; the foetid refuse stagnant over the surface. An external standpipe, the water on only for one hour in twenty-four, supplies water to an entire court with many tenants; tubs, mugs, pots, pans, and troughs, being placed in yards, on stair-landings, or in the filthy rooms, to absorb all the deleterious gases of the places.'

The appalling sanitary conditions were made worse still by the number of animals that lived and died in the Victorian cities. Rapid growth had created vast urbanized spaces but within them various forms of animal husbandry persisted; sheep were still driven through the streets to market. With no refrigeration, livestock had to be slaughtered close to where their flesh was to be consumed, and the slaughterhouses were inevitably located where the poor had their homes. A medical officer in London's Whitechapel, one of the city's most ill-famed districts, reported to the local Poor Law authorities that he had personally seen Rose Lane, one of Whitechapel's better streets, 'completely flooded with blood from the slaughter house'. In addition to the blood and offal from slaughterhouses and knackers' yards literally tons of animal dung also accumulated on the streets, from the millions of horses that pulled carts, cabs, and omnibuses, and from urban cow yards and pigsties jumbled in among the houses. The poet Robert Southey spoke of the 'stench of animal putrefaction' lingering over the poorer districts of early nineteenth-century Manchester, while the Central Board of Health for the City of York noted in one of its reports that during the cholera epidemic of 1831 there were 'slaughter-houses, dung-heaps, pig-sties' situated in the 'heart of the town', all of them 'pouring their foetid contents into open drains'. Dr James Kay explained how in parts of some cities the residents were paid by local butchers to house pigs on little patches of open land surrounding their homes. These open areas he reported were 'immediately covered with pigstyes, and converted into a dung-heap and receptacle of the putrescent garbage, upon which the animals are fed, as also of the refuse which is now heedlessly flung into it from all the surrounding dwellings.' The journalist Angus Reach described how, in the Leeds of 1849, 'A short walk from the Briggate, in the direction in which Deansgate branches off' lay 'a perfect wilderness of foulness'. There 'mud lay in wreaths from wall to wall; and across open spaces, overlooked by houses all round, in which the pigs, wandering from the central oasis, seemed to be roaming through what was only a large sty. Indeed, pigs seem to be natural inhabitants of such places. I think that they are more common in some parts of Leeds than dogs and cats are in others.'

In some areas the danger to health posed by the animals and animal waste was accentuated by the fact that some of the residents of cellars and courts shared not just their streets but even their homes with livestock, which were valuable possessions to people so impoverished. A Leeds doctor told Edwin Chadwick's sanitary commissioners that he had 'seen a cellar dwelling in one of the most densely-populated districts of Leeds in which were living seven persons, with one corner fenced off and a pig in it; a ridge of clay being placed round the fence to prevent the wet from the pigsty running all over the floor, and to this cellar there was no drainage.'

The vast accumulations of animal and human waste that gathered in the streets and around the homes of the Victorian poor had nowhere to go. The system of privies and night-soil men that had developed in pre-industrial times was simply overwhelmed by the extraordinary urban growth of the nineteenth century. In the middle of that century there were five thousand cesspools in London which in theory were to be regularly emptied by the night-soil men, and the waste therein sold to farmers who used it as fertilizer. However in some tenements, as the numbers dwelling in them had increased, cellars were converted into cesspits in which literally tons of human waste gradually accumulated, sometimes up to a depth of several feet. Robert Rawlinson reported that in Leeds 'there are upwards of one thousand inhabited rooms which have middens, privies, and cess-pits beneath them.' A survey of two London houses in the 1840s reported that their cellars were full of sewage to a depth of three feet, which for years had been permitted to accumulate. The watery effluence from urban cesspools seeped into the ground water and contaminated the very soil.

In city after city, rivers that had run fresh when populations had been counted in mere tens of thousands became open gutters. Alexis de Tocqueville spoke of the 'fetid, muddy waters' in 1830s Manchester that were 'stained with a thousand colours by the factories they pass'. In 1800 Lord Byron had been in the habit of going for a morning swim in the Thames at Westminster Bridge. Half a century later the river had become a vast sewer, its ebb and flow incapable of flushing away the waste of so vast a metropolis. In a poem of 1819, Byron's friend Percy Shelley wrote, 'Hell is a city much like London – A populous and a smoky city'. By the middle of the century Shelley's verse appeared prophetic. The water in their rivers and the earth under the feet of the city dweller were fast becoming as polluted as the air they breathed. The inevitable consequence of so profound a collapse in public sanitation and so vast and rapid an accumulation of impoverished people in such small and concentrated areas was a public-health disaster: the outbreak of epidemic disease.

By the 1840s it was evident that the unprecedented wealth and material progress brought about by the industrial harnessing of coal and steam had come at a cost. The conditions that had been permitted to develop within the homes of the industrial workers, as well as those found within the factories and mills themselves, had resulted in the improvements in life expectancy that had been won over earlier decades being thrown into a shocking reverse. Although the statistics for the early decades of the century have to be treated with caution, the national death rate before 1831 was probably something around 19 per 1,000. By 1838 it had risen to 22.4. In 1849, in the aftermath of the second of the Victorian cholera epidemics, it had increased to 25 per 1,000. These national figures disguise the fact that mortality was concentrated in the poorer districts of the industrial cities. In the cholera epidemic of 1832 the death rate in the city of Glasgow reached a catastrophic 49 per 1,000. Central to this terrifying decline in the health of the industrial working class were the insanitary and overcrowded conditions in which so many people were forced to live. For the poor the home itself had become the incubator of disease.

The long struggle to address the housing crisis and the health crisis it facilitated began with the work of the various sanitary and public-health reformers. As the mechanisms by which diseases like typhus, smallpox, measles, scarlet fever, and above all cholera were transmitted remained unknown or misunderstood, those who like Dr James Kay were medically trained, rather than offering diagnoses, gathered information. What the reformers accumulated was a vast body of facts and statistics – adult and child mortality rates, population densities, and other metrics. Their reports and investigations made stark and evident the link between infectious disease and poor sanitation, bad house design, shoddy construction, inadequate ventilation, and chronic overcrowding. The creation of the Poor Law Commission in 1832 and the General Register Office for England and Wales in 1837 helped bring this information together. The key document that linked diseases to the conditions within the home was Edwin Chadwick's 1842 *Report on the Sanitary Conditions of the Labouring Population of Great Britain*, in which he argued that the health crisis was also a housing crisis, one that could be solved by the creation of proper sewers and controls on how homes were constructed. Chadwick's report was so influential that, incredibly for an official publication, it became a minor bestseller, with a hundred thousand copies sold. Yet change came only gradually, partly because the solutions involved spending public money on an enormous scale – building sewers and improving houses. To this, in an era in which many were dedicated to the principle of *laissez-faire* capitalism, there was inevitably much opposition. While defenders of individual liberty denounced the work of Chadwick and others as an infringement upon their rights, an unknown discontent in Leeds complained of the reformers that, 'All they want is to expend other people's money and get popularity by letting what they may call poor have the water for nothing and also accommodating themselves and tenants at other people's expense.' *The Times* in 1854 went as far as saying, 'We prefer to take our chance with cholera than be bullied into health. There is nothing a man hates so much as being cleansed against his will or having his floor swept, his hall whitewashed, his dung heaps cleared away and his thatch forced to give way to slate.'

The various public health and sanitation acts of the 1840s and 1850s gave local councils the power to act but did not compel them. Liverpool, regarded as among the most insanitary cities in the country, became the first to make serious efforts to tackle the problem and successfully navigated the Liverpool Sanitary Act through Parliament in 1846. This empowered the council to appoint an Inspector of Nuisances (i.e. dangers to the community), a Borough Engineer, and a Medical Officer of Health, the highly efficient Dr William Henry Duncan. With new powers they set about improving conditions in the city. Other authorities were far more tentative and achieved far less. Yet by 1853 local Boards of Health had been established by over a hundred and sixty towns and cities.

Throughout this period of sanitary and housing reform one disease above all others gave impetus to the struggle to both improve the conditions in which the poor lived and halt the public-health catastrophe. Cholera first came to Britain in 1832, brought ashore by a sailor who landed in Sunderland. From that bridgehead the disease tore across the country. In that first epidemic thirty-two thousand people died. The shocking visceral speed with which cholera drew the life from its victims, and the evident inability of the authorities and the experts to control its spread, made it 'King Cholera', the most dreaded of all the infectious diseases. When cholera returned in 1848 it took sixty-two thousand lives. The epidemic of 1853–54 took another twenty-three thousand. When cholera returned for a fourth time in 1865 it harvested another twenty thousand souls. Among the victims of the third epidemic was John Bowes, who lived at 62 Falkner Street in Liverpool with his wife Elizabeth. As the house had a reliable supply of clean water it is unlikely that he contracted cholera at home. His profession was listed on his death certificate as 'wine merchant', a job which took him to the Liverpool docks, where the worst of the courts and cellar dwellings were located. It is likely that it was while there, or in some other insanitary district of the city, that he drank cholera-infected water. As was typical he succumbed quickly. Continuing on a business trip, until the effects of the disease incapacitated him, he died in Poulton-le-Sands, then a

An 1866 depiction of 'King Cholera' dispensing contaminated water to the poor. The image appeared at around the time that Dr John Snow demonstrated that the disease was transmitted through drinking water.

village near Morecambe sixty miles north of Liverpool. His death forced his widow Elizabeth to become a boarding-house keeper and rent out rooms at number 62.

In 1872 a new Public Health Act carved the country into sanitary authorities, and obliged each to appoint an Inspector of Nuisances and a Medical Officer of Health, who between them were responsible for improving public health. Speculative builders still found ways to squeeze as much profit out of every square foot of land and continued to cut corners where they could. However in 1875 a second Public Health Act was passed by the Conservative government in which Benjamin Disraeli was Prime Minister. The new act consolidated earlier laws but went further in improving housing stock. Rather than permitting local authorities to use byelaws to control the building of terraced houses and ensure they met minimum requirements of sanitation and ventilation, it obliged them to do so. The 1875 Act also regulated the use of cellars as dwelling places. The Artisans' and Labourers' Dwellings Act of the same year empowered local authorities to condemn and replace homes deemed to be insanitary.

In response to the 1875 Public Health Act a new type of working-class housing emerged, the byelaw terrace. These were two-storey homes whose layout and dimensions adhered to the stipulations laid down in the 1875 Act. Their rooms were larger and they were lit by taller sash windows that improved both lighting and ventilation. They had enclosed private yards and private earth-closet privies on the back wall. The demands of the new act forced builders to lay the new streets in what became the almost ubiquitous grid-iron pattern, with each street serviced by an alleyway behind. In 2011 it was estimated that around 15 per cent of the UK's housing stock was made up of byelaw terraced houses.

One of the heroes of Disraeli's novel *Sybil* (1845), the aristocratic Charles Egremont, gradually becomes awoken to the terrible injustices of his age and appalled by the ways in which the labouring poor are mistreated by his own class and indeed his own family. Sybil herself, the woman of the book's title, reveals to him the miserable conditions in which industrial workers are trapped and helps him formulate ways by which relations between the 'two nations' might be improved and national unity attained, even in the midst of runaway industrial expansion and urban growth. Disraeli's other hero is Mr Trafford, a factory owner whose social conscience leads him to ensure that his vast factory is well lit and well ventilated to improve the health of the workers. Under his paternal care and watchful eye they enjoy better health than those employed elsewhere and the number of industrial accidents is reduced. In his ultimate act of benevolence Trafford builds a model village close to the factory, in order to house his workers in clean and sanitary conditions. 'When the workpeople of Mr Trafford left his factory', wrote Disraeli, 'they were not forgotten. Deeply had Mr Trafford pondered on the influence of the employer on the health and content of his workpeople. He knew well that the domestic virtues are dependent on the existence of a home, and one of his first efforts had been to build a village where every family might be well lodged . . . In every street there was a well; behind the factory there were the public baths.'

Although the plot of *Sybil* proposes a Romantic and idealized relationship between the classes, Disraeli had no delusions as to the reality of life for the industrial poor. He had toured the industrial regions of the north and while researching and writing the novel he read the reports of the various parliamentary commissions established to examine the conditions of the industrial poor. Disraeli's fictional depictions of the 'wretched tenements' in which the workers were 'obliged to sleep, without distinction of age, or sex' differ little from the documentary accounts of Chadwick, Gaskell, and Rawlinson. Likewise the solutions that Trafford arrives at for bridging the chasm separating rich from poor, and elevating the working class were drawn from contemporary reality.

By the 1850s a number of Victorian industrialists were using their enormous wealth and access to capital to build houses and model villages for their own workers. The most famous of this breed of philanthropic mill and factory owners was Titus Salt, who after taking over his family's wool and textile business in 1824 became the richest man in Bradford. In the 1840s, when serving as Bradford's mayor, Salt witnessed the effect that a cholera epidemic had upon the industrial poor of the town. In 1850 he set about building a single enormous mill to the north of Bradford that was designed to replace all five of his existing mills. The site selected was away from the pollution and dirt of Bradford, a town that in 1845 had been pronounced 'the most filthy' in the country by James Smith in his *Report to the Health of Towns Commission*. Combining his family name with that of the River Aire, which ran through the site of his new mill, he called it Saltaire. In 1853, the year Saltaire opened, he also began work on a model village to house his employees adjacent to the mill. When completed Saltaire Village consisted of eight hundred homes spread over some fifty acres. Many were simple two-up two-down terraces, others were larger homes, and they were allocated to workers according to the size of their families and their ability to pay the rent. By the standards of 1850s Bradford they were luxurious. Each had its own supply of cold water and its own outside toilet. Each had its own backyard and some came with small front gardens. There was also a large dormitory block for single people. In addition to the houses, Salt built an almshouse for the elderly, public baths, a public dining hall, washhouses, an infirmary, and a school. There was also a library, churches, and a public park. The one form of recreation that was not catered for at Saltaire was drinking alcohol. Titus Salt, a devout Congregationalist and teetotaller, insisted that no pubs or 'beer-shops' were built in the village. By 1871 the population of Saltaire was over four thousand. Similar model villages were created by other philanthropic industrialists. William Hesketh Lever, later first Viscount Leverhulme, built Port Sunlight across the Mersey from Liverpool. The village had communal gardens, and later an art gallery, and housed the workers employed in his factory producing Sunlight soap. The Cadbury family built Bourneville, a model settlement constructed on a hundred and twenty acres of land near the Cadbury factory outside Birmingham. It was designed, as George Cadbury wrote, so that 'each man could have his own house, a large garden to cultivate and healthy surroundings'.

Both Saltaire and Bourneville still exist. The houses built by their philanthropic founders are still inhabited. Saltaire is one of Bradford's heritage sites; the great mill built by Titus Salt is now an art gallery. Not far away, in the centre of Birmingham, a very different heritage site can be found. On Hurst Street stand a cluster of early nineteenth-century back-to-back houses, the last in the city to have survived. Built in 1802 they were converted into shops and a warehouse, which enabled them to survive the slum clearances that by the 1970s had eradicated back-to-back houses from the cityscape. Rediscovered in the 1980s they were granted listed status and restored in a project funded by English Heritage. Today they are run by the National Trust and open to visitors.

To the modern visitor what is shocking about the Birmingham back-to-backs is just how tiny they are. Their rooms, even when compared to modern city-centre studio flats or micro-apartments in London, New York, or Tokyo, are diminutive. The staircases that are pushed into a corner of each room spiral up so steeply that to climb them is almost like climbing a vertical ladder. The lack of light that is an inevitable feature of a home enclosed on three sides is palpable and oppressive. Yet despite the houses and the court they are clustered around having been carefully restored, it remains difficult to imagine what it was to like to live there. No heritage site can evoke the smells of Victorian privies, the smoke and pollution that hung in the air of the great coal-fired metropolis of the nineteenth century, or the suffocating and overwhelming overcrowding that blighted the lives of the poor. Our ancestors endured life with little personal space, without the privacy we take for granted. They were constantly surrounded by the dozens of others with whom they shared not just the courtyard but the facilities within it. The notion that in order to go to a toilet the occupants of the street-facing houses of back-to-back terraces had to leave their homes, walk along the public street, through a brick passageway, and across the communal courtyard – day or night, rain or sun – is almost unimaginable. As is the cold that made life more difficult still in homes that were draughty and uninsulated, heated only by tiny coal fires and an iron cooking range.

The Birmingham back-to-backs are relics from one of the great political struggles of the nineteenth and twentieth centuries: a battle that was fought by social reformers, politicians, and the poor themselves to improve the standards of housing in which the industrial workers, the men and women whose labour transformed Britain, were forced to lived. But for millions of people they are also a window into the lives of our working-class ancestors. People for whom grand houses like 62 Falkner Street, 5 Ravensworth Terrace, or 10 Guinea Street were never intended.

CHAPTER FIVE

THE DEVIL'S ACRE

The Crisis of the Slums

In the 1840s Friedrich Engels suggested that Manchester was 'peculiarly built', because 'a person may live in it for years, and go in and out daily without coming into contact with a working people's quarter or even with workers, that is, so long as he confines himself to his business or to pleasure walks. This arises chiefly from the fact, that by unconscious tacit agreement, as well as with outspoken conscious determination, the working people's quarters are sharply separated from the sections of the city reserved for the middle-class'. Whatever the peculiarities of Manchester in the 1840s the segregation of the rich and the poor into distinct districts became a standard feature of Britain's larger cities during the nineteenth century. In London the poor and the rich often lived surprisingly close to one another, sometimes in adjacent or parallel streets – grand terraces in one, squat rows of miserable mews houses in the other – isolated from one another. In *Oliver Twist* Charles Dickens classified the slums at Rotherhithe by the Thames as one of the 'many localities that are hidden in London, wholly unknown, even by name, to the great mass of its inhabitants.' The sanitary reformer J. R. Martin put it more succinctly: 'the rich know nothing of the poor', he wrote in his report on the state of English towns in the 1840s. 'The mass of misery that festers beneath the affluence of London and of the great towns', he continued, 'is not known to their wealthy occupants.'

With unprecedented, polychromatic clarity the philanthropist Charles Booth who we first met in chapter one revealed how the rich and poor were distributed across the capital. His famous colour-coded maps pinpointed the exact streets and even the individual homes within which wealth accrued or poverty festered. In Booth's cartography, which began in the 1880s, the squares and terraces that had been laid out by Georgian speculative builders and in which the upper middle classes remained encamped were marked in yellow. The homes of the well-to-do, middle classes in red. At the opposite end of both the social scale and Booth's colour spectrum were the warrens of streets in which the people he described as the 'lowest class' resided. Their homes he marked in black. Within such districts lived the residuum of Victorian society. Of them he wrote: 'Their life is the life of savages, with vicissitudes of extreme hardship and their only luxury is drink.' At street level the homes of the poor were more difficult to locate. The frontages lining the main streets were those of fine buildings. But behind them were the stinking courts and the grimy brick-lined passages that led to them. 'The most lordly streets are frequently but a mask for the squalid districts which lie beyond them', wrote Dickens in his magazine *Household Words* in 1850. The slums were concealed but present; a national secret yet infamous and much discussed. George Godwin of the *Builder* magazine was undoubtedly correct in 1854 when he noted, 'Few persons venture into these haunts besides the regular inhabitants, the London missionaries, the parish surgeon, and the police, and thus the extent of this great evil is imperfectly understood'. Yet while contact between those who lived in the golden squares and the multitudes who loitered in the black labyrinths of winding lanes and slept in dank garrets was constrained even the most unworldly among the wealthy could not fail, on occasion, to catch fleeting glimpses of the slums. The hovels of the poor could be spied at the end of dark streets and passageways by the wealthy through the misty windows of their carriages. If they could not see the slums from time to time they could not help but smell them.

When the railways began to gouge great caverns through the poorest districts of Britain's cities, the wealthy were presented with new vistas from which to examine what had previously been concealed. At that moment, from the 1830s onwards, the middle classes were suddenly able to see not just the poor – beggars, mudlarks, costermongers, crossing-sweepers, bone-grubbers, pure-finders, flower-girls, and prostitutes – but the hovels in which they lived. In 1872, when Gustave Doré drew his famous image of slum houses packed tightly together in a sweeping curved terrace, their yards thronging with people, he set the scene beneath the arches of one of London's railway viaducts. High above the miserable abodes a train is rushing past, conveying its middle-class passengers to more salubrious parts of the city. In *Dombey and Son* Dickens imagines a similar scene but in reverse. As his train cuts through the city Mr Dombey, heartbroken at the recent loss of his son, looks down from the window of his train carriage to see the slum houses.

> Everything around is blackened. There are dark pools of water, muddy lanes, and miserable habitations far below. There are jagged walls and falling houses close at hand, and through the battered roofs and broken windows, wretched rooms are seen, where want and fever hide themselves in many wretched shapes, while smoke and crowded gables, and distorted chimneys, and deformity of brick and mortar penning up deformity of mind and body, choke the murky distance.

One oddity revealed by Booth's maps was that many of Britain's most overcrowded and insanitary streets were the mews where the wealthy kept their horses and coaches, literally around the corners from the most expensive addresses. Yet despite this the attention of the middle classes was focused on the larger and more infamous slums, especially those associated with crime and criminality. This was particularly the case in London. Dr Henry Julian Hunter, who investigated housing conditions for the Privy Council Medical Committee, concluded in 1865 that there were around twenty areas of the capital in which people lived in conditions worse than those found anywhere else in England. The residents of those districts became the objects of a titillating fascination and a fathomless dread. In the twilight zones into which the wealthy never ventured, people they little understood existed beyond their influence or control. In London alone they were said to number one hundred thousand. The thought of so vast a number of people, unknown and yet close by, preyed upon the minds of the elite.

Fascination with the slums was fed by a constant stream of books and newspaper reports, written by men who had penetrated the darkness of the poor districts and encountered the strange races that resided there.

This new genre of literature, 'urban exploration', grew in popularity as attention was drawn away from the conditions in the mills and factories and towards the slums. After 1850 those concerned about the living conditions of the poor no longer bought copies of Chadwick's *Report on Sanitary Conditions* but instead read Henry Mayhew's *London Labour and the London Poor*, or *How the Poor Live* by George R. Sims. The Congregational

Gustave Doré's Over London By Rail, 1872, reveals how the Victorian railway boom had cut canyons through the slums of terrace houses.

minister the Reverend Andrew Mearns added to the genre with *The Bitter Cry of Outcast London*. It was perhaps inevitable in an age of imperial expansion that the abyssal depths of the most impenetrable slums would be compared to the rainforests of 'Darkest Africa', and the slum dwellers classified as another type of 'native', as William Booth, the founder of the Salvation Army, did in his book *In Darkest England and the Way Out*, written in 1890. George Godwin took the colonial metaphor further by adding a racial dimension. 'To investigate the condition of the houses of the very poor in this great metropolis is a task of no small danger and difficulty', he claimed, because to do so it was 'necessary to brave the risks of fever and other injuries to health, and a contact of men and women often as Lawless as the Arab and the Kaffir.' Perhaps unsurprisingly, as Godwin confessed, 'There is amongst the very poor a strong feeling against intrusion.'

Who were the people who lived in slum housing in the age of Victoria? Many of the reformers who investigated conditions in the slums were particularly disturbed by the answer. In the overcrowded tenements people whom they regarded as the 'honest poor' were thrown together with the worst of the so-called 'criminal race'. Hector Gavin, author of the 1840s study *Sanitary Ramblings*, drew a clear distinction between the criminal poor and what he called 'the honest, labouring poor', and believed the former corrupted and contaminated the latter. The immoral section of the poor who resided in 1840s Bethnal Green, he wrote, were those with 'an utter defiance of all the laws of health, and the complete disregard of all the characteristics of civilization.' It was this class of people he argued who 'supply our courts with criminals, our gaols with convicts, our charities with paupers, and our hospitals with the sick and diseased'. The Select Committee on the Health of Towns was informed by one witness in 1840 that the inhabitants of the St Giles Rookery, London's most infamous slum, were 'most intolerably filthy; they are the lowest description of Irish, many Germans, and many Jews, and they are, of all the people in the world, the most filthy'. George Godwin agreed, believing the slum dwellers were 'the poorest Irish lodging-house keepers, tramps, costermongers, thieves, and the lowest class of street-walkers. In addition to these there are small shopkeepers, receivers of stolen goods, brokers, and publicans.'

Every form of immoral behaviour was said to take place in the slum tenements. In decaying houses men and women slept in the same rooms and cohabited in ways that were anathema to middle-class Victorian sexual morality. Drunkenness, violence, and theft were endemic; even incest was said to thrive in the worst of the hovels and tenements of the rookeries. All these vices were amplified by the sheer weight of numbers. As the cities grew so did the numbers squeezed into the slums. Many impoverished districts were hemmed in on all sides by better parts of town, and the slums had no way of expanding to reduce the density of population. In 1858 Dr Conway Evans, the medical officer for the

Strand District of London, listed the multiple effects that overcrowding had on the lives of the slum dwellers he examined.

> The evil consequences of this overcrowding are manifold . . . the duration of life generally is shortened and health impaired . . . these effects, though manifest when looked for . . . in persons of adult age, are far more readily discoverable in the case of infants and young children. But the evil consequences of overcrowding [are] not limited to the impairment of health, or even to the destruction of life . . . but by its action not only are the bodily powers prostrated and sapped, but the moral life is also degraded and debased; and ignorance, indecency, immorality, intemperance, prostitution, and crime, are directly or indirectly fostered and induced. The mode in which prostitution originates in overcrowding is but too frequently illustrated in this densely peopled district; indeed, cases occasionally come under my observation in which this vice cannot but be regarded as the necessary and inevitable result of the indiscriminate manner in which the sexes are huddled together . . . So long as twenty, thirty, or even forty individuals are permitted – it might be said compelled – to reside in a house originally built for the accommodation of a single family or at most two families, so long will the evils pointed out in regard of health, of ignorance, of indecency, immorality, intemperance, prostitution, and crime continue to exist unchecked.

Robert Rawlinson, the famous health inspector, recognized the same vices outside the capital.

> The social and moral abominations resulting from over-crowding in room-tenements may be found described in sanitary and police reports; the sexes, adults and children, having often no means of separation. A midnight inspection of such dwellings is an awful spectacle.

The disastrous effects of overcrowding and insanitary conditions within the Victorian slums were known not just to public health and housing reformers but to those who read their reports or any of the multiple accounts of their work in the newspapers. Similar observations filled the pages of the more sensational books written by the 'urban explorers'. Yet throughout the Victorian nineteenth century the overcrowding was allowed to increase and conditions worsen as new forces changed the urban landscape.

In the 1850s Robert Rawlinson had written about the Pipewellgate and Hillgate slums of Gateshead, areas blighted by tenements whose walls had been 'discoloured with age, damp, and rot'. Conditions there were in many ways typical of the mid-nineteenth-century slum tenements. Pipewellgate and Hillgate were situated in the historic centre of town, in a district that had fallen from favour as the well-to-do moved away from the pollution of industry; which, in Gateshead, meant fleeing from the glass works and the ceaseless industrial and maritime clamour of the Tyne Valley. Yet what also condemned the once luxurious houses on the banks of the Tyne to subdivision and decay was the arrival of a force that was central to the industrial and commercial success of Gateshead, Newcastle, and the other settlements along the river.

Even before the main railway lines had been cut through Gateshead and Newcastle, the wealthier residents of both towns had begun moving out of the Tyne Valley and into new terraces and villas on the high ground behind. Ravensworth Terrace was built in the 1820s as a secluded middle-class refuge from the overcrowding and pollution of the Newcastle quayside. The coming of the railways in the 1830s and 1840s accelerated that process. When the main lines were laid through Gateshead, linking up to the new High Level Bridge (built in 1849), both Pipewellgate and Hillgate were cut off from the rest of the town by the tracks and high embankments; both districts were now literally on the wrong side of the tracks, squeezed between the river and a screen of brick arches. Multiple factors had contributed to their decline but after the coming of the railways it was complete. Through this form of geographic strangulation, as the historian J. R. Kellett has explained, railways could play a role in the wrecking of an urban district's fortunes and the formation of a new slum. Yet the railways were just as adept at destroying slums as creating them.

The Victorian railway companies were hungry for urban land on which to lay their tracks and erect their stations, sheds, carriage-works,

The rapid growth of Newcastle in 1830 (above) and 1849 (right). Ravensworth Terrace is in the top left of each map.

loading yards, and warehouses, and all together they consumed around 800 acres in central London during the nineteenth century. While the coming of railways – as we shall see – encouraged the construction of new homes in new out-of-town suburbs, within the poor districts of the inner cities they often had the opposite effect. The land commandeered during the railway revolution was almost always taken from those least able to assert their tenure – the poor. Whole districts in which the poorest sections of the working class had found shelter were swept away. The so-called 'Demolition Statements' that were submitted by the railway companies in advance of these clearances repeatedly classified the properties that

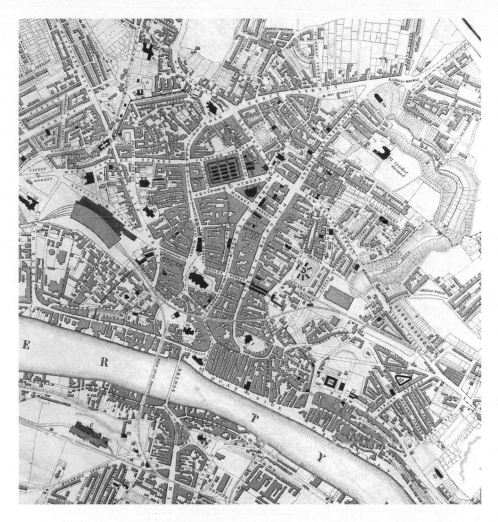

had been earmarked for demolition as being the homes of the 'labouring classes'. In London alone private railway companies building their lines, terminals, and depots between 1840 and 1900 drove as many as a hundred and twenty thousand people from their homes. Owners of land and property were compensated but their tenants usually received nothing, and many slum dwellers were given little notice of their impending eviction. There was also an inbuilt economic incentive to drive the lines through areas of cheap, low-quality housing and avoid the expensive homes of the wealthy and the premises of profitable businesses to whom the courts were likely to award considerable compensation.

One victim of the railways and their hunger for urban land was Agar Town in London, a Victorian slum built on land owned by a wealthy lawyer named William Agar. It lay north of where St Pancras Station now stands and consisted mostly of ramshackle houses for the poor that had been built cheaply on land that had been leased for a mere twenty-one years. Also squeezed into Agar Town were houses of an even lower quality. The poorest labourers who had settled there, many of them Irish, had constructed homes for themselves and their families out of whatever materials they could obtain. These were some of the shanty houses of Victorian London that housing reformers reported finding across the city. The sanitary reformer Hector Gavin came across simple wooden sheds in Bethnal Green that were home to poor people despite being only the size of 'a large dog-kennel'. Agar Town had no sewers and was unlit. Dickens described the streets as 'a complete bog of mud and filth with deep cart-ruts, wretched hovels, the doors blocked up with mud, heaps of ash, oyster shells and decayed vegetables, the stench on a rainy morning is enough to knock down a bullock.'

When the railways arrived in London, Agar Town's fetid streets, self-built shanty towns, and jerry-built terraces along with their impoverished inhabitants were regarded as eminently expendable. In 1851 the Midland Railway Company bought the land and on it built its enormous warehouses. An 1870s history of London was less than sentimental about Agar Town's demise.

Those who knew this district at that time have no regret at the change. Time was when the wealthy owner of a large estate had lived here in his mansion; but after his departure the place became a very 'abomination of desolation.' In its centre was what was termed La Belle Isle, a dreary and unsavoury locality, abandoned to mountains of refuse from the metropolitan dust-bins, strewn with decaying vegetables and foul-smelling fragments of what once had been fish, or occupied by knackers'-yards and manure-making, bone-boiling, and soap-manufacturing works, and smoke-belching potteries and brick-kilns. At the broken doors of mutilated houses canaries still sang, and dogs lay basking in the sun, as if to remind one of the vast colonies of bird-fanciers and dog-fanciers who formerly made Agar Town their abode; and from these dwellings came out wretched creatures in rags and dirt, and searched amid the far-extending refuse for the filthy treasure by the aid of which they eked out a miserable livelihood; whilst over the whole neighbourhood the gas-works poured forth their mephitic vapours, and the canal gave forth its rheumatic dampness, extracting in return some of the more poisonous ingredients in the atmosphere, and spreading them upon the surface of the water in a thick scum of various and ominous hues. Such was Agar Town before the Midland Railway came into the midst of it.

The homes of the very poorest of the Victorian working class were often wiped off the map with shocking alacrity, the fate of those rendered homeless of little concern to either the railway companies or the city authorities. In the case of Agar Town its destruction arrived a mere two decades after its initial construction. The extension of the Midland Railway Company into London also led to the demolitions of homes in Somers Town and Camden Town. According to one report the railway was responsible for the demolition of four thousand houses that had been home to thirty-two thousand mainly working-class people. The district and its displaced inhabitants are today remembered in the name Agar Grove, a street north of St Pancras Station, and the expensive apartments of the Agar Grove Estate. The area's only famous son was Tom Sayers, the legendary Victorian bare-knuckle prizefighter who, despite being a mere five feet eight inches tall, became English Heavyweight Champion from 1857 to 1860. Before embarking upon a life in the ring Sayers contributed, in a small way, to the establishment in London of the force that led to the demolition of his home and his neighbourhood. He is said to have discovered his potential as a pugilist during a fight with a supervisor while he was a labourer working on the building of King's Cross Station.

The arrival of the railway in one part of a Victorian city increased overcrowding elsewhere, as the inhabitants of the demolished homes had to find rooms in nearby districts, leading to further subdividing and sub-letting. While the railways reduced what few choices the poor had to find accommodation, they created new possibilities for the middle classes by making life in distant suburbs possible. Indeed there was something of a feedback loop. Enthusiastically the middle class left behind the poor, huddled ever tighter in a shrinking number of slums, over which they were carried on high railway viaducts, as they moved back and forth between city and suburb. When the same forces encouraged armies of lower-middle-class clerks and later thousands of skilled artisans to migrate to newer suburbs, the wealthy moved even further afield.

Edwin Chadwick was convinced that in the poorer areas of the nation's cities overcrowding increased over the course of the century. The Royal Commission on the Housing of the Working Classes of 1885 came to the same conclusion. To take one local example, in 1841 there were 655 people living in a small cluster of twenty-seven houses on Church Lane in Westminster. Six years later 1,095 people were crammed into the same twenty-seven properties.

Yet the railways were merely one of a number of forces that led to the demolition of houses occupied by the poor. Ceaseless population growth and continuing urbanization remained consistent background factors, but the homes of the poor were almost casually consigned to history whenever they got in the way of any number of the schemes for urban 'improvement', a generic term applied to building new streets, widening others, or constructing new docks or other facilities. In London, for example, the land required for the St Katherine's Dock in the 1820s was acquired by making 1,033 poor people homeless. 'Improvement' could also mean building new civic amenities – town halls, libraries, concert halls, police stations, and court houses, which were clustered in the city centres. In Liverpool, St George's Hall, a vast neoclassical building that contained both a concert hall and court house, was built on land that had been occupied by the poor. Among the grandest neoclassical buildings ever constructed, St George's Hall was perhaps the most spectacular expression of Victorian Liverpool's growing civic pride and commercial power. Yet the vast sums spent on its construction were regarded by some as an outrage. One commentator in the *Leisure Hour*, a popular campaigning magazine, complained in 1853:

> Many millions have been lavished in some of our largest cities in improvements . . . while the condition of their back streets is a disgrace to any civilized community. In Liverpool a magnificent structure has lately been reared. One's heart swells with patriotic emotion in contemplating such a glorious monument . . . Yet

while standing in front of St George's Hall, and giving way to this enthusiasm, is there nothing chilling in the thought that of all who are born beneath its stately shadow 53 per cent are consigned to the grave within five years of their birth? . . . Might not more lowly, but more useful labours, undertaken . . . in those back-slums and alleys where every breath of air is pestilence and where fever has taken up its fixed abode.

Edwin Chadwick expressed similar views and condemned Liverpool's business and civic elite for spending enormous sums on St. George's Hall while so many of the city's poorer inhabitants still lived in the dank courts and underground cellars of the dockside slums. He accused the city fathers of 'A parsimony for objects of such importance as the saving of pain and misery would ill become Liverpool, where there is in course of expenditure, for splendour, on one single edifice, St. George's Hall, upwards of £100,000; a sum which would, if so applied, serve to sweep and cleanse in perpetuity, and make decent, the filthy by-streets of upwards of 23,000 houses, out of the 45,000 houses, which are under the corporation jurisdiction.' But such improvements always had their supporters. In his 1828 book *Metropolitan Improvements* the architect James Elmes predicted:

Among the glories of this age, the historian will have to record the conversion of dirty alleys, dingy courts and squalid dens of misery and crime . . . into 'stately streets', to 'squares that court the breeze' to palaces and mansions, to elegant private dwellings, to rich and costly shops, filled with the productions of every clime, to magnificent ware-rooms, stowed with the ingenious and valuable manufactures of our artisans and mechanics, giving activity to commerce with all the enviable results of national prosperity.

The 'improvements' that led more than any other to the demolition of dirty alleys and dingy courts involved building new roads. The sites of many of Victorian Britain's most infamous slums are today entombed under acres of tarmac as over the course of the century new thoroughfares were carved through acres of slum housing. The slums were targeted for multiple reasons. As they were characterized by narrow alleys and lanes through which traffic could not easily pass, they increasingly became obstacles to the flow of people and goods around the expanding cities, and thus a constraint on the proper operation of commerce. The maps of Charles Booth revealed not just where the rich and the poor resided, but how the physical layout of the streets they occupied differed. The streets and squares of the wealthy were broad and straight, laid out in rectilinear patterns. The courts, alleyways, and passages inhabited by the poorest Londoners followed the chaotic lines of older, medieval street patterns: narrow labyrinths compressed together, full of tight turns and dead ends. One effect of urban growth was the inevitable increase in circulating traffic as the invention of the omnibus and the popularity of hansom cabs among the rich put increasing numbers of vehicles on city roads. This inevitably led to longer travel times and growing calls for better roads, particularly in London. By crashing straight modern roads through the sprawling slum districts, these winding passages and narrow lanes could be replaced. The same improvements would allow for better drainage and sanitation and new homes and shops to line the new boulevards. Crucially they would also have the effect of bringing the slum dwellers out into the open, where they could be better placed under the surveillance of the authorities and reformed by the influence of respectable society. In 1800 C. G. Stonestreet, a resolute supporter of street improvements, published a pamphlet entitled *Domestic Union, or London as it Should Be* in which he complained of the mazes of streets that 'form a cover and shelter for people of the worst casts in society'. Stonestreet was pleased to reassure his readers that any slum could be destroyed 'by carrying through the midst of it a free and open street with buildings suitable for the industrious and reputable orders of the people', which would 'let in that eye and observation which will effectively break up their combinations [conspiracies]'. Without regard to the fate of those whose homes were to be destroyed, Stonestreet called for the 'perforation of every such nest'. Almost four decades later the same debate was still raging. In 1838 the report of the Metropolitan Improvement Select Committee warned:

> There are some districts in this vast city through which no great thoroughfares pass, and which being wholly occupied by a dense

population, composed of the lowest class of labourers, entirely secluded from the observation and influence of wealthier and better educated neighbours, exhibit a state of moral and physical degradation deeply to be deplored . . . The moral condition of these poorer occupants must necessarily be improved by immediate communication with a more respectable inhabitancy; and the introduction at the same time of improved habits and a freer circulation of air, will tend materially to extirpate those prevalent diseases which are now not only so destructive among themselves, but so dangerous to the neighbourhood around them.

The new roads that the committee recommended would open the poor up to the influence of their betters and would supposedly reduce the risk of disease by allowing air to better circulate around the city. The destruction of whole streets and neighbourhoods in which the poor resided was therefore seen not as an unfortunate by-product of necessary street improvements but as an ancillary benefit, and at times slum clearance was a prime motivation. After having been presented with extensive evidence as to the conditions that prevailed in London's rookeries the committee concluded that 'the most important improvements . . . are in direct proportion to the degree in which they embrace all the great purposes of amendment in respect of health and morals . . . by the removal of congregations, vice and misery, and the introduction of a better police'. In 1861, with the process of improvement well underway, *The Times* rationalized the policy: 'As we cut . . . roads to our forest so it should be a policy to divide district jungles of crime and misery. Much has already been done to tempt these people to cure and better habits'.

One of the areas most enthusiastically targeted during London's extensive programme of street improvements was St Giles, a huge eight-acre rookery in Holborn that included what is now Bloomsbury and Tottenham Court Road. The St Giles Rookery had been a legendary locus of poverty and criminality for longer than anyone could remember. It was there that William Hogarth had set *Gin Lane*, his infamous 1751 depiction of the calamitous social effects of the Georgian gin craze. By the middle of the nineteenth century this small area was still among London's most desperate slums, described by one writer as a 'great maze of narrow crooked paths crossing and intersecting in labyrinthine

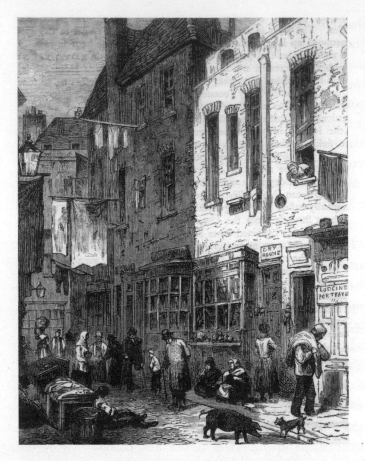

A view of the infamous Rookery at St Giles in London, a labyrinth of narrow streets and slum houses near to where Centre Point now stands.

convulsions, as if the houses had been originally one great block of stone eaten by slugs into innumerable small chambers and connecting passages'. Within St Giles, he explained, 'There is no privacy here for any of the over-crowded population; every apartment in the place is accessible from every other by a dozen different approaches . . . Hence whoever ventures here finds the streets (by courtesy so called) thronged with loiterers, and sees through the half-glazed windows the rooms crowded to suffocation.'

By the 1840s the population of St Giles had been swollen by the arrival of thousands of poor Irish migrants, their presence bequeathing the district the nickname 'Little Ireland'. They endured suffocating levels of overcrowding, multiple families living in each house, often large properties that had originally been built for the middle classes but that had long ago slipped into decay and disrepair. Friedrich Engels vividly described them as 'tall, three- or four-storied houses, with narrow, crooked, filthy streets'. What had originally been the back gardens of these middle-class homes had become decayed and filthy. These houses were 'occupied from cellar to garret, filthy within and without, and their appearance is such that no human being could possibly wish to live in them'. According to Engels the terrible conditions within these large subdivided houses was

> nothing in comparison with the dwellings in the narrow courts and alleys between the streets, entered by covered passages between the houses, in which the filth and tottering ruin surpass all description. Scarcely a whole window-pane can be found, the walls are crumbling, door-posts and window-frames loose and broken, doors of old boards nailed together, or altogether wanting in this thieves' quarter, where no doors are needed, there being nothing to steal. Heaps of garbage and ashes lie in all directions, and the foul liquids emptied before the doors gather in stinking pools. Here live the poorest of the poor, the worst paid workers with thieves and the victims of prostitution indiscriminately huddled together, the majority Irish, or of Irish extraction, and those who have not yet sunk in the whirlpool of moral ruin which surrounds them, sinking daily deeper, losing daily more and more of their power to resist the demoralizing influence of want, filth and evil surroundings.

Such conditions were not unique to St Giles. Local medical officers and sanitary reformers recorded a similar picture wherever the poor were forced to live in subdivided homes built for the rich. However, the authorities found the existence of the St Giles Rookery particularly troubling because of its proximity to London's wealthy districts. As Engels explained, 'St Giles is in the midst of the most populous part of the town, surrounded by broad, splendid avenues in which the gay world of London idles about, in the immediate neighbourhood of Oxford Street, Regent Street, of Trafalgar Square and the Strand.' Engels was pleased to report in 1844 that St Giles was 'at last, about to be penetrated by a couple of broad streets.'

The architect appointed to design New Oxford Street was James Pennethorne, a protégé of John Nash. His preferred plan involved the comprehensive demolition of the entire slum, so as to socially cleanse the area of the poor and increase the value of the new shops and business premises that were to be built. Financial constraints meant that he was only permitted to demolish parts of the rookery, along the line of two of its main streets. The work was completed in 1847, by which time perhaps as many as five thousand people had lost their homes. In the spring of that year the *Illustrated London News* noted:

> It is curious to observe what various impressions different persons are apt to receive from the progress of the improvements of our Metropolis. The visitor to the great town, at this gay season of the year, rejoices in the widening of streets and the cleansing of roadways, for personal convenience. Another, by aid of the last published map, and the recollection of paragraphs in the newspapers, picks out the lines of new streets in progress, and is almost lost in self-glorification at the sweeping away of so many vile courts and alleys – 'rookeries' of vice and crime – to make room for architectural displays of sumptuous character, though intended only for commercial purposes. Then, perchance, arise reflections of the vast sums of money expended in these improvements, calculations as to their investment for profit, and other speculations of a mercenary class. It has, probably, occurred to few such observers to inquire what has become of the poor persons who have become unhoused by these great changes?

The answer was that the improvement plans had contained no provisions for the poor slum dwellers or given any thought to their fate once their homes had been destroyed. A few years later in his book *The Rookeries of London: Past, Present, and Prospective*, Thomas Beames wrote of St Giles, 'The Rookery is no more! A spacious street is in its stead.' But who, asked Beames, had benefited from the clearing away of the homes in which so many had found shelter? 'Will you tell us that any poor man has gained by the change; that any section of the working class has reaped an advantage?' The demolition of parts of St Giles had not resulted in the 'clearance' of the slum, but merely the displacement of many of its desperate occupants. By reducing the number of tenements and rooms available for rent in St Giles, the building of New Oxford Street had increased demand elsewhere, which in turn led to even greater overcrowding as the former inhabitants of the demolished streets, now refugees, migrated to other parts of St Giles in search of rooms or space in shared rooms. This pattern enabled the exploitative landlords of the rotting houses and stinking courts that had escaped the attention of James Pennethorne to charge higher rents. There were reports of rent increases of up to 50 per cent.

In the view of Thomas Beames the construction of New Oxford Street and the clearing of parts of St Giles could only 'falsely' be called 'improvements'.

> The expelled inhabitants cannot, of course, derive any advantage from new erections, and are forced to invade the yet remaining hovels suited to their means; the circle of their habitations is contracted while their numbers are increased, and thus a large population is crowded into less space . . . The conclusion is obvious: if Rookeries are pulled down, you must build habitable dwellings for the population you have displaced, otherwise, you will not merely have typhus, but plague; some fearful pestilence worse than cholera or Irish fever, which will rage, as the periodical miasmata of other times were wont to do, numbering its victims by tens of thousands!

Dickens was of a similar view in 1851. 'Thus, we make our New Oxford Streets, and our other new streets, never heeding, never asking, where the wretches whom we clear out, crowd.' He wrote in *Household Words*, the magazine he edited, 'What must be the result of these London improvements, when the roofs of a hundred wretched people are pulled down to make room for perhaps ten who are more prosperous?'

Proof that the improvements did nothing to improve the lives of the slum dwellers arrived two years after New Oxford Street had been completed. It came directly from the people of St Giles, who in 1849 sent the editor of *The Times* a remarkable letter. Beyond the conversations with mudlarks and beggars that were transcribed and published by Henry Mayhew we rarely hear the direct voice of the Victorian poor. Their suffering is more usually relayed to us through the reports of concerned middle-class reformers or self-promoting 'urban explorers'. The letter of 1849 arrived addressed to *'THE EDITUR OF THE TIMES PAPER'* and was accompanied by a petition containing fifty-four signatures.

Its authors were residents of Church Lane and Carrier Street in the St Giles Rookery. Although understandably written in muddled prose and peppered with misspellings the message that the slum dwellers sought to convey, their cry of despair, was clear enough:

Sur, – May we beg and beseech your proteckshion and power. We are Sur, as it may be, livin in a Wilderniss, so far as the rest of London knows anything of us, or as the rich and great people care about. We live in muck and filth. We aint got no priviz, no dust bins, no drains, no water-splies, and no drain or suer in the hole place. The Suer Company, in Greek St., Soho Square, all great, rich and powerfool men, take no notice watsomdever of our complaints. The Stenche of a Gully-hole is disgustin. We all of us suffer, and numbers are ill, and if the Colera comes Lord help us. Some gentlemans comed yesterday, and we thought they was comishioners from the Suer Company, but they was complaining of the noosance and stenche our lanes and corts was to them in New Oxforde Strect. They was much surprized to see the seller in No. 12, Carrier St., in our lane, where a child was dyin from fever, and would not believe that Sixty persons sleep in it every night. This here seller you couldent swing a cat in, and the rent is five shillings a week; but theare are greate many sich deare sellars. Sur, we hope you will let us have our complaints put into your hinfluenshall paper, and make these landlords of our houses and these comishioners (the friends we spose of the landlords) make our houses decent for Christions to live in. Preaye Sir com and see us, for we are living like piggs, and it aint faire we shoulde be so ill treted. We are your respeckfull servents in Church Lane, Carrier St., and the other corts. Teusday, Juley 3, 1849.

In the same decade that New Oxford Street was being cut through St Giles, a new road to link Westminster to Pimlico, Victoria Street, was being built. It now reaches all the way up to Victoria Station. To ensure that the new thoroughfare cut through Old Pye Street, which lay at the centre of Westminster's infamous slum the Devil's Acre, the trajectory of Victoria Street was deliberately angled in that direction by the architect in charge of the project, who once again was James Pennethorne.

The Devil's Acre was one of Victorian London's most shameful secrets, a maze of alleys and courts concealed behind Westminster Abbey. The conversion of Buckingham House into Buckingham Palace, and its establishment in the 1830s as the main London residence of the royal family, added new impetus to the campaign to improve the area between the new royal abode and Westminster. The horrors of the Devil's Acre, situated so close to Westminster Abbey and Parliament, had inspired Dickens to describe it as the worst of the capital's many slums.

> . . . the blackest tide of moral turpitude that flows in the capital rolls its filthy wavelets up to the very walls of Westminster Abbey; and the law-makers for one-seventh of the human race sit, night after night, in deliberation, in the immediate vicinity of the most notorious haunt of law-breakers in the empire. There is no district in London more filthy and disgusting, more steeped in villany and guilt, than that on which every morning's sun casts the sombre shadows of the Abbey, mingled, as they soon will be, with those of the gorgeous towers of the new 'Palace at Westminster'.

Those who lost their homes when Victoria Street was ploughed through the Devil's Acre included a number of people who had only recently moved there, having been displaced from St Giles Rookery. They and the older residents were now harried across the capital. Many were forced to crowd into what remained of the Devil's Acre or seek new rooms in nearby districts. According to the Bishop of London three-quarters of the five thousand people who were displaced by building Victoria Street migrated to desperately poor areas on the south side of the Thames, districts that now groaned under the pressure of even greater levels of overcrowding. 'In many instances', he wrote, 'where one family had a house before there were now three or four families in it.' Victoria Street, the 'improved thoroughfare', wrote John Hollingshead in his 1861 book *Ragged London*, 'was ploughed through to Pimlico', but the 'diseased heart' of the Devil's Acre slum was merely 'divided in half – one part was pushed on one side, and the other part on the other'. The 'chief result', Hollingshead concluded, 'has been to cause more huddling together.' The investors in the improvement scheme had succeeded in breaking up the old slum but failed to make the return on their investments that they had hoped for. As Hollingshead noted, Victoria Street became a 'nightmare street of unlet palaces . . . waiting for more capital to fill its yawning gulf and a few more residents to warm its hollow chambers in to life', while elsewhere 'the landlords of the slums were raising their rents; and thieves, prostitutes, labourers, and working women were packed in a smaller compass.'

At Devil's Acre, as with St Giles Rookery, the improvements had failed to comprehensively sweep away the slum. After the building of Victoria Street, Gustave Doré produced an image, albeit a stylized one, of a group of slum houses in the Devil's Acre (see the plate section). It appears in *London: a Pilgrimage*, a collaboration with the journalist William Blanchard Jerrold. Doré depicts the surviving court as a cluster of miserable and tiny dwellings, with low ceilings and patched-up walls, built around a communal yard. The land around them is littered with piles of ash and dust across which shrouded figures wander. To one side are the better-constructed buildings that face the main road and conceal the horrors of the slum from general view. Westminster Abbey is seen behind in the distance. The accompanying text, written by Jerrold, again stresses how the world of the slum dwellers and that of the wealthy and powerful existed side by side: 'The Solemn and Venerable is at the elbow of the sordid and the woe-begone. By the noble Abbey is the ignoble Devil's Acre, hideous where it now lies in the sunlight!'

The drive to replace London's narrow lanes and alleys with wide thoroughfares like Victoria Street and New Oxford Street continued unrelentingly. By the middle of the century Regent Street had displaced the old rookery at Soho, Victoria Street had punctured the heart of the Devil's Acre, Commercial Street had torn through the slums of Whitechapel, the Farringdon Road had cut through the Saffron Hill Rookery, and tens of thousands of the poorest Londoners had lost their homes. In 1854 *Punch* magazine in an article entitled 'The Battle of The Streets' felt the need to ask once again the question Thomas Beames had asked in 1852: if slum houses are demolished, where are their residents to go? If their narrow lanes are to be demolished to build broad new streets, can space not be found for them within the new cityscape? The article appeared under an illustrated cartoon showing grand civic buildings and the mansions of the wealthy charging across the cityscape driving out the ramshackle homes of the poor, like knights on horseback. The author of the article warned:

> the contest between broad and narrow – is revolutionizing the metropolis. Unfortunately for the narrow, the broad carries, or rather knocks down everything before it. We shall soon be utterly without a lane or alley throughout the whole of London; while as to architecture, the old brick and tile order will be utterly superseded by the modern stuccoite. It is all very well to enlarge the streets if we can sufficiently enlarge the means of the people to live in them; but if the habitations of the poor are superseded by palaces, while pauperism still remains we would simply ask what on earth is to become of it. The old police principle of 'move on', 'you can't stop here', seems to be now generally applied to those of humble means, and the question is, 'where are they all to go to?' So as they are got rid of somehow, this is a question which gives little trouble to those who are bent on 'improving' a neighbourhood.

The demolition of houses in the city centres disproportionately affected the Victorian poor as it was essential that they lived near their places of employment. This was especially true for those in trades such as dock work, where employment was short-term, temporary, and precarious. Many were hired by the day, some even by the hour. In the mid-1860s it was estimated that there were six hundred and eighty thousand casual labourers in London alone who relied on short-term bouts of casual work and had to be on the spot and able to respond quickly to offers of very temporary employment. Long shifts and the physical nature of much of the work also made it unfeasible for the poor to expend additional time and energy walking long distances from home – their wages, and even those of working people in more regular employment, did not permit them to use the expanding network of omnibuses to travel to work. In 1861 *The Times* summed it up: 'The dock and the wharf labourer, the porter and the costermonger cannot remove. You may pull down their wretched homes: they must find others, and make their dwellings more crowded and wretched than their old ones. The tailor, shoemaker and other workmen are in much the same position.'

Victorian street improvements entailed not just the demolition of the homes of poor families but the break-up of their communities. Although slums were miserable places of habitation, they were neighbourhoods to which even the poorest of people had evident bonds and strong attachments. There is evidence also to suggest that within some slum districts the population was more settled and stable and less transient than is often imagined. Made refugees by the ceaseless waves of so-called improvements that characterized the entire Victorian age, and forced into unplanned urban migrations, thousands of poor people were desperate to remain within the district they understood and felt connected to for personal, familial and sentimental reasons, as well as practical ones. As familiar streets and sometimes whole districts of the large cities were wiped off the map to make way for the new roads, Charles Dickens, as ever the chronicler of his age, captured the bewildering sense of displacement that was felt by so many. *The Old Curiosity Shop*, set in the 1820s but written in the early 1840s, ends with the narrator discussing Kit Nubbles' habit of taking his children to see the site of the curiosity shop where Nell Trent, the book's tragic heroine, had lived.

> He sometimes took them to the street where she had lived; but new improvements had altered it so much, it was not like the same. The old house had been pulled down, and a fine broad road was in its place. At first, he would draw with his stick a square upon the ground to show them where it used to stand. But, he soon became uncertain of the spot, and could only say it was thereabouts, he thought, and that these alterations were confusing.

This vision of the city undergoing rapid and disorienting transformation was so potent, to both rich and poor, that Dickens included a similar passage in *Dombey and Son*, in which Paul Dombey makes a pilgrimage to Staggs Gardens, six years after having first visited, only to discover it 'vanished from the earth.'

> Where the old rotten summer-houses once had stood, palaces now reared their heads, and granite columns of gigantic girth opened a vista to the railway world beyond . . . The old by-streets

now swarmed with passengers and vehicles of every kind: the new streets that had stopped disheartened in the mud and waggon-ruts, formed towns within themselves, originating wholesome comforts and conveniences belonging to themselves, and never tried nor thought of until they sprung into existence. Bridges that had led to nothing, led to villas, gardens, churches, healthy public walks. The carcasses of houses, and beginnings of new thoroughfares, had started off upon the line at steam's own speed, and shot away into the country in a monster train.

Edwin Chadwick and the other sanitary reformers had stressed that the conditions within the homes of the poor could only be improved if they were connected to proper sewers, drains, and water supplies. They also recommended a vast programme of paving and a new municipal culture of street cleaning. Yet to properly confront the reality of the slums even more was required: huge numbers of existing dwellings had to be improved and new homes built in great numbers. Among those resistant to calls for housing reform and sanitary improvements were those unwilling to countenance the accompanying bill, one that would inevitably arrive at the door of the local ratepayer. It was more convenient therefore to regard the slums as the physical manifestation of the character defects and immorality of their inhabitants, rather than as the consequences of low wages, unplanned urban growth, and a failed housing market: environment was the consequence of character and not the other way around, it was claimed. The answer to the slums thus lay in the moral reformation of the poor and the improvement of their personal habits rather than their abodes. Yet in the latter half of the nineteenth century such views increasingly clashed with the growing religiosity of Victorian society and with a developing belief in the sanctity of the family. Without a safe and sanitary home, without separate sleeping accommodation for adults and children, without the capacity to keep their homes, their clothes, and themselves clean, how could the 'heathen' slum dwellers possibly better themselves or even begin to follow modes of living that conformed to middle-class notions of respectability? Without privacy how could the poor learn to privilege the family unit over other more communal and gregarious forms of association that were anathema to middle-class values? 'It is no use preaching religion, or making education cheap, or founding ragged schools, while the present state of things in this respect exists', argued a correspondent to the *Builder* in 1855. 'Give to the poor man a cleanly and cheerful home at a price his means will bear and then order and sobriety will ensue'. As the home was the crucible of the family, and the family was the fundamental building block of society, the crisis of overcrowded and insanitary slums dwellings was a potential threat to social order and perhaps public order. 'The strength of the people rests upon the purity and firmness of the domestic system', wrote the social reformer Lord Shaftesbury. 'If a working man has his own house I have no fear of revolution.'

The crisis of the slums was of such a magnitude that some believed it called into question Victorian Britain's claim to be the first among the great nations of the world. 'The condition of the poor of the City cries shame on our boasted civilization and our undeniable opulence, and demands immediate reformation', thundered the *City Press* newspaper in 1857. The *Pall Mall Gazette* in 1880 concluded that the focus of Liberal politics should be the civilization not of the 'heathen who dwell . . . on other distant shores, but the civilisation of our own flesh and blood, of the heathen who dwells in St Giles, in Spitalfields, in Bethnal Green'. In *The Masses Without!*, a near hysterical pamphlet by the preacher John Knox, the author judged the slums a national disgrace. The pamphlet was subtitled *On the Sanitary, Social, Moral and Heathen Condition of the Masses Who Inhabit the Alleys, Courts, Wynds, Garrett Cellars, Lodging-houses, Dens and Hovels of Great Britain* and identified eight 'Prominent Evils of Society', the first of which was the 'Shocking Sanitary Condition of the Masses'. Drawing links between poor housing, ill health, and the preponderance within the slums of what he regarded as immoral behaviour, he wrote:

> If we look to Edinburgh, Liverpool, Manchester, and many other
> places, we find that the homes and houses of the masses are in
> a wretched condition – bad air – bad water – bad light – bad
> ventilation – bad drainage – bad domestic arrangement; and the
> sad consequences are disease, premature death, drunkenness, and
> moral corruption! When their homes are bad, it too frequently
> happens that their hearts correspond!

Although on a national level the number of houses built in the Victorian period largely kept pace with population growth, enough even to allow for a decline in the overall figure of numbers per household, such progress failed to percolate down to the slums. As the very poorest among the urban working class – the casual labourer, the impoverished weaver, the starving seamstress – could barely afford the rent charged for single rooms in ghastly tenements, how could clean and sanitary homes be constructed that were within their reach? Speculative capital could usually be found for ever more ambitious and expansive house-building schemes in the suburbs. Yet as long as landlords and investors could make greater returns by building commercial premises or homes for the rich, they had no incentive to provide the slum dwellers with homes that were an improvement on their current accommodation at rents they could afford to pay. The poor were thus beyond the reach of Victorian capitalism. The problem of the slums appeared intractable, if the housing of the poor was to remain subject to the same market pressures as every other commodity. If this were the case, then should and could another provider, not solely reliant upon the profit motive, intervene?

In the same decade that the missionaries and Bible societies rushed to minister to the 'heathens' of the slums, a movement emerged dedicated to building model homes on new estates that were within reach of the poorer working-class families and in which they could live moral as well as healthy lives. In 1841 the Metropolitan Association for Improving the Dwellings of the Industrious Classes was founded with the declared aim of 'enabling the poorer classes to obtain comfortable habitations at moderate rents'. It described itself as an association 'formed for the purpose of providing the labouring man with an increase of the comforts and conveniences of life, with full return to the capitalist' and became the model for other commercial philanthropies. Their business model was to limit profits to a maximum of 5 per cent (some never reached this threshold) and seek to attract investors who would contribute to the betterment of the poor while making a reasonable return, and a 5 per cent return was reasonable for the 1840s. The idea became known as 'five per cent philanthropy', although the Society for Improving the Condition of the Labouring Classes, founded in 1844 by Lord Shaftesbury with the Prince Consort as its president, insisted on a return of 6 per cent. Its first model dwellings, the Bagnigge Wells buildings, were built on King's

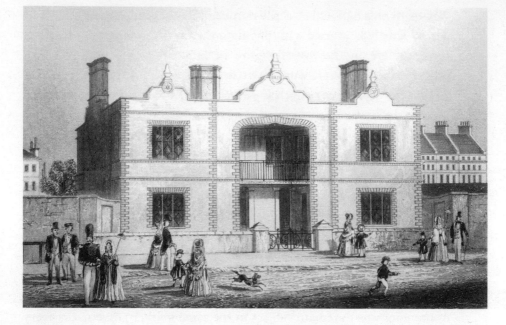

Cross Road and comprised two rows of two-storey houses facing one another. Then in 1847 a new block near St Pancras was erected and a year later saw another block of model houses off New Oxford Street in St Giles. Many of the homes had two bedrooms and their own water closets. In 1850, in his capacity as President of the society, Prince Albert and the society's Chief Architect, Henry Roberts, designed a plan for 'Model Houses for Four Families' and built an example at the Great Exhibition in Hyde Park the following year. The design did not catch on.

Prince Albert's model dwelling for the labouring classes, built for the Great Exhibition of 1851.

When, in 1858, Robert Rawlinson published a paper entitled *On House Accommodation: Its Social Bearing, Individually and Nationally*, he began by flattering the prince for his efforts to encourage the building of 'model houses' and 'improved cottages', but then proceeded to warn his readers that, 'To remedy all existing defects in houses of the poor in such manner is, however, too much for isolated individual enterprise, and far too vast even for a free government. How, then, must the work be done?' More was needed and new philanthropic builders who worked on a larger scale emerged in the 1850s and the 1860s. The Improved Industrial Dwellings Company was founded in 1863 by Sydney Waterlow, the Lord Mayor of London, with an initial capital of £50,000. Among its investors were members of parliament and leading builders and merchants. Ultimately thirty thousand people were housed in dwellings built and managed by the company. Waterlow's ideas were copied elsewhere. The Newcastle-upon-Tyne Improved Industrial Dwellings Company was established after its founders had visited Waterlow in London. The model blocks it built at Garth Heads are still standing. The company adhered to the general mantra of 5 per cent philanthropy, stating it had been 'formed for the purpose of supplying an improved class of dwellings, suitable for the working classes, as a rental that will allow for a fair return to the investor'.

Ultimately more than thirty housing charities built model dwellings in London alone in the second half of the nineteenth century. The most famous were those created by George Peabody, the wealthy American merchant and banker who donated a total of half a million pounds to build housing for the working class in London. The first Peabody estate was built in Spitalfields in London in 1864, followed by another in Islington in 1865. The nineteen Peabody estates completed by 1885 consisted of blocks between three and six storeys in height, usually grouped around a central courtyard (see the plate section). The individual flats contained one to four rooms. The residents shared water, laundry, and toilet facilities. To ensure that environment reformed character the Peabody Trust imposed strict rules regarding behaviour, monitored by a resident superintendent who collected the rent, processed new applicants, and ensured that the long list of rules was adhered to. These stipulated that: 'The passages, steps, closets, lavatory and lavatory windows must be washed every Saturday and swept every morning before 10 o'clock. This must be done by the tenants in turn. Washing must only be done in the laundry . . . Refuse must not be thrown out of windows . . . Tenants are required to report to the superintendent any births, deaths or infectious disease occurring in their rooms. Any tenant not complying with this rule will receive notice to quit'. Drunken or disorderly tenants were given immediate notice to leave and as the rules stated, 'No application for rooms will be entertained unless every member of the applicant's family has been vaccinated and in the case of those past childhood revaccinated.' By 1882 the Peabody Trust housed 14,600 residents in 3,500 dwellings in blocks that are still scattered across the capital.

The critical question was whether such schemes were large and ambitious enough to even begin to alleviate the crisis of the slums, by addressing the overcrowding that had been so exacerbated by the programme of urban 'improvements'. John Hollingshead, author of *Ragged London* (1861), carried out a detailed analysis of the tenants who had been given homes within the housing blocks built by a number of model housing companies. He began his research in St Pancras, where the poor clung on in what little was left of Agar Town, and in the Chapel Street and Somers Town districts, 'the worst parts of the parish' according to him. The model dwellings he examined there were those of the Metropolitan Association for Improving the Dwellings of the Industrious Classes. By the late 1850s the assocation had housed nearly two thousand people. What Hollingshead found in St Pancras however was that 'the occupants are chiefly the higher class of labourers and artisans' rather than the desperately poor, who remained in the squalor of the local tenements. Looking at Bethnal Green, where the Metropolitan Association for Improving the Dwellings of the Industrious Classes had built another block of model housing on Albert Street, he found much the same and concluded that rents demanded for the flats within the model dwellings constructed by the various well-meaning charities were beyond the capacity of the slum dwellers to pay. They therefore excluded those in greatest need and did almost nothing to forestall the decline in living standards and the increase in overcrowding within the slum districts. He wrote:

> The Bethnal Green population – the low and really poor – are housed even more badly now than they were before the society started in philanthropic business. They have been pushed on one side, compelled to crowd closer together, because their huts have been pulled down for 'improvements' and new buildings, and are looked upon by the managers of model houses with ill-concealed contempt. Even in the family houses at the side of these club-chambers, no weaver or street hawker is to be found; the rents, although unremunerative, are pitched too high for such people, and there are standing rules to keep them out . . . At St. Pancras, they have done nothing for the worst class in Somers Town and Agar Town, and they have wasted their means on a class who are well able to help themselves. I can find hundreds of tenants

who are attracted to these houses from all sides by the low
artificial rents, who have no more right to be pensioners of a half-
benevolent society than I have. The costermongers – the street
hawkers – the industrious poor, are still rotting up their filthy,
ill-drained, ill-ventilated courts, while well-paid mechanics,
clerks, and porters, willing to sacrifice a certain portion of their
self-respect, are the constant tenants of all these model dwellings.

Hollingshead then examined another block of model houses in Bethnal
Green that had been built in the 1850s by the philanthropist Angela
Burdett-Coutts, of the famous banking dynasty and once described as
the 'richest heiress in England'. It lay in an area known as Nova Scotia
Gardens where an infamous child murder had taken place in the 1830s.
Among Burdett-Coutts's associates who assisted in the acquiring and
development of the model dwellings were the public-health reformer Dr
Thomas Southwood Smith and her friend and correspondent Charles
Dickens. Hollingshead carried out a survey of its inhabitants and found
that rather than being members of the insecure, working poor from
the many slum tenements in the immediate vicinity, they were better-
off skilled labourers and artisans; in some cases men who, if judged by
their occupations, might even be classified as among the lowest of the
lower middle classes. These residents, he believed, had been drawn to
the building by the offer of low rents and had secured tenancy. Better
educated, better presented, and more worldly, they had been easily able
to satisfy the managers of the building that they were of good character.
His detailed analysis of the population of one wing of the building
showed that among the tenants were:

A clerk, employed in the city, who came here from Hoxton;
a warehouseman, employed in the city, who came here from
Clerkenwell; a workman, employed at Woolwich, who runs
up and down by the Eastern Counties' Railway; a compositor,
employed in the neighbourhood, who came here from the city;
a railway guard employed at the railway; the family belonging to
the mate of a ship who is in the East Indies; a working cooper,
who came here from St. Luke's parish; two or three more
warehousemen and clerks.

His reluctant judgement on the model dwellings schemes of the 1850s was that:

> Whatever good such buildings may do, they can never improve the neighbourhood they stand in. They fly over the heads of those who are most in want of improvement, instead of burrowing under their feet. They attract a crowd of sharp-sighted tenants from outside districts who are a little more advanced in cleanliness and civilization, and are quick to see where ten shillings' worth of comfort is selling at less than half-price.

Outside the slums, by the last quarter of the nineteenth century the standards of working-class housing and urban sanitary conditions were rapidly improving. Rates of dysentery and typhoid were in decline and 'King Cholera' did not return after his fourth visitation in 1865. These improvements were largely due to the enormous progress made in the construction of drains and sewers. These were the critical measures that reformers like Edwin Chadwick and James Kay had called for in the 1830s and 1840s. Cesspits were becoming less common and water closets were being rapidly adopted. Decade by decade more effective public-health legislation was not only being introduced by central government but increasingly adopted and acted upon by local councils. Sanitary and housing legislation no longer empowered councils to act but compelled them. However, these measures, like building model dwellings by the philanthropic societies, had little impact in the slums. Those blighted, miserable districts shrank each year, as the land under the slum dwellers' feet was taken from them by schemes for urban 'improvement'; yet for those crowded into what remained of the rookeries life remained much as it had been for the residents of St Giles who had written in desperation to the editor of *The Times*, forty years earlier.

By the 1880s the slums were no longer an open secret or a concealed national shame; they were the focus of constant debate and discussion. It was in the 1880s that Charles Booth and his team of researchers carried out their research and drew their extraordinary map of London's archipelagos of misery. Their findings were first published in 1889 as *Life and Labour of the People*. Six years earlier in October 1883 the penny-pamphlet *The Bitter Cry of Outcast London: An Inquiry into the Condition of the Abject Poor* appeared, initially under anonymous authorship. The response to this slight, cheaply printed account of life in London's slums was extraordinary and unprecedented. For months the pamphlet was the subject of intense debate in the newspapers and learned journals. It garnered far more attention and inspired far more discussion than much longer, more detailed studies. The debate the pamphlet sparked had an influence on the establishment of the Royal Commission on the Housing of the Working Classes the following year. When the author finally came forward he was revealed to be the Reverend Andrew Mearns, secretary of the London Congregational Union. Mearns had been assisted by two colleagues, James Monroe and W. C. Preston.

Of all the chroniclers and campaigners who spoke on the issue of the Victorian slums, none did so with more explicit urgency than Mearns. As the historian Anthony S. Wohl has pointed out, little of the information in the pamphlet was new and its exceptional impact has to be partly put down to an accident of timing: it arrived at a moment when large numbers of people were willing to consider the plight of those trapped in the slums in ways that had not been the case in earlier decades. Yet the visceral power of Mearns' prose and the forthright way in which he made a call for action were also critical to the pamphlet's success. Among those inspired by Mearns' writing was W. T. Stead, the legendary editor of the *Pall Mall Gazette*. Just nine days after the pamphlet appeared the *Gazette* opined, 'The die is cast, and henceforth the Housing of the Poor takes its place in the front rank of the political questions of the day'.

The central plea of *The Bitter Cry of Outcast London* was for the acceptance of a fundamental reality. Under the heading 'What It Is Proposed To Do', Mearns made an argument that would not be accepted until the twentieth century: that the crisis of the slums was of such a magnitude that the only power that could possibly address it was that of the state.

> We shall be pointed to the fact that without State interference nothing effectual can be accomplished upon any large scale. And it is a fact. These wretched people must live somewhere. They must live near the centres where their work lies. They cannot afford to go out by train or tram into the suburbs; and how, with their poor emaciated, starved bodies, can they be expected – in

addition to working twelve hours or more, for a shilling, or less, – to walk three or four miles each way to take and fetch ? . . . Large spaces have been cleared of fever-breeding rookeries, to make way for the building of decent habitations, but the rents of these are far beyond the means of the abject poor. They are driven to crowd more closely together, in the few stifling places still left to them . . . because the poor must have shelter somewhere, even though it be the shelter of a living tomb. The State must make short work of this iniquitous traffic, and secure for the poorest the rights of citizenship; the right to live in something better than fever dens ; the right to live as something better than the uncleanest of brute beasts.

CHAPTER SIX

LIFE AT
'THE LAURELS'

The Victorian Suburbs

As we have seen, the same fate befell all three houses featured in *A House Through Time*. Unable to attract the sorts of wealthy residents for whom they had originally been built, they were subdivided and became home to multiple individuals and families who were drawn from the lower ranks of Victorian society. Although situated in three different cities whose economic fortunes followed different trajectories, each of them underwent the same decline and fall, as did hundreds of thousands of houses like them across Britain during the latter half of the nineteenth century. Several factors explain this recurring pattern, but the decline in the fortunes of 62 Falkner Street, 5 Ravensworth Terrace, and 10 Guinea Street was partly caused or exacerbated by the emergence of new suburbs to which the expanding middle classes were inexorably drawn. Out of favour and out of fashion our houses, like the city-centre districts in which they stood, attracted new residents, working people with modest incomes, people who the builders of our houses never imagined would cross the threshold other than to work as servants. Yet similar presumptions were shared by the builders of the new homes in the new suburbs, houses that for the most part were squarely aimed at the expanding ranks of what in the Victorian age was sometimes called the 'great middle class'.

* * *

The suburbs came of age during the reign of Queen Victoria but they had existed, in a different form, for centuries. In earlier times suburbs had been those areas just beyond a city's gates to which the sick, the poor, and the criminal were banished and to which the most noxious industries were consigned. The word suburb was in use in the 1380s and the adjective suburban can be found in 1583. They were often literally sub-urban, in that as well as being beyond the city walls they were on lower ground, as so many cities had been built on hills or high ground for defence. In their own way those pre-modern suburbs had been slums of sorts, semi-urban twilight zones. During the eighteenth century the suburb was radically reimagined as a desirable place of residence, a refuge for those who harboured dreams of escaping from the rapidly industrializing cities and the festering slums within them. The new suburbs and the suburban home became intimately linked to the story of the rise and growth of the middle classes.

It was not until around the 1820s that a distinct British middle-class identity began to emerge. By the middle of the nineteenth century the middle classes were estimated to represent about 15 per cent of the population of England and Wales. That figure had grown to 17 per cent by 1881 according to some readings of the census of that year, and 20 per cent by the end of the century. Defining who was and who was not a member of the middle classes was never a simple task, and remains a complex and contentious exercise today. Many nineteenth-century commentators felt that the middle classes represented so broad a swathe of the population that in order to be properly understood they needed to be divided up into subcategories. At the top were the upper middle classes. They were wealthy industrialists, merchants, and bankers, families like the self-satisfied Burlings in J. B. Priestley's play *An Inspector Calls*, with their grand home built on the profits that flowed from a large family business. The very wealthiest members of the upper middle class drew vast incomes, thousands of pounds a year, from their firms and investments and were wealthier than some of the old aristocracy. To show off that wealth they occupied substantial town houses in exclusive districts but, as we shall see, many moved to the suburbs and large villas with extensive gardens. Below them were the middle and lower middle classes. This group made up the vast bulk of the middle class and included members of the respected professions but also, on the lower rungs of the ladder, shopkeepers, book-keepers, and especially clerks, one of the fastest growing occupations in the second half of the nineteenth century. They were men like Mr Pooter, the unlikely hero of George and Weedon Grossmith's 1892 comic novel *The Diary of a Nobody*, perhaps the most influential pastiche of suburban life ever written.

While the story of the suburbs began with the upper middle class, by the second half of the nineteenth century the groups most firmly associated with life in suburbia and the clichés that accrued around it were the middle and lower middle classes. Many earned just enough to keep them and their families above the line that separated the poorest of the middle classes from the best off among the working classes. In the mid-nineteenth century this meant a wage of around £150 per annum. Anthony Trollope, for example, began his working life as a junior clerk in the General Post Office and the starting salary was just £90 a year, barely enough for him to claim even lower-middle-class status. After seven years' service his wages had increased to £140, which still left him on the precarious borders of class status. Yet the demarcation between the bottom of the lower middle class and the top of the working class was as much about manners and expectations as about earnings. While an engineer with specialized and sought-after skills might well earn as much as or even more than a junior clerk, what ensured the engineer remained firmly within the ranks of the working classes was the nature of his work. Unlike our clerk, an engineer worked with his hands rather than with a pen and paper. Rather than generating words and numbers, his labour was physical and he was thus a worker.

What also marked a family as being of the middle classes was their having an income large enough to allow for at least one live-in domestic servant. The presence of a domestic servant within the middle-class home not only advertised a certain income, it was sometimes felt that it was essential if the woman of the house were to become the 'lady' of the house, even if the house in question was relatively modest. Middle-class ladies were of course expected not to have careers of their own or engage in any work outside of the home. Servants were so fundamental to middle-class status and identity that even when confronted by financial crises many middle-class families remained determined to retain them and made financial sacrifices elsewhere. In 1898 when Emmeline Pankhurst lost her husband and hence much of her family income she

'The Laurels', Brickfield Terrace, Holloway, home of Mr Pooter and his wife Carrie in George and Weedon Grossmith's 1892 comic novel *The Diary of a Nobody*.

was forced to move out of the wealthy suburbs and into a smaller house in a more built-up area of Manchester. Despite this profound reduction in her circumstances she refused to dispense with the services of her servant Ellen. It was likewise critical to the fictional Mr Pooter, whose six-roomed, semi-detached suburban home 'The Laurels' on Brickfield Terrace, Holloway, was the focus of his life. Mr Pooter struggled to maintain his tenuous grip on lower-middle-class status and to afford the services of Sarah, the Pooter family's domestic servant. Shared cultural expectations and a powerful sense of respectability and religiosity united everyone from the wealthy industrialist to the likes of Mr Pooter into a single if broad social class.

While no single force accounts for the flight of so large a number of people from the cities to the suburbs it was, in part, a pragmatic and understandable response to the social and environmental problems that blighted the cities of Britain's industrial age. Rapid urbanization, as we have seen, led to overcrowding and high population densities. Urban overcrowding was of course most devastating for the poor but even the wealthier residents of the Georgian cities lived at increasingly high densities. The Georgian terrace had, after all, been designed to allow speculative builders to pack as many homes as possible onto the valuable plots of urban land over which they obtained leases. For all their grandeur the squares and crescents of London, Edinburgh, Bristol, Liverpool, and elsewhere still represented high-density, vertical living. While the private parks at the centre of the better squares offered access to open spaces and brought a little of the countryside into the city, private domestic gardens were a luxury for only the wealthiest residents of the very grandest of homes.

Beyond the desire for more personal space and greater contact with nature there were other, starker aspects of nineteenth-century urban life that became what the historian H. J. Dyos termed 'centrifugal forces'; push factors that led millions to seek an escape from Britain's great towns. The Victorian city dweller lived constantly with pollution, not just from hundreds of thousands of domestic fires but also from urban industries – large mills and factories, as well as smaller but equally noxious establishments, such as tanneries, dye-works, glue factories, bone-boilers, grease-makers, and glass works, that discharged their effluence into the streets and rivers and sent clouds of smoke and dust into the sky. The middle-class Victorian city dwellers, whose working life or social engagements took them away from the home, out into the streets across various urban districts, were daily assaulted by foul smells that emanated from the cellars and the courts of the slums and had to navigate filthy, dung-strewn streets. As it was generally (though wrongly) believed that diseases like cholera were transmitted via the air through foul smells and miasmas, the stench of the city was thus regarded not just as a nuisance but as literally life-threatening. In addition to this there was a desire for privacy, an escape from the urban multitudes. The suburban home, from the very beginning, was both designed and lived in with privacy a central preoccupation.

For some the raucous attractions of city life and the business opportunities it offered were worth all the inconveniences and dangers. Others however were eager to find or invent a new form of living. Inevitably this meant looking to areas further from the city centres and then as now the educated and wealthy people, whose privilege gave them choices, were well aware that the money that bought only modest living space in the city could yield far more on the rural fringes.

From the perspective of the speculative builder, rather than the city dweller, the rise of the suburban house in the second half of the nineteenth century was the inevitable consequence of the long period of urban expansion. In many places, by the middle of the century the bulk of the urban sites upon which new homes could be built had been consumed. Extension into the countryside, where new land was not only available but also cheap, was the only viable mechanism by which the nation's ever-expanding urban populations could be housed. This was particularly true of London. According to the 1841 census the capital began the Victorian era with a population of around 2,235,000. The census of 1901 revealed that it began the twentieth century with a population of 6,581,000. In one sense, therefore, the suburbs were the inevitable consequence of population growth and continued urbanization. Yet it was not the speculative builders of the later Victorian era who initiated the 'flight to the suburbs'. The first steps in that direction had been made in the early decades of the eighteenth century, long before Britain's cities had begun to run out of land for development.

The pioneers of suburbanization were members of the wealthy eighteenth-century merchant class. It was they who resurrected and reclaimed an old Roman idea, that of the villa, a large house within its own large gardens (sometimes very large), although the eighteenth-century villa was little like its classical predecessor. That the modern suburbs began with the villa is fitting, as the concept of the suburbs and the etymological roots of the word itself are both also Roman in origin. The men who built the new villas were merchants, bankers, and early industrialists, members of what would come to be seen as the upper middle classes, who wanted luxurious second homes that were close enough to the cities to allow them easy access to their offices, factories, and warehouses – the sources of their great wealth. Travelling around Britain in the 1720s, Daniel Defoe noticed that the grand homes of Tottenham, then a settlement outside London, were 'generally belonging to the middle sort of mankind, grown wealthy by trade, and who still taste of London; some of them live both in the city, and in the country at the same time: yet many of these are immensely rich.' Although often grand and imposing, these early villas were not country houses: they were smaller and usually had no land to cultivate and manage. They were conspicuously built to advertise the wealth of their owners but were always conceived as homes for single family units, a fundamental principle that was to remain central to the idea of the suburban home.

When not resident in their villas, the wealthy men who built them lived in urban townhouses, as was the case with Thomas Goldney II, a Bristol merchant who had made enormous profits in the slave trade and was an investor in Abraham Darby I's experimental iron works at Coalbrookdale in Shropshire. Goldney's city residence was a townhouse on Bristol's High Street, not far from Guinea Street; but in the 1720s, on land in Clifton that had been bought by his father, he built the imposing Goldney Hall. From there he had easy access to the city of Bristol and its busy port but was equally able to enjoy the relative seclusion of Goldney Hall and its large gardens. (The version of Goldney Hall seen today 'encased' the original one in the Victorian period when Goldney's son did major remodelling.) Another early villa was Marble Hill House, near Twickenham. It was commissioned by Henrietta Howard, who obtained the land in 1724 with money gifted to her by her lover, the Prince of Wales, later King George II. Set back from the Thames, then a busy waterway, and approached from the river via an avenue of chestnut trees that cut through fine lawns, Marble Hill was intended as a leafy retreat within which Henrietta could escape from her hectic life at court. It was only when she retired from court in 1735 that she made Marble Hill her main residence. With such wealthy clients it is hardly surprising that some of the grand villas of the mid-eighteenth and early nineteenth centuries were designed by celebrated architects, men whose services were in high demand. Childwall Hall near Liverpool was the work of John Nash, later responsible for Regent Street and Park Crescent in London and Ravensworth Castle outside Newcastle, after which Ravensworth Terrace was named.

In the second half of the eighteenth century the number of new villas began to increase as more of the wealthy elite set out to create their own suburban sanctuaries. In a way that felt novel, the borders between city and countryside became less clear and obvious. In 1789 a contemporary writer described the roads leading from London as being lined with 'scattered villas and genteel houses, in the manner of a continuous, and rather elegant village . . . for three, five or seven miles out of London.' Half a century later in 1848 a correspondent to

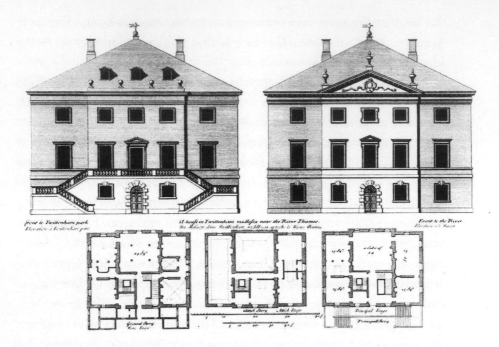

the *Builder* was still speaking of a 'villa mania' that 'is everywhere most obtrusive'. The villa boom was partly explained by the fact that by the end of the eighteenth century, villas, rather than being second homes, were increasingly becoming the primary residences of their wealthy owners, some of whom commuted daily to their city offices in their carriages. As demand for this new

The plans of Marble Hill House in Richmond, built during the suburban villa boom of the early eighteenth century.

suburban mode of life increased it was no longer enough for individual wealthy owners to purchase land and commission single houses built to their specifications. Instead landowners near the cities began to plan suburban estates made up of multiple dwellings laid out to a plan, just as had been the case when the Georgian terraces of London, Glasgow, Bath, and elsewhere had first been built.

One of the first was undertaken by the Eyre family, who in 1794 set out their *Plan for the improvement of the freehold estate call'd St John's Wood*, an area they had acquired and that was then open farmland. Unlike most of the families who owned land around London, the Eyres, who had been merchants from Wiltshire and the owners of plantations and enslaved people in Antigua, were members of the upper middle class rather than the aristocracy. In their 1794 plan Henry Samuel Eyre and his brother Walpole Eyre envisaged forty-two modest-sized villas with gardens across an estate. The homes were arranged along broad streets that represented the wholesale rejection of the angular grid patterns of the Georgian terraces that stretched over much of west London. The streets were laid out in great sweeping curves and there was a large circular street at the centre of the development. Another break with tradition was that each house was oriented to face the garden rather than the facade of the house opposite it. This was intended to create a sense of distance and rustic privacy, something that was not possible even in the grandest city terraces. *The Times* described the new suburb as being 'most obviously suitable for the erection of Residences of such novel description, as will unite the beauty and pleasure of a Country-House, with the convenience and advantage of a town one'. The Eyres then leased plots of their land to speculative builders who were instructed to build according to the original plan.

Three decades later in Manchester the civic architect Richard Lane created another exclusive suburban estate. In 1836 he presented a plan for a new development named Victoria Park, after the future queen, then the heir presumptive. The new suburb was to be built in the township of Rusholme, two miles south of the city, an area the developer's prospectus stressed was 'in the immediate neighbourhood of the great and increasing town of Manchester'. Victoria Park, its promoters promised, would provide 'an adequate number of first-rate dwelling houses' and in so doing would fill a gap in the market created, as the prospectus explained, by the 'want of private residences of this description' within the rapidly industrializing Manchester of the 1830s, caused in part it was claimed by 'the rapid conversion of dwelling houses into warehouses'. The homes were to be 'handsome villas; protected from every nuisance, and each residence so placed as to command an advantageous prospect, without interfering with those around it'. The new homes were to have access to 'the best roads', which allowed them, according to another account, 'the advantage of a close proximity to the town' and 'the privacy and advantage of a country residence'. While conveniently near to Manchester the exclusive homes in Victoria Park were to be 'free from any possible nuisances that in other situations may arise from the vicinity of smoke and manufactures'. Victoria Park was exclusive in a literal sense; great efforts were to be made to ensure that members of the lower

classes were actively excluded. Like London's Regent's Park and several other garden suburbs created during the middle of the century, Victoria Park was what today would be called a gated community. Among the first bricks laid were those of the walls that surrounded the development and lodges that flanked the entrance gates.

A gated entrance to Manchester's Victoria Park, a suburban estate laid out in the 1830s and later home to the novelist Elizabeth Gaskell.

In the same years that Victoria Park was being built another smaller scheme was underway in Aigburth, on the outskirts of Liverpool. In 1839 the brothers William and Alexander Smith, two Liverpool merchants, purchased a thirty-six-acre parcel of land at Fulwood Park. Their plan was to sell off individual plots upon which high-quality houses could be built, again within a gated community. Fulwood Park was intended to be a true garden suburb. Only thirty houses were planned, less than one per acre, an exceptionally low density of housing even for an exclusive suburb in the 1830s. In the end some purchasers bought more than one plot and the density of housing turned out to be even lower than planned. To ensure the houses were fitting for their location, covenants attached to the plots insisted that the minimum that could be spent on the building of each house was £1,500, a large sum for the day.

By 1847 several of the homes had been completed and were occupied by precisely the class of owners the Smiths had had in mind. Among those first residents were a barrister, a wealthy clergyman, and a town councillor. Other later residents described themselves as merchants working in shipping, the cotton importation industry, and the East India trade. Small as it was, with only nineteen houses at the time of the 1871 census, Fulwood Park became a template for larger estates in Liverpool like Grassendale and Cressington Park, which were developed in the 1850s. Among the promoters of the Cressington Park scheme was Thomas Doran, an accountant who operated out of offices on Falkner Street, not far from the house in the first series of *A House Through Time*.

One of the main complaints levelled against the suburbs in the last decades of the nineteenth century was that they were dull and monotonous, that in the great seas of semi-detached villas that spread themselves across the fields surrounding Britain's cities each house looked exactly like its neighbour, and individuality and self-expression were absent. In the garden suburbs of the early and middle decades of the nineteenth century the opposite was true. There on the fringes of the city where land was cheap, the economic laws that had dictated the uniformity of the urban terrace were absent and speculative builders were able to construct homes that consumed large chunks of land but in different styles and layouts. They did this to stay up to date with the shifting tides of fashions and to build homes that were affordable to each of the sub-categories within the expanding middle classes. Every gradation of wealth and status among the new suburbanites was given solid form in brick, stone, and mortar. The decision to break away from the conventions of the terraced Georgian townhouse was conscious and deliberate. Suburban villas, such as those in St John's Wood, Victoria Park, and elsewhere, were set back from the road and those roads were often curved, undulating, and frequently lined with avenues of trees. The cliched description of the suburbs as 'leafy' was always justified. But the other break with the terrace was the rejection of uniformity, both of style and layout. The same was true for the later, less exclusive, Victorian suburbs in which a huge range of house styles and sizes – villas, detached homes, semi-detached, and what were misleadingly called 'cottages' – was built.

The emergence of new styles of home and new options for decoration were enhanced by the repeal of various taxes that had influenced house-building during the Georgian era. In 1850 the brick tax was abolished, helping to make bricks, particular decorative ones, more popular as a design feature. This change, along with a new interest in Venetian architectural styles, popularized by the art critic John Ruskin and his influential 1849 book *The Seven Lamps of Architecture*, gave rise to the use of bricks of various different shades to create colour – known by architects as polychromatic. Variously coloured bricks were arranged into bands or diagonal patterns, adding not just decoration but also individuality to new suburban homes. The styles and sizes of windows were also transformed by the repeal, in 1851, of the much-hated window tax, which had sat on the statute books for a hundred and fifty-six years. Combined with innovations in the manufacture of plate glass, the end of the window tax allowed Victorian builders to create homes with far larger windows and more of them. The new technologies also meant that the individual panes of glass could be larger, again increasing the potential for individualization. The new glass-making technology, the growing demand for ornamentation, and the Victorian desire for privacy combined together in fascinating ways. One result was the development of the textured, opaque, and coloured types of glass that were used in thousands of suburban Victorian homes in the second half of the century, increasing the scope of decoration while maintaining the home as a private space shielded from the gaze of neighbours or passers-by.

As well as new materials there was an explosion of new styles in which suburban homes could be built. These were set out in popular pattern books, bound and illustrated volumes that offered inspiration and instruction to architects and their clients and practical instruction to builders. Pattern books also served to spread new designs and fashions and thousands of them were published in the eighteenth and nineteenth centuries. In the Georgian era they had enabled builders to remain within the accepted conventions of style; for the Victorian suburbs they became catalogues that laid out in often beautifully illustrated detail the expanding range of styles available. In 1836, the year the plans of Manchester's Victoria Park were published, the architect P. F. Robinson published a pattern book entitled *Designs for Ornamental Villas in Ninety-six Plates*. Speaking up for his profession Robinson complained of the worrying 'absence of taste' that marred many 'modern buildings' and that was particularly marked in those for which 'the aid of the architect had not been sought in creating them'. After all he explained 'the mere builder cannot be supposed to possess that refinement of art which the man regularly educated, and with perhaps the advantage of having visited other countries should enjoy'. He then set out designs and specifications for villas in Grecian (inspired, he said by 'the fortunate acquisition of the Elgin marbles'), Palladian, Castellated, Anglo-Norman, Elizabethan, and Old English Style. He also included plans for 'A residence in the decorated style of Henry the seventh's time'. In *Suburban & Rural Architecture, English & Foreign*, another pattern book written in the late 1860s, E. L. Blackburne, the author, offered up an even wider range of designs for suburban homes. Starting with a detached villa in the English Domestic Gothic style, Blackburne presented detailed illustrations and plans to help builders construct villas – both detached and semi-detached – in the following styles: German, French Gothic, Italian, Anglo-Italian, Tudor Gothic, Swiss, and Italianized-Gothic. The author was careful to delineate which styles were appropriate for suburban locations and which should only be built in 'a more strictly rural locality'. The fashion for 'historic' styles of architecture that subtly suggested old money and inherited wealth revealed that while the Victorian middle classes were often critical or even dismissive of the old aristocracy they still deferred to them on matters of taste. For their part the aristocracy, the so-called 'Upper Ten Thousand', looked with alarm upon the unstoppable spread of the suburbs, a dramatic sign of the expanding size and economic power of the middle classes.

One effect of this growing Victorian desire for choice and individualism was that by the 1850s the elegant symmetry of houses like 62 Falkner Street and 5 Ravensworth Terrace had begun to lose some of its appeal. The change in tastes was not sparked by the rise of the suburbs but had begun earlier, as Georgian styles were slowly supplanted by new styles emerging from a Romantic revival. Back in 1807, the Romantic poet Robert Southey had dismissed the Georgian terraces as 'extended brick walls, about forty feet high, with equally extended ranges of windows and doors, all precisely alike, and without any appearance of being distinct houses. You would rather suppose them to be hospitals or arsenals or public granaries, were it not for their extent.'

Even in cities like Bath, Cheltenham, and Brighton, where the grand terraces were to remain a defining feature and a symbol of civic pride, the new styles gradually began to take over. Worcester Terrace, designed by architect Charles Underwood, was the last of the Georgian terraces built in Clifton, Bristol's exclusive suburb. After it was completed in 1853 the further expansion of Clifton and the development of nearby middle-class suburbs like Redland was achieved through the building of semi-detached villas and mansions, some of them on a vast scale.

However, the grandeur and appeal of the very finest Georgian terraces never entirely faded. John Haberfield, who as a young man in the early nineteenth century had lived with his family at 10 Guinea Street, had moved to Royal York Crescent in Bristol's elite suburb of Clifton by the time he was the city's mayor in the 1850s. He regarded his fine home there, with its extraordinary views over the city, as entirely fitting for a man of his status. In London and in inner-city districts elsewhere, where the high price of land meant that the original economic rationale behind the terrace remained unchanged, the age of the narrow-fronted, standard-plan terraced home rumbled on.

Yet the change in styles can be seen clearly in the development of the suburbs of Bristol and in the careers of the individuals who were behind them. In the 1830s the area was mainly rural with scattered suburban villas built by wealthy members of Bristol's merchant class. In 1842, when the last of the Georgian terraces of Clifton were still under construction, Benjamin Stickland acquired nine acres of land in Redland, a largely rural area to the east of Clifton. Stickland was able to acquire this land outright, not on lease. He then conveyed individual plots to builders who were to carry out the construction of the new homes, without employing any architects. The first houses he built on this land were narrow-fronted three-storey houses with basements, little different to some of the terraced houses in nearby Clifton and typically Georgian in style. But Stickland was one of the developers who could see that tastes were changing. By 1851 the homes he had hired builders to construct in the rest of the street were semi-detached villas. The earliest of these villas were given Georgian facades but the later ones were given bay windows, gables, and other classically Victorian features. The street itself was named Hampton Park Road, thereby conferring upon it the connotations of leafy suburban exclusivity that the word 'Park' had by then come to denote. These new suburban homes attracted the sorts of professional families who in earlier decades might have been eager to live in city centre districts like Redcliffe where 10 Guinea Street stands. To walk along Hampton Park Road today is to pass physically through the change in suburban styles, from terraced to semi-detached, from archetypically Georgian homes to clearly Victorian ones.

Many of the Victorian-era houses built on Hampton Park Road were what we today would call semi-detached. This was one of the great innovations of the suburb. There had been workers' cottages built in pairs in the past but the suburban semi was in many ways new; yet it began in the city. In 1825 John Claudius Loudon, one of the most famous and influential nineteenth-century voices on taste and domestic life, built himself what he referred to as a *double-detached* house in then suburban Bayswater (see p. 190). His intention, as he explained, was to create 'two small houses which should appear as one, and have some pretensions to architectural design'. By creating a domed, semicircular entrance porch that concealed the fact that there were two separate front doors, Loudon, as he himself said, was able to 'give dignity and consequence to each dwelling by making it appear to have the magnitude of two houses.' Loudon's grand Palladian mansion still stands on Porchester Terrace in Bayswater, now one of the most expensive streets in London. But it was away from the city, in the suburbs, that the idea of the double-detached house, what we today call a semi-detached, really took off. Semi-detached villas, as the historian Geoffrey Best has pointed out, 'were the next best thing to wholly detached ones . . . they cost less than the detached houses, were nearly as private, and gave the casual passer-by an impression of being grander than they actually were'. John Ruskin, the great Victorian art critic, described semi-detached houses as homes that had been 'fastened in a Siamese-twin manner together by their sides and each couple has a Greek or Gothic portico shared between them, with magnificent steps, and highly-ornamented capitals'. Today almost one in three houses in the UK are semi-detached, a result more of the post-1945 period than the Victorian suburban boom, as between 1945 and 1964 more than 40 per cent of all new homes were semi-detached.

The transition from one type of home to another and from urban to suburban modes of life can be seen not just when walking along certain

Victorian streets but also through the biographies of many of the most eminent Victorians. The trajectories of their domestic and family lives speak to the rise of the suburbs and the power of their appeal. The family of John Ruskin, for example, were early adopters of the suburban experiment. Ruskin's father was a wine merchant and in some ways typical of the kinds of people who first rejected the Georgian terraces that had delighted earlier generations. When John was born in 1819 his parents were living in a substantial brick-fronted Georgian terraced house in London's Brunswick Square, bought on a sixty-three-year lease for £2,192. In his not entirely reliable autobiography *Praeterita* Ruskin explained that his family left their large urban home in a desirable part of town and moved to one of London's new suburbs. 'When I was about four years old', he wrote, 'my father found himself able to buy the lease of a house on Herne Hill, a rustic eminence four miles south of the "Standard in Cornhill", of which the leafy seclusion remains in all essential points of character unchanged to this day'. The new residence, 28 Herne Hill, was part of a small suburban development near the village of Camberwell, to the south of London. From it the young Ruskin could see St Paul's Cathedral and ships on the River Thames – such panoramas are difficult to envisage today. Of 28 Herne Hill he wrote:

> Our house was the northernmost of a group which . . . consisted
> of two precisely similar partner-couples of houses, gardens and all
> to match; . . . three-storied, with garrets above . . . It had front and
> back garden in sufficient proportion to its size; the front, richly set
> with old evergreens, and well-grown lilac and laburnum; the back,
> seventy yards long by twenty wide, renowned . . . for its pears and
> apples . . .

What Ruskin quaintly calls 'partner-couples of houses' were semi-detached villas. He lived there until he was twenty-one. It was while at Herne Hill that he wrote much of his first book, *Modern Painters*, and it is clear from the fondness with which he wrote about his childhood home that it fulfilled his family's aspirations for a new mode of living. The house and its garden, he later wrote, 'answered every purpose of paradise to me.' In 1842 the family took a further step up the ladder of Victorian home ownership, moving into a detached house in Denmark Hill, about a mile from Herne Hill. The Ruskins' new home (now demolished) represented the realization of their suburban ambitions. Situated within a garden of seven acres it was far larger than their previous home, with enough rooms to house the seven servants who were employed to cater for a family that consisted merely of Ruskin and his parents.

While the Ruskins were happily ensconced in Denmark Hill, the author Elizabeth Gaskell and her husband the Reverend William Gaskell were living in a large terraced house on Upper Rumford Street in Ardwick, on the outskirts of Manchester. In 1850 Reverend Gaskell received an inheritance that enabled the family to make the move to 42 Plymouth Grove (now no. 84), a large detached house within the exclusive gated suburb of Victoria Park, which was by then well established. (See the plate section.) The Gaskells moved to their new home in June 1850, not long after Elizabeth's novel *Mary Barton* had been published. Her excitement at the prospect of living in such a luxurious property is palpable in a letter she wrote to her friend Eliza Fox just after arriving. 'And we've got a house. Yes! We really have, And if I had neither conscience nor prudence I should be delighted for it certainly is a beauty'. The Gaskells' Greek Revival-style detached villa had been built just a few years earlier in 1838 as part of the Victoria Park scheme. It contained twenty rooms arranged over two floors, including seven bedrooms, a drawing and a dining room, and a coach house. For this grand residence the Gaskells paid an annual rent of £150, half her husband's salary and a sum that Elizabeth found daunting. In the same letter to Eliza Fox she predicted (wrongly) that the house would ruin them: 'a year and I dare say we shall be ruined; and I've already asked after the ventilation at the new Borough Gaol.' Charlotte Brontë visited the Gaskells in Victoria Park on three occasions between 1851 and 1854 and described their home as 'a large, cheerful, airy house . . . a garden surrounds it, and as in this hot weather, the windows were kept open – a whispering of leaves and perfume of flowers always pervaded the rooms'. Critically, Charlotte Brontë explained, the house was 'quite out of Manchester smoke'. The cost of running Plymouth Grove meant that when the Gaskells moved in with their four children and five servants they could not afford to do much in the way of renovations. Elizabeth, who loved to travel in the countryside of North Wales and the Lake District, did however make the most of Victoria Park's open spaces and rustic pretensions by growing vegetables in her large garden and also keeping pigs, poultry, and even a cow. It was while living there that she wrote both *Cranford* and *North and South*.

The life of Charles Dickens, more than either Ruskin or Gaskell, was marked by social mobility, a journey that can be read in the succession of homes he bought. Dickens' childhood was blighted and ultimately foreshortened by his father's indebtedness, which forced the family into poverty and drove the teenage Charles to find work in Warren's Blacking Warehouse, a shoe-polish factory where he worked attaching labels on pots of polish, for which he earned a shilling a week. Those experiences shaped his character and left him with a deep and lifelong appreciation of how debt could send a member of the middle classes down into the abyss of poverty and even destitution. Social mobility operated in both directions. Perhaps influenced by his childhood experiences of poverty, Dickens had an acquisitive and materialistic nature manifest at times in his relationship with the homes he acquired over the decades. As a bachelor and later a newlywed he had lived in apartments in Furnival's Inn, Holborn, where he paid an annual rent of £35. But on the birth of their first child, Charles and his wife Catherine began the search for a family home. In 1837, with the income he was earning from his journalism and increasingly popular sketches he was able to purchase the lease on 48 Doughty Street, a terraced house on a private, gated road, in genteel Bloomsbury. The lease had an annual rent of £80. With its twelve rooms Dickens rather grandly described it as a 'first class family mansion'. He spent two years in this Georgian terrace with his wife, child, his younger brother, and servants. But when his third child was born in 1839 his financial position had so improved following the publication of both *Oliver Twist* and *Nicholas Nickleby* that he was able to make the decisive move to 1 Devonshire Terrace, just outside suburban Regent's Park. From the first moment Dickens viewed his future home he became desperate to secure the lease on what he called 'A house of great promise (and great premium), "undeniable" situation and excessive splendour . . . I am in ecstatic restlessness.' The 'premium' he referred to was an annual rent of £160 for which he got a large secluded garden, a coach house, and thirteen rooms.

For Dickens, Ruskin, and Gaskell, moving to the fashionable new suburbs was an exhilarating and affirming experience. Other notable

The great women's suffrage campaigner Emmeline Pankhurst, another resident of Manchester's Victoria Park.

Victorians left accounts of journeys made in the opposite direction. Being forced to abandon suburbia was painful and unsettling, and came to represent sliding down the ladder of wealth and status. Emmeline Pankhurst, who was from a middle-class and politically active family in Manchester, married Richard Pankhurst, a barrister with a social conscience and unfulfilled political ambitions, in 1878. The couple lived in a terraced house in London's Russell Square. In 1893 they moved to Manchester. Their new home was 4 Buckingham Crescent (now Daisy Bank), another villa in Victoria Park. The Pankhursts' house, far less grand than that to which Elizabeth Gaskell had moved four decades earlier, had a small walled garden and more land at the front. There, within its comforts, Pankhurst's political activism flowered. However, in 1898 Richard died and the family income contracted, forcing Emmeline to leave Victoria Park and move back into the city. 62 Nelson Street, off the busy Oxford Road, was a modest red-brick semi-detached two-storey house, located in the Chorlton–Medlock area of Manchester (see the plate section). One of Pankhurst's biographers described how difficult this slide down the property ladder was:

> At the time the short half mile that separated Buckingham
> Crescent from Nelson Street looks like a yawning social gulf
> between the comfortable bourgeoisie on the one hand and the
> precarious lower middle classes on the other. This perception that
> she had become downwardly mobile for the first time introduced
> an unwelcome element of insecurity into Emmeline's life, and one
> which remained with her . . .

The first suburbanites, the wealthy men who built villas along the roads into London, on the hills overlooking Bristol, and elsewhere, were able to travel between city and suburb at ease and in style as they were rich enough to afford their own horse-drawn carriages. This carriage-owning class, the upper stratum of the upper middle classes, represented a small fraction of the population. Those slightly less well-off made their daily journeys between the city and their suburban homes in horse-drawn hackney cabs. However, in the decades immediately before Victoria came to the throne, a new mode of transport emerged. It was cheap enough and reliable enough to enable a broader range of people to hold down jobs in the commercial centres of Britain's cities and have their homes in the suburbs. This in turn led to acceleration in the growth of the suburbs themselves. The vehicle responsible for this revolution was not the train. It was later in the nineteenth century that the railways and the suburbs became synonymous with one another: in the early decades of the century railways focused largely on the transportation of industrial raw materials and finished goods, and this freight traffic was often prioritized over passengers. In the 1820s and 1830s it was the horse-drawn omnibus, a vehicle whose story is often overshadowed by that of the commuter train. The age of the omnibus was critical to the development of the Victorian city and its suburbs, but its significance was not lost on people at the time. In 1849 the *Athenaeum*, an exclusive literary magazine, carried an article entitled 'The Age of Cheap Conveyance'. Its author confidently asserted that the horse-drawn omnibus was one of a handful of 'social conveniences' that had 'revolutionised all the chief capitals of Europe'.

The London omnibus was pioneered by George Shillibeer and created a transport revolution that allowed the middle classes to travel from the suburbs to the city.

'Few things in modern times', he explained, 'have been such influential agencies as the omnibus.'

Omnibuses were enclosed carriages driven by teams of horses, at least two but sometimes three or four. The carriages themselves were fitted with seats for between twelve and twenty-two passengers – around fifteen was typical in London. In addition, others had seats fitted to the roof. The driver sat high up on a seat at the front of the carriage, as with a stagecoach, and had to brave the elements. Arguably the first omnibus service in Britain was launched in 1824 by John Greenwood, a tollgate keeper in Pendleton, a Regency-era suburb near Salford that was favoured by the merchant class. Greenwood ran his primitive omnibus between there and Manchester. What distinguished it from the well-established stagecoaches was that passengers did not have to book a seat in advance – Greenwood and later pioneers allowed them to get on and off wherever they liked along the route. After initial success Greenwood started services to other suburbs and villages around Manchester, including Rusholme where the Victoria Park suburb was being built. Rival omnibus companies sprang up quickly and by the end of 1830s Manchester had a whole omnibus network. The omnibus came to the capital in 1829 after the London coachmaker George Shillibeer was commissioned by a French company to build omnibus coaches for Paris. Shillibeer decided to build coaches for himself and start operating a service in London. His omnibuses were pulled by three horses and had seats for twenty-two passengers. The first ran four times a day from Paddington (not yet home to a railway station), along the busy Marylebone Road to the Bank of England and the City. Others recognized the potential and launched rival services. Among them were the Wilson family, who operated Wilson's Omnibus Services from the 1830s until the 1850s, linking the recently built suburbs in North London, places like Islington and Highbury, to the centre of town. They took on many of Shillibeer's carriages and routes when his business failed and later Wilson's itself was absorbed into the London General Omnibus Company, which went on to dominate London's omnibus trade. Shillibeer himself fell into bankruptcy and was sent to a debtors' prison. After his release he became an undertaker, having converted an omnibus into a hearse. Within ten years of their arrival in the city there was a regular omnibus service linking the elegant villas built by the Eyre family in St John's Wood to the commercial centres of the capital. As London's omnibus services expanded they allowed the wealthy owners of suburban villas to abandon their horses and rely on the new form of public transport; even for the wealthy the cost of maintaining horses, coaches, and stables was not insignificant. By the middle of the 1850s it was estimated that around twenty thousand people commuted into London on horse-drawn omnibuses. Only six thousand at this point travelled by rail, and a further fifteen thousand travelled into the city by steamship, making use of London's oldest thoroughfare, the Thames.

The journalist Max Schlesinger, author of the 1853 classic, *Saunterings In and About London*, wrote that 'Among the middle classes of London, the omnibus stands immediately after air, tea, and flannel, in the list of the necessaries of life. A Londoner generally manages to get on without the sun; water he drinks only in case of serious illness . . . But the Omnibus is a necessity; the Londoner cannot get on without it.' The *Athenaeum* in 1849 claimed that the omnibus was not simply a form of transport but rather a 'health-giving instrument', because 'by its help all the world is able to live out of town'. By 'all the world' the author evidently meant only the middle classes. What the omnibus had done for them was to make their migration to the suburbs logistically feasible, as 'Barristers, merchants, artists, and men of letters, who formerly crowded the narrow courts and passages of Fleet-street and Cheapside, live now', thanks to the omnibus, 'in snug suburban cottages in Norwood, Hampstead, Putney or Blackheath.' The *Athenaeum* article noted that property prices and rents tended to increase 'wherever a good and cheap service of omnibus is established'. The relationships between the success of a suburb and the availability of a reliable omnibus service was so marked that on occasion property owners themselves established services, to increase the value of their property. By 1900 the number of omnibuses passing London's Bank Station each hour was 690.

As the number of omnibuses on the streets of Britain's cities increased, competition between the various companies, combined with other factors, led to a reduction in fares. Omnibus services that had initially been aimed at merchants were now available to ordinary clerks and other members of the lower middle classes who were able to commute to jobs in the city centres for sixpence and live in the suburbs. It was 'the quarter-to-nine 'bus to the City' that enabled Mr Pooter from *The Diary of a Nobody* to work in London while living at 'The Laurels', Brickfield Terrace – his semi-detached, suburban Eden. Mr Pooter only used the railway when going on holidays to the coast, or when visiting relatives out of town. It did however intrude into his life, as the track of the Great Northern Railway ran along the bottom of his garden, indicating that his home was one of the least desirable in Brickfield Terrace, undermining his sense of suburban seclusion and causing a crack to develop in the garden wall. Its proximity was one of the factors that encouraged him to nurse dreams of moving to a leafier, more exclusive garden suburb that perpetually remained beyond his means.

The link between the omnibus and suburban life was so well understood that the authors of more serious novels were able to construct their plots around it. As a youth in the late 1830s Wilkie Collins took the omnibus to get from his childhood home in suburban Regent's Park to his school in Highbury. In his 1852 novel *Basil: A Story of Modern Life* the eponymous central character is captivated by a woman he encounters on an omnibus heading out of London and up to the suburbs north of Regent's Park, then being constructed. 'We had nearly arrived at the last point to which the omnibus would take us, when she and her companion got out. I followed them . . . at some distance . . . They went on, until we reached a suburb of new houses, intermingled with wretched patches

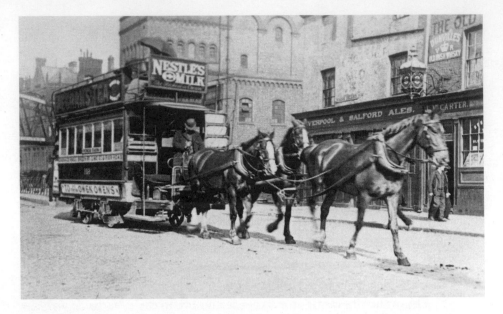

of waste land, half built over. Unfinished streets, unfinished crescents, unfinished squares, unfinished shops, unfinished gardens, surrounded us . . .'

A horse-drawn tram emblazoned with advertisements travels the streets of Liverpool in the 1890s.

The omnibus revolution had begun in the suburbs around Manchester and by 1831 it had arrived in Liverpool. New companies began by offering services that enabled the city's bankers and traders to travel from the suburbs to the Liverpool Exchange, the centre of commercial and banking activity in the city. The Liverpool North and South Omnibuses Company, for example, ran a service from the suburb of Aigburth to the exchange. The company's advertisements that appeared in the *Liverpool Mercury* carried an illustration of their omnibus carriages and detailed listings of the route and table of fares. Local landowners and speculative builders quickly recognized the omnibuses as a force that could attract buyers and tenants and make new suburban developments viable. Advertisements from the time that list land being sold for property development are careful to make potential buyers aware that the new homes would be near an omnibus route. A 'to be let' advertisement for 'a good house' in New Brighton, a suburb on the Wirral, that appeared in the *Liverpool Standard and General Commercial Advertiser* on 29 May 1838 explained that the property came with its own stable and coach house, yet stressed that 'the Seacombe omnibus passes the door'. In the mid-1840s competition between Liverpool's omnibus operators led to a considerable reduction in fares which opened up the possibility of moving to a suburban home to a wider swathe of the middle classes. While exclusive new suburbs like Grassendale Park and Cressington Park were being developed primarily with the wealthy carriage class in mind, advertisements for homes there were careful to mention that they were close to an omnibus station, which would be convenient if not for the wealthiest owners then for their servants and the tradesmen upon whom they relied to clean and maintain their large homes. By 1859, as the contemporary historian Thomas Baines recorded, there were twelve omnibus lines running from the centre of Liverpool to various middle-class suburbs. One of Liverpool's most successful omnibus operators was William Busby, whose company operated daily services in and out of the city and played a role in the development of suburbs like Everton.

The horse-drawn omnibus opened up suburban life to huge numbers of people, but not everywhere. Although horse-drawn omnibus services were introduced in Newcastle in the 1830s they were seen as overpriced and somewhat eclipsed later that decade by more affordable railways. In Bristol the omnibus offered only limited services and by 1849 was primarily functioning to connect the wealthy suburb of Clifton to the city's new railway station to the east of the city. The omnibus there was rather undone by the topography, Bristol's middle-class suburbs being on a plateau only accessible up steep hills that all horse-drawn vehicles struggled to ascend. Bristol's omnibuses were often only able to complete their journey by changing horses partway up the hill.

In Liverpool another form of commuting developed that allowed for even more distant suburbs to develop around the city. From the 1817 onwards it was possible to commute from Birkenhead, on the southern side of the vast River Mersey, into the heart of the second city of the Empire via steamship. That year the *Etna*, the first ship on the new ferry service from Birkenhead to Liverpool's Queen Docks, entered service, making it possible to live on one side of the Mersey and work on the other. Before the steam ferry the journey across the river was only possible on sailing ships that were too unreliable and weather-dependent for a regular commuting journey. The census of 1811 had shown that the population of Birkenhead had declined in the preceding ten years, while that of Liverpool had increased by about twenty thousand. Two years after the ferry service began a new church was built in Birkenhead and the town began to expand, as middle-class residents of Liverpool were increasingly drawn to the open country and fresh air away from the pollution of Liverpool, and the spectacular views across the Mersey. In 1801 Birkenhead had a population of not much over a hundred; by 1841, it had become a commuter town with a population of 8,227 and 1,256 houses. In the following decades the polluting industries that the suburban commuters had been keen to escape also began to establish themselves in the town.

The omnibus, despite the fall in the cost of fares, remained largely the preserve of the middle classes, a means by which clerks and shopkeepers could live in the suburbs closest to the city centres. The wealthier so-called 'respectable working classes' favoured the trams, which were far cheaper. Trams, like omnibuses, were at first horse-drawn and later electrified. In recognition of the fact that it was the working classes who used the trams, considerable efforts were made in London to ensure that they did not come into the centre of the city and instead disgorged their passengers on the edges of the central zone. The journalist A. H. Bevan noted in 1901 that the 'bringing of these lines to the centre of London has always been . . . rigorously opposed . . . on the plea that it lowers the character of the thoroughfare.'

The last home of Charles Dickens was Gad's Hill Place, a Georgian villa in the country near Rochester in Kent, originally built for a mayor of Rochester. Although grand and expensive (it cost Dickens £1,790 in 1856) it was not a house he considered exceptionally stylish. But among its many saving graces was that it was conveniently close to Higham railway station on the North Kent Line into London. By 1870, when Dickens died, the relationship between the railways and the suburbs was taking on the form it has maintained ever since. New suburbs were mushrooming around the cities and new commuter lines were being built to serve them. Often it was the emergence of new suburbs that inspired the building of the new commuter lines, rather than the other way around, but the relationship was often symbiotic, particularly around London. *The Suburban Homes of London*, an 1881 guide book to the suburbs of the capital written by William Clark, described 'the stream of arrivals from the country and from all parts of the world who are seeking a home near London either as a matter of taste or through business necessity.'

The ranks of these would-be suburban commuters had expanded, he concluded, 'now that railway and other means of communication have left the choice of situation so free'. With so many people looking to move to one of London's many suburbs, Clark had spotted a gap in the market for a 'compact impartial Handbook of the Suburbs', that carefully listed the advantages and disadvantages of each of London's eighty-nine suburbs, giving special attention to the local railway stations and the train services that operated from them. The inner suburb of 'Stratford New Town' was, Clark told his readers, 'a thriving place in a commercial view, and not rough in its manners'. The whole area, he reported, was a 'creation of the railway junction, and the works connected with the Great Eastern Railway.' When it came to more distant Greenwich and Blackheath, Clark felt that the homes that could be found on Burney Street, Brand Street, and Blissett Street were 'comfortably-arranged houses of modern style' and that they were 'not only desirable in themselves, but from the contiguity to the railway convenient to the inhabitants whose business is in London will render useful assistance.' When it came to London's original garden suburb of St John's Wood, laid out almost a century earlier by the Eyre family, Clark advised would-be residents that the area was fortunate to be served by both the railways and an omnibus service. 'No better-appointed conveyances enter London', claimed Clark. St John's Wood was the point of departure for Shillibeer's first omnibus, which went 'from the Eyre Arms to Baker-street, and along the New-road and City-road to the City, at a fare of 1s. 6d. The journey either way is now only 6d., and the omnibuses are greatly improved.' Even in the midst of the railway boom a reliable omnibus service was still a huge benefit to a suburb.

The inner suburbs grew not only by simple expansion beyond the cities' limits but also through infilling. The main roads were the first to be developed, then streets were laid out in the fields behind them as more land was purchased, until all the green spaces were consumed. Victorian infilling also captured some of the older and more exclusive suburbs, such as Newcastle's Ravensworth Terrace and the other late Georgian terraces surrounding Summerhill Square as industry spread along the banks of the Tyne and the city's westward expansion continued. The loss of the rural settings in which these early suburbs had been built inspired a great deal of unhappy grumbling, much of it inflected with class prejudice, and also led some of the wealthy residents to move further away, into new and more rustic suburbs or into the countryside itself.

John Ruskin, whose parents had been among the early suburban pioneers, became a vocal opponent of infilling and the expansion of the suburbs of south London. He was particularly unhappy about the building of new semi-detached homes in Sydenham Hill in the 1850s as they encroached on his childhood home at Herne Hill, blocking the panoramic views he had known as a child. Yet Ruskin was one of the authors of his own misfortune. His enormously influential writings on architecture, particularly his popularizing of Venetian Gothic styles, had inspired features within the design of polychromatic brickwork and decorated porches in the seemingly endless rows of villas and terraces that sprawled over the green spaces of his youth. Aware of the irony, he wrote, 'One of my principal notions for leaving my present house is that it is surrounded everywhere by accursed Frankenstein monsters of, indirectly, my own making'. Rejecting suburbia completely, in 1871 he purchased a large house called Brantwood in the Lake District, in which he lived out his later years, although he retained a room in his Denmark Hill house for visits to London.

While new more distant suburbs were being planted in the countryside around London, the city's industrial heart was itself expanding. This meant that some of the first suburbs that had been built closest to the city, the districts in which the genteel middle classes of the early nineteenth century had sought sanctuary from industry and pollution, were overtaken by the forces they had attempted to out-run. This process was poignantly described in *The Little World of London*, a book of novelistic essays written in 1857 by Charles Manby Smith, a now obscure writer who described himself as a 'Journeyman Printer'. Smith follows the story of his fictional Strawberry Street, in the suburb of Islington, from the 1820s when it was first built to the 1850s, by which time its demise was complete.

> When Strawberry Street first rose into being, which it did very gradually – taking between two and three years to complete its double row of two-storied dwellings – it was, to all intents and purposes, a suburb of London, and like other suburbs, shrank

from being swallowed up in Babylon's bosom, and clung with considerable tenacity to rural associations and characteristics. It retained for some years a strip of grass between the footpath and roadway, and boasted a tree or two, almost amounting to a row, on the eastern side. In lieu of pavement, the footpath was laid down with gravel, and the roadway was neatly macadamised; and, as all the front-parlours were fenced off from curious eyes by iron railings four feet at least from the windows, the street wore an undeniably neat and respectable appearance. And genteel it undoubtedly was – for a time. It became very early the abode of professional ladies and gentlemen, whose neat brass-plates informed you that they taught drawing and painting, and japanning, and French, Italian, and German, and the pianoforte and singing, and the practice of all kinds of musical instruments. Then there were clerks, managers, and responsible persons employed in the city, who came home to their families in Strawberry Street, as regular as the clock, about seven in the evening; and, besides these, a number of persons of independent property, of the staid and sober sort . . .

As London expanded, the genteel two-storey dwellings of Strawberry Street, rather like the very real houses of Liverpool's Falkner Street and Newcastle's Ravensworth Terrace, began a precipitous fall, until eventually industry itself – noisy, polluting, and corrupting – invaded.

The palmy days of Strawberry Street were now passing away, and its pretensions were evidently on the decline. The professional ladies and gentlemen moved by degrees further north, and their places were supplied by a new class – by tradesmen's clerks, by foremen and overseers of workshops, men of a hundred a year and no leisure, who came home at all hours of the night, and let themselves out in the dark mornings of winter long before sunrising, and who let lodgings to help to pay the rent . . . And now long ranks of cottages, not twenty feet apart, sprung up like mushrooms in the waste ground on the eastern side. These were inhabited almost as soon as built, by a class who did not trouble their heads about gentility at all . . . Suddenly, one winter's morning, the tall chimney, from which the scaffolding had disappeared a few days before, began sending forth a volume of black smoke, which darkened the whole neighbourhood . . . in less than a couple of years from the erection of the tall chimney, the whole street on both sides of the way, with the exception of a very few houses was transformed into a third-rate business street, and had lost all trace of its original neatness.

Within thirty years Charles Manby Smith's Strawberry Street went from being a new inner suburb, 'the abode of quiet and ease-loving', to become home to 'the toiling and struggling . . . its grass and trees all gone'. Finally the street was 'blessed with a gin-shop – that modern climax of civilisation'.

Even some of the more exclusive garden suburbs, in London and elsewhere, that had been designed to be leafy, low-density developments, experienced a degree of infilling. The land within Manchester's Victoria Park had been 'tied' by the developers, to prohibit any dwelling with a rental value of less than £50 a year. But in 1889, the building tie on the land within the park was repealed, following pressure from one of the major landowners who wanted to build new homes at higher densities for lower-middle-class residents. The result was that rows of modest terraces were erected on the field opposite 42 Plymouth Grove, where Elizabeth Gaskell had kept her cow, bringing to an end the sense of rural seclusion that Charlotte Brontë had commented upon. Fulwood Park in the Aigburth suburb of Liverpool had had similar covenants attached to the plots which were intended to prevent the building of new houses and maintain the suburb's exclusivity. The Fulwood Park covenants that stipulated that only one house was permitted to be built in each acre of land were never relinquished and remain in place today.

CHAPTER SEVEN

A HOME IN SUBURBIA

The Expanding Middle Class

What did a home in the suburbs mean to the Victorians who occupied it? Not just the wealthy merchants who since the eighteenth century had had the means to build villas in empty fields and commute to town in private carriages, but the great mass of the middle class who were enabled by omnibus and then the railways to move away from the cities and begin new lives in suburbia. What new modes of life, what new pleasures and pursuits were millions able to enjoy in suburbia that had been impossible within smaller, more densely packed city homes?

It was the separation of the home from the place of work, one of the great social transformations born of the age, that made the suburbs possible. Middle-class families who in earlier decades would have been content to live above the shop, in homes that were also places of manufacture or business, had come to demand something different. Once that rupture had taken place and the world of work had been detached from the home the remaining question was how great could the distance between the two be extended? In suburbs that were linked to the cities, by first the omnibus and then the train, the middle classes found their answer. The suburbs, by placing distance and travel time between the two spheres of life, further sharpened the divisions between work and play, weekdays and weekends; lines that in the twenty-first century, with the revival of home working, are becoming blurred once again.

The suburban home was a new space in which free time could be enjoyed. Behind their garden gates and screens of evergreen shrubs the suburbanites were granted new levels of domestic privacy, unavailable to all but the very rich within the dense cities. It was within the suburban home that the values of the great middle class were fully expressed. The communality that was a feature of working-class domesticity, with families sharing single dwellings or packed close together in small terraced houses, was anathema to the new mode of life. The home was private space, distant from the outside world and neighbours. The vibrant street life that was a feature of many European capitals was absent in the suburbs, to the bemusement of numerous foreign observers. In his 1904 book *The English House*, Hermann Muthesius, a Prussian architect who became the cultural attaché at the German Embassy in London, wrote perceptively and in exhaustive detail about the British and their love of domesticity. 'The great store that the English still set by owning their home', he observed, 'is part of this powerful sense of the individual personality. The Englishman sees the whole of life embodied in his house. Here in the heart of his family, self-sufficient and feeling no great urge for sociability, pursuing his own interest in virtual isolation, he finds his happiness and his real spiritual comfort.' Identifying trends that had already become a concern to some, he noted that the home-centred family-focused life of the suburbs was preferred over 'the hubbub of the metropolitan streets, a visit to a Bierkeller or a café'. Muthesius's observations here were of the British middle classes; the working classes had no choice but to engage with the streets and sought out the comforts of the pub whenever they could to escape the cold and the dark of the back-to-backs.

The homes built in the late Georgian and Victorian suburbs became the refuges within which the middle classes forged new identities and new modes of living. Their individuality could be expressed through the wide range of styles in which suburban homes could be built and reinforced through home decoration. Those houses and their gardens reflected all the gradations of wealth and status that characterized the broad span of the middle classes.

What made the home was cleanliness, which was essential to respectability. Along with the separation of work and home came the separation of the sexes within the home. Women were to be dominant within the home: their essential work was its maintenance and thus for them the house was a place of residence and a place of work. And within the private home the virtues of self-sufficiency, discipline, and respectability were nurtured. The different relationship to the home of the two sexes was perhaps best expressed by John Ruskin in his famous essay *Of Queen's Gardens*, in 1865. After describing the virtues of man – that of 'the doer, the creator, the discoverer, the defender' – he outlined the nature of women (hardly his area of expertise) and their relationship to the home. 'Her great function', he wrote, 'is Praise . . . within his house, as ruled by her, unless she herself has sought it, need enter no danger, no temptation, no cause of error or offense. This is the true nature of home – it is the place of Peace; the shelter, not only from all injury, but from all terror, doubt, and division. In so far as it is not this, it is not home'.

In her 1888 guide *From Kitchen to Garret: Hints For Young Householders*, Jane Ellen Panton, an enormously popular and prodigious author, offered up 'the benefit of the experience that has been bought by me, occasionally rather dearly, in the course of some eighteen or twenty years' to 'young housekeepers, just launching their bark on the troubled seas of domesticity'. The advice on domestic management set out by Mrs Panton, daughter of the Victorian painter William Powell Frith, covered everything from arranging a kitchen to establishing a nursery, managing servants, and decorating the home. It was, in the first instance, directed towards an imaginary middle-class couple, whom she rather quaintly named Edwin and Angelina. Young, soon to be married, moderately well-off, but not yet able to afford a comfortable life, they were, in her mind at least, archetypal. In order to find domestic happiness in the early years of their marriage Mrs Panton advised Edwin and Angelina in the following terms.

> I would strongly recommend a house some little way out of London. Rents are less; smuts and blacks [smoke pollution] are conspicuous by their absence; a small garden, or even a tiny conservatory (the joys and management of which ought to have a chapter all to themselves), is not an impossibility; and if Edwin has to pay for his season-ticket, that is nothing in comparison

with his being able to sleep in fresh air, to have a game of tennis in summer, or a friendly evening of music, chess, or games in the winter, without expense.'

In addition to these advantages Mrs Panton suggested that 'Another reason for choosing the suburbs at the commencement of married life is that in this case the rival mothers-in-law and the rival families will not be running in and out perpetually'. As to which of the many suburbs Edwin and Angelina should select, she wrote, 'while I most emphatically taboo those on the north side, I can as emphatically recommend those on the south. Bromley, Beckenham, Shortlands, and all the Crystal Palace districts are to be spoken well of'. Addressing Angelina, the author warned that as she will no longer be living in the city, and as Edwin will be at work most of the week, she had to guard against the bad habit of 'always contrasting the old ease, plenty, and amusements in her sisters' lives . . . with the somewhat straitened and monotonous existence that she must put up with until Edwin has made a mark in the world, and is able to keep his carriage and live in style.' Even in the late 1880s being able to afford a carriage, horses, and stables was the ultimate marker of genteel middle-class status. A decade after its first publication *From Kitchen to Garret* was still in print, by then in its eleventh edition, and was one book in a whole genre of guides to domestic management, many of which espoused the advantages of the suburbs for couples starting out in life.

Although the suburban home was the sphere in which the enclosed lives of middle-class women were lived, the physical structure of the house was to be maintained and improved by their husbands. The suburban home became the focus of a cult of home improvement. This shaped the lives and attitudes of the fictional Mr Pooter and his wife Carrie – who became for many the literal stereotypes of the Victorian suburbanite. 'After my work in the City, I like to be at home', wrote Mr Pooter in his diary.

What's the good of a home, if you are never in it? 'Home, Sweet Home,' that's my motto. I am always in of an evening. . . . Carrie and I can manage to pass our evenings together without friends. There is always something to be done : a tin-tack here, a

Mr Pooter painting the washstand in the servant's bedroom.

Venetian blind to put straight, a fan to nail up, or part of a carpet to nail down – all of which I can do with my pipe in my mouth; while Carrie is not above putting a button on a shirt, mending a pillow-case.

The suburban garden, every bit as much as the suburban home, was counted among the consolations of life outside the city. Nothing confirmed an individual's escape from the city's pollution had been realized more than the fresh air and birdsong of the garden. For those who had migrated to the suburbs from the country, as a great many did, the garden offered the link back to a surrendered rural way of life. The essential guide available to those who had freshly arrived in suburbia was written by John Claudius Loudon, who in 1825 had designed the prototype semi-detached mansion at Porchester Terrace in Bayswater. He was assisted in the writing of his many books by his equally energetic and prolific wife Jane Webb Loudon, who was herself a knowledgeable horticulturalist, the author of nineteen books and a pioneer of nineteenth-century science fiction and Gothic horror. John Claudius Loudon's most influential book was *The Suburban Gardener and Villa Companion*, published in 1838. In exhaustive detail it presented to the reader the many possibilities contained within the modest suburban garden. Like many mid-nineteenth-century books it had a long subtitle, which advertised

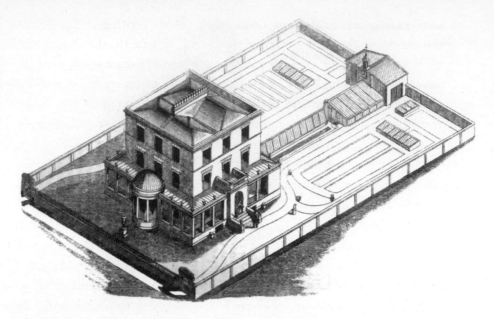

the book as 'Comprising The Choice Of A Suburban Or Villa Residence, Or Of A Situation On Which To Form One; The Arrangement And Furnishing Of The House; And The Laying Out, Planting And General Management Of The Garden And Grounds; The Whole Adapted For Grounds From One Acre to Fifty Acres And Upwards In Extent; And Intended For The Instruction Of Those Who Know Little Of Gardening And Rural Affairs And More Particularly For The Use Of Ladies.' The Loudons, both John Claudius and Jane Webb, were committed to the task of empowering women to become knowledgeable gardeners and to derive joy from their plots of suburban land. In the introduction, John Claudius Loudon promised his readers that he would 'prove, in this work, that a suburban residence, with a very small portion of land attached, will contain all that is essential to happiness'. The garden, he promised, would offer its owner 'health, which is the result of temperance and exercise; enjoyment, which is the possession of something which we can call our own and on which we can set our heart and affections; and the respect of society, which is the result of the favourable opinion of our sentiments and moral conduct'.

John Claudius Loudon's 1825 semi-detached mansion at Porchester Terrace in Bayswater.

Beyond the suburban home and its garden lay the suburb itself and further beyond that the countryside and the many leisure activities that became linked to the notion of a suburban life, as living in the suburbs also made access to the true countryside easier. Writing in 1877, near the height of the boom years of the Victorian suburb, the American-born novelist Henry James described the essential nature of the English suburb as 'the mingling of density and rurality, the ivy-covered brick walls, the riverside holiday-making, the old royal seats at an easy drive, the little open-windowed inns, where the charm of rural seclusion seems to merge itself in that of proximity to the city market'.

Both the suburb and the suburban home, distant from work and the city, were places of recreation and relaxation. Whereas the Georgian middle classes who had lived their lives in the grand terraces had tended to socialize out of the house, at theatres and so on, the suburban Victorians socialized much more within their homes. With larger houses and gardens they had more rooms for entertaining. Safe and secure in their rustic and mock-rustic retreats, the suburban middle classes increasingly regarded the inner-city slums – which they now saw only from the viaducts that carried their trains into the great cities – with continued horror. Indeed for some middle-class suburbanites their escape from the city had been made possible by the income they received in rent from the working-class people packed into decaying tenements in the declining city-centre slums.

Until the middle of the eighteenth century houses in both the cities and countryside were given names rather than numbers. As homes in pre-industrial Britain were very often also places of work, signs were often added to identify them to potential customers. In a largely illiterate society these signs often showed pictures rather than text. In London in the 1760s house names began to be abandoned in favour of numbers – the most notable exception being public houses. Other towns and cities then followed the capital's lead. But in the countryside houses retained their names and the builders of suburban villas sought to emphasize their suburban, semi-rural status by privileging names over numbers.

Where suburban homes developed along major roads out of the city, names were preferred over numbers for a different reason. As it was often obvious that more houses were soon to be built along a particular road, it made little sense for the speculative builder to number a completed property as the numbers would have to change – as was the case with number 62 Falkner Street in Liverpool, which began its life as number

58. One way around this was for a builder to give the houses he had constructed names. At other times new suburban houses along a road were given both names and numbers. Yet there were other reasons why speculative builders often gave newly built suburban homes names rather than numbers. As the flight to the suburbs was partly inspired by the urge to escape the city and a romantic longing for the country, builders attempted to emphasize or exaggerate the semi-rural character of the homes they built and the suburbs in which they sat by naming newly built houses after plants or other features of the natural world. For people who hoped that a move to the suburbs might allow them to be closer to the country and to nature, names like Rose Cottage, Oak House, Laburnum Lodge, Magnolia House, Orchard Villa, and of course The Laurels were potentially alluring, tapping as they did into the growing Victorian passions for nature and natural history. The intense Victorian fashion for collecting and growing ferns, the Victorians' somewhat staid and dour equivalent of the Tulip Mania of the Dutch Golden Age (the craze for ferns was dubbed *pteridomania* in 1855 by Charles Kingsley, 'pterido' being Latin for ferns), inspired house names such as Fern Cottage, while the gardening fashion for evergreen trees and shrubs, the greenery that provided suburban homes with year-round privacy, lay behind house names such as The Firs, The Shrubbery, and The Cedars. Such names could also subtly signal status, as only a decent-sized garden could accommodate a mature cedar tree.

Names could be used not just to stress the supposedly bucolic character of a suburb or a suburban home but also as a way in which builders could signal to potential residents that the houses in question were fashionable and modern. This could be achieved by naming them after recent events of national or international importance. The many thousands of Alma Villas and Cottages dotted across the UK were named in remembrance of the Battle of Alma, a victory for Britain and her allies over the Russians during the Crimean War in 1854, and began to appear in 1855. Similarly countless Victorian homes built in both the suburbs and in the cities were named after Lord Raglan, the commander of British forces at Alma and later battles in the Crimea. Naming homes after British military victories and victorious generals also tapped into the patriotism of the age. Victorian literary culture was another source of inspiration. The huge and enduring popularity of the novels of Sir Walter Scott through much of the Victorian era inspired numerous Waverley Cottages. Other suburban homes were named after Scott's celebrated novels *Ivanhoe* and *Kenilworth*, while Abbotsford, the name of his family home by the River Tweed, became another firm favourite.

The word 'villa' also had particular appeal, harking back as it did to the earlier, more exclusive days of the first Georgian suburbs. *Matthews's Bristol Street Directory* for 1871 identifies twenty-eight houses on Hampton Park, in the expanding suburb of Redland, that had been defined as 'villas'. The semi-detached houses on Hampton Park were substantial homes, but as the pace of suburban development quickened, builders increasingly assigned the word villa to almost any dwelling. Soon the more discerning were discreetly renaming properties, dropping 'villa' in preference for 'house' or 'lodge'. The term 'villa' fell out of fashion in part because it became one of a growing number of suburban affectations that attracted mockery. In 1847 a writer for the *Kentish Mercury* concluded that the names of suburban villas offered insights into their inhabitants. Under the headline 'The "Natural History" of Suburban Villas', the writer put forward the following theory.

> Among the notables of suburban neighbourhoods are the names of the houses of which they are composed. After a profound investigation into this novel branch of natural history, we are able to divide these into five categories – the floral, the geographical, the nominal, the religious, and the miscellaneous. Of the floral class there is Violet Cottage, Rose Villa, Laburnum Lodge, and Magnolia House. This class is generally inhabited by flower loving ladies, who blush fuchsia and smell verbena. . . . . The second class into which the names of suburban houses divide themselves is the geographical. Of this class is Worcester Villa, Hanover House, Cambridge College . . . Of the third category, the nominal class, there are more various inspirations. An old commodore retires upon his pension and inhabits Nelson House or Navarino Lodge. A half-pay major fights over again his battles in Wellington Villa, or Blenheim Cottage . . .

* * *

'There is a great flood . . . which has overtaken London and our great cities with houses and dwellings for the middle and working classes.' So said the *Building News* in 1900. 'Go where we will – north, south, east, or west of this huge overgrown metropolis – the fungus-like growth of houses manifests itself, stretching from town to suburb and village . . . In every direction we see the same outward growth of dwelling-houses of a small and unpretending class – generally a repetition of a type of house that has been found to meet the requirements of the middle class and artisan. The larger and more commodious residence of fifty years ago is being pulled down, or swamped by this tide of small houses; where one large house existed, ten or a hundred or more have been built, absorbing the acres of gardens and private parklands. This is one of the social revolutions of the age . . .'

The suburbs of London were some of the most rapidly growing areas of late-nineteenth-century England, expanding by 50 per cent each decade between 1861 and 1891. Between 1891 and 1901 the ring of suburbs that had come to encircle the capital grew by 45 per cent. There was more modest growth around Birmingham, Manchester, Leeds, and elsewhere. No two suburbs were the same and even within suburbs there was huge variation in the styles and costs of houses and the status of residents. What they had in common was an astonishing pace of growth that was shocking to many. In an essay written for the *Contemporary Review* in 1891 Sidney Lowe, the editor of the *St James's Gazette*, summed up their seemingly unstoppable growth. 'The centre of population is shifting from the heart to the limbs. The life-blood is pouring into the long arms of brick and mortar and cheap stucco that are feeling their way out to the Sussex Moors, and the Essex Flats and the Herefordshire Copses. Already "Outer London" is beginning to vie in population with the "Inner Ring".' Lowe and others argued that the rise of suburbia had become one of the great revolutions of the age and that it represented not merely the expansion of the nation's cities but the creation of a new zone that would eventually surpass them. 'The Englishman of the future', he suggested, 'will neither be a dweller in the country nor a dweller in the town. He will be a suburb-dweller. The majority of the people of this island will live in the suburbs; and the suburban type will be the most widespread and characteristic of all, as the rural has been in the past, and as the urban may perhaps be said to be in the present.' It was as Lowe was writing in the 1890s that the word 'suburbia' came into common usage.

Part of the concern among the elite about the suburbs stemmed from the fact that the omnibus and the railway had made them accessible to lower-middle-class families. In 1904 *The Times*, the traditional organ of the English establishment, ran an article entitled 'The Formation of the Suburbs' in which it attempted to sum up the suburban revolution that had begun in the eighteenth century when the first merchants had built villas on the outskirts of cities. In the past, *The Times'* writer stated, 'the manner of suburban extension seemed to affect mainly the middle classes': now, with Victoria's reign over, 'The habit of living at a distance from the scene of work has spread from the merchant and the clerk to artisan. And one has only to observe the substitution of small houses for larger in the older suburbs, and the streets of cottages in new extensions, to realise that the suburb is now mainly the residence of the family of small means'. 'Every suburban extension', it warned, 'makes existing suburbs less desirable'. *The Times* complained that the 'vast acres' of suburban streets served to make suburbia 'a district of appalling monotony, ugliness and dullness'. Yet it was the residents of those monotonous houses as much as their appearance that bothered the wealthy.

In 1871 the number of men in white-collar jobs in Britain was 262,084. By 1891 there were 534,622 and 918,186 by 1911. In 1891 they made up around 5.5 per cent of the male workforce, 10 per cent in London. The transition from a Dickensian world of counting houses to the late-nineteenth-century world of the office came about as an increasingly technical and technocratic economy demanded literacy and numeracy, even at junior levels. The Education Act of 1870, the year that Dickens died, helped create new generations of young men who had these skills. Those who, in need of further vocational qualifications, such as accountancy, attended private commercial schools, like the one opened at 10 Guinea Street by the entrepreneurial twenty-one-year-old William R. Martin in the 1870s.

The job of clerk, once a middle-class occupation, became opened up to boys whose fathers were skilled manual workers. Many late-Victorian clerks were young men (their youth often counting against them in popular portrayals) who had done well at school and dreamed of getting on in life, but whose family backgrounds were working class. However,

A typical suburban semi-detached house of the 1890s with two children standing outside.

the position of clerk was regarded as lower middle class and junior clerks were very often not paid enough to afford the necessary trappings of middle-class life. While the better-off bank clerks could earn a respectable middle-class salary, junior commercial clerks might earn just £80 a year, far below what was needed to be comfortably middle class, and not much more than the wages of a skilled labourer. Educated but underpaid clerks came to be seen as working-class upstarts with pretensions to middle-class status. They were dismissed in commentaries and in novels from the time as young men with middle-class aspirations but working-class salaries, forever short of money but determined to seize all the trappings of middle-class status. The clerk was seen as obsessed with keeping up appearances and emphasizing his imagined social status. He was, in short, a figure of derision, and the semi-detached house in the suburbs was regarded as the most overt way in which he telegraphed his middle-class pretensions. There were those who celebrated the rise of the educated, literate clerk as a clear manifestation of Victorian social mobility. E. M. Forster portrayed the clerk and his precarious position sympathetically, through the tragic figure of Leonard Bast, the young insurance clerk with a home in the suburbs in *Howards End*. Others, however, motivated by snobbery, derided the clerk and the suburbs where he increasingly came to live. When George and Weedon Grossmith made Mr Pooter a clerk who lived in a suburban semi-detached house, and punctuated his story with faux pas and moments of social embarrassment, they were tapping into exactly this stereotype and drawing upon the condescending class-consciousness that underwrote it.

Worse still for the reputation of the suburbs in the last quarter of the nineteenth century, the middle classes were joined in suburbia by members of the wealthiest sections of the working classes. The railways were encouraged to provide special workmen's trains. Permissions granted by Parliament to the private railway companies to build new stations in London came with stipulations to put on special services into and out of the city with low fares for working people. Thus the railway companies built more stations and drew more people out of the crowded city centres and into less congested areas such as Edmonton, Walthamstow, and Stratford. The Cheap Trains Act of 1883 formalized this, requiring railway companies to provide such 'proper and sufficient workmen's trains . . . for workmen going to . . . and returning from their work . . . between 6 o.c. in the evening and 8 o.c. in the morning as appear to the Board of Trade to be reasonable', and abolished the passenger duty on these trains. The suburbs, to which the middle classes had rushed in order to escape the pollution of the city and the working classes, became places to which the working classes, particularly skilled artisans, could now aspire to live. In 1891, Sidney Lowe noted that 'The new suburbs which show the largest increase are those in which a considerable proportion of the inhabitants are artisans and mechanics.' Looking ahead to the coming twentieth century, he predicted:

> Not one but a dozen Croydons will form a circle of detached
> forts round the central stronghold. The clerk and the small trader

will move onto remote suburban villages, as the merchant and the stockbroker go further afield to the Sussex downs and the Hampshire commons; and cheap trains will whirl the artisan daily from Rickmansworth or Romford as they now bring him in from Stratford or Canning town. What is happening in London will take place elsewhere. Liverpool, Manchester, and Birmingham are also approximating to the type of suburban town community. They too will have their central area, in which people will work and buy and sell, and perhaps learn and teach and to a certain extent amuse themselves; and their outer belt of residential satellites, in which their citizens will live and sleep. It is in such communities that the majority of Englishmen in the future seem likely to pass their lives.

By the last years of the nineteenth century it was fashionable to sneer at the suburbs and furtively mock those who lived in houses with names such as Rose Villa, Laburnum Lodge, or The Laurels. All were deemed pretentious and tasteless, as were many of the suburban home's architectural flourishes. In his 1905 book *The Suburbans* the poet T. W. H. Crosland wrote that 'in the whole arid area of Suburbia you shall not find a building that meets the eye graciously, or that does not bespeak a vile taste and a stingy purse.' By the end of the century even the term suburban itself had become pejorative. 'To the superior mind, in fact, "suburban" is a sort of label which may be properly applied to pretty well everything on the earth that is ill-conditioned, undesirable, and unholy. If a man or a woman have a fault of taste, of inclination, of temperament, of breeding, or even of manner, the superior mind proceeds, on little wings of haste, to pronounce that fault suburban', he proclaimed. Not only did the suburbs appear tasteless to those he felt were of 'superior mind', many commentators believed that they represented the ascendancy of the home over the city, the triumph of domestic life over social obligations. The Victorian age, during which Britain became the first-ever majority-urban society, with three-quarters of the population living in cities by 1901, an epoch defined by the growth of London into an unprecedented megacity and Manchester into industrial 'cottonopolis', had ended, it seemed, with millions who wanted little more than the comfort of their semi-detached 'villas'. The suburbanite who rushed home each night engaged with the city only as much as his work and his journey to and from it demanded. The civic life of the city and the civic responsibility of the citizen had, many feared, been jettisoned by a great swathe of the middle classes who spent their evenings and weekends pottering in suburban gardens or carrying out minor 'Pooterish' home repairs rather than attending public meetings or sitting on committees and councils.

In his 1909 book *The Condition of England* the Liberal politician C. F. G. Masterman wrote of the 'miles and miles of little red houses in little silent streets, in number defying imagination'. He examined their inhabitants and drew a damning conclusion. Every one of those suburban homes 'boasts its pleasant drawing-room, its bow-window, its little front garden, its high-sounding title – "Acacia Villa" or "Camperdown Lodge".' Victorian Britain's lower-middle-class white-collar workers, Masterman believed, had forged themselves into a new social subclass, obsessed with respectability and determined to cling onto the essential benefits of middle-class status. They were, he argued, profoundly conservative and had a tendency towards political as well as civic disengagement beyond what was necessary in order to maintain their standing. Rather their attention was focused on the many consolations of suburban life, 'a greenhouse filled with chrysanthemums, there a tiny green patch with bordering flowers; a chicken-house, a bicycle shed, a tennis lawn. The women, with their single domestic servants, now so difficult to get, and so exacting when found, find time hangs rather heavy on their hands. But there are excursions to shopping centres in the West End, and pious sociabilities, and occasional theatre'. Masterman regarded the Victorian suburb-dwellers as having created 'a homogeneous civilisation – detached, self-centred, unostentatious . . . a life of Security; a life of Sedentary occupation; a life of Respectability'. They were a class of people who 'do not strive or cry; and for the most part only ask to be left alone. They have none of those channels of communication in their possession by which the rich and the poor are able to express their hostility to any political or social change.' Consequently, he concluded: 'No one fears the Middle Classes, the suburbans and perhaps for that reason, no one respects them.'

The great irony attached to the history of the British suburban home, with its bay windows and garden, is that while to the Victorian city-dweller it was a place of escape, in the last years of the nineteenth

and throughout the twentieth centuries, those safe, comfortable semi-detached homes became everything later generations sought to escape in their turn. The generations who were brought up in the suburbs began to see suburban life in much the same terms C. F. G. Masterman had done – homogeneous, unostentatious, sedentary, and respectable. They sought refuge from such drabness in exactly the place from which their parents and grandparents had fled – the inner city, with all its vibrancy, dirt, and energy.

H. G. Wells lived in the London suburb of Bromley and depicted suburban life in a number of his novels.

One notable critic of suburbia was H. G. Wells, the son of a lower-middle-class shopkeeper who grew up in the London suburb of Bromley. Wells wrote often about the suburbs and the lives that were lived there. He decried Bromley's 'jerry-built unalterable houses' that formed 'a morbid sprawl of population'. Literary critics have often speculated on the degree to which his attitudes towards the suburbs – both conscious and subconscious – were reflected in his books. In his 1910 novel *The History of Mr. Polly* his central character is a suburban shopkeeper who comes to despise his dreary life in the imaginary suburban town of Fishbourne: to awaken from the suburban torpor he dramatically abandons his shop, his wife, and the suburbs, and runs off with another woman. The suburbs are also the backdrop for Wells' most famous novel, *The War of the Worlds*, written at the end of the nineteenth century when Wells himself was a reluctant resident of 'a small resolute semi-detached villa with a minute greenhouse' in the town of Woking. It is on common land near Woking that Wells had his invading Martians land. From that bridgehead they march on London, striding through the Surrey countryside in their fearsome tripods. On their way to the capital the invaders use their deadly heat rays to destroy, one by one, each of the suburbs they pass through – Weybridge, Shepperton, Leatherhead, Putney – what the narrator of the novel describes as 'the little world in which I had been living securely for years'.

Even now, almost a century and a half since Mr Pooter first moved to 'The Laurels', the suburban home remains the butt of knowing jokes and cultural snobbery; attitudes that became even more pronounced over the course of the twentieth century, as new waves of Britons migrated from the cities to pursue happiness amidst the great inland seas of semi-detached villas. Yet the millions of homes built within Britain's suburbs by our Victorian ancestors have proven incredibly popular and remarkably adaptable. Millions of us happily live in them, from time to time wondering about the lives of those who tended their gardens and slept in their bedrooms.

CHAPTER EIGHT

HOMES FOR HEROES

A Semi-Detached Britain

The semi-detached homes of suburbia were the subject of further derision long past the Victorian age. In his book *The Castles on the Ground*, written in 1946, the distinguished architect James Richards pondered the revulsion he and others felt about the suburban estates built between the wars which had encircled all the major cities in the country: 'We well know the epithets used to revile the modern suburb – "Jerrybethan", and the rest – and the scornful finger that gets pointed at spec-builder's Tudor with its half-inch boards nailed flat to the wall in imitation of oak timbering, though perhaps we should not criticize so fiercely the architectural idiom the suburb has adopted as its own if we understood the instincts and ideals it aims to satisfy, and how well, judged by its own standards, it often succeeds in doing so. If democracy means anything, it means deciding – for a change – to pay some attention to the expressed preference of the majority, to what people themselves want.'

What people wanted at the dawn of the twentieth century was an escape from the worst horrors of the Victorian city, the prospect of fresh air, and, in their wildest dreams, a garden. Modernist architecture was irrelevant: the abiding image was of the 'cottage', now with all modern conveniences. That this dream was fulfilled for so many in just twenty years between the end of the First World War and the outbreak of another was, in retrospect, a remarkable achievement.

Before the outbreak of war in 1914 some local authorities such as Liverpool, Newcastle, and London attempted to alleviate the ills of poverty by providing low-rent housing for the people living in the worst slums, but they did not have the funds to do much before the demands of war intervened. The belief that the private sector and charity could provide adequate housing for the working classes had been challenged. Estimates of the scale of the problem varied, but there seemed to be a consensus that when the war was over half a million new homes would have to be built.

After four years of savage warfare soldiers began to return home, many of them still armed, and there were real fears that there might be an insurrection. The Revolution in Russia in 1917 was in the minds of politicians when a general election was held in 1918, a month after the signing of the Armistice. The wartime Coalition Government with David Lloyd George as Prime Minister won a resounding victory.

On the campaign trail on 23 November, Lloyd George was invited to speak at the Grand Hotel in Wolverhampton, and was cheered as a war hero. He spoke with passion: 'Had it not been for millions of our men, who came from humble homes and laid their lives on the altar for their country, the British Empire might have been cowering at the feet of the most arrogant masters that ever bullied the world . . . The work is not over yet – the work of the nation, the work of those who have sacrificed. This is the appeal I make. Our task is to make Britain a country fit for heroes to live in.'

The Coalition Government of 1918, though predominantly Conservative, was led by senior Liberals who promoted the Housing and Town Planning Act of 1919. This embodied the historically momentous decision that central government would invest directly in subsidized housing. Previously local authorities were simply 'permitted' to provide council housing. Now government would underwrite the cost of building, making up the shortfall between income from rents and rates and the cost of raising the funds. This began two decades of house-building on an unprecedented scale.

Though the number of council houses built under this act fell woefully short of the promised half million, it led to the creation of 'cottage' estates on the fringes of all the major towns and cities in the country. Government funding fell back sharply in 1923 and gradually the building by private companies of what became known as 'semi-detached' suburbia outpaced council building, providing cheap housing for the more affluent working classes. Between 1919 and 1939, taken together, 4,200,000 new homes were built in England and Wales. By the outbreak of war in September 1939 this vast suburbia amounted to one-third of all houses then standing.

The man in charge of the creation of the post-1918 council estates was Christopher Addison. After a distinguished career in medicine, Addison devoted his life to politics and social reform. He was Minister for Health in the Coalition Government at a time when housing the working classes was considered a health issue. The Housing Act became known as the 'Addison Act', drawn up to fulfil Lloyd George's promise.

In June 1919 Addison dug the first sod on a site on the edge of Bristol to mark the beginning of the local authority's building programme at Sea Mills. The Lady Mayor planted a tree on the spot, which is there today and known locally as Addison's Oak. It was a contender in 2019 for the Woodland Trust's English 'Tree of the Year'. Sea Mills estate is now a conservation area, a rare accolade for a council estate.

Local authorities had little experience of house-building: some had attempted to emulate the charitable housing tenements of the Victorian era. But in terms of solving the housing problem this was negligible. Now councils had a kind of carte blanche to construct thousands of houses. The earliest housing built under the Act was often idealistic, almost Romantic: for inspiration they had the utopian vision of the 'garden city' movement, which dated from the late nineteenth century. Published in 1898, *Garden Cities of Tomorrow* imagined a future in which the benefits of both town and country might be enjoyed in one carefully planned, low-density settlement isolated from the Victorian towns.

The author was not an architect nor a planner but a stenographer called Ebenezer Howard. At the age of twenty-one Howard had left his work in the City of London and with two friends attempted to set up as a farmer in America, working a hundred and sixty acres in Howard County, Nebraska. After one winter the farm was abandoned and Howard moved to Chicago. Here he learned of 'garden cities', which were being created after the great fire of 1871. He began to read the writings of radical Americans, and on his return to London joined a philosophical society where he rubbed shoulders with the likes of George Bernard Shaw.

Howard pondered the relative advantages and disadvantages of town and country living. While the town was exciting and stimulating, living conditions were likely to be unhealthy. The countryside might be dull but the air would be clean. Reasoning in this way he imagined a garden city that had it all. He could not get government support for his ideas but he was able to raise private capital to buy land for a pioneer scheme. His first garden city was built at Letchworth in Hertfordshire, thirty miles from London. His second was begun at Welwyn, fifteen miles to the south, in 1920. Howard did not make much money but as Bernard Shaw said he was 'one of those heroic simpletons who do big things whilst our prominent worldlings are explaining why they are Utopian and impossible. And of course it is they who will make money out of his work'. He was knighted in 1927, a year before he died.

Howard's concept of a garden city separated from the older town by a green belt was theoretical, a sketch of plans of the layout of streets showing the proposed low density of housing. It was greatly modified and given more substance by Raymond Unwin, author of *Cottage Plans and Common Sense*, and Barry Parker, who both had been involved in the design of Letchworth and went on to express their own ideas of rustic urban dwellings in the creation of Hampstead Garden Suburb in 1905. Unwin was appointed to the committee chaired by the Paymaster-General, Sir Tudor Walters, which recommended a high standard of building that was adopted as a model for the Addison Act.

With a utopian vision for their pioneer council-funded cottage-estate schemes, local authorities began by buying large tracts of land on the outskirts of their Victorian cities. In Bristol the Sea Mills estate, described in the local papers as a 'garden city' when the first houses were completed in August 1920, was as close as any came to Unwin and Parker's dream. When he was making some recordings for the BBC the poet John Betjeman, noted for his love of Victorian architecture and his distaste for modern buildings, remarked of Sea Mills: 'a surprising beauty showing off in the evening sunlight; and vistas of trees and fields and pleasant cottages that that magic estate has managed to create.'

Between the wars Bristol built fifteen thousand council houses on nine new estates, which was 40 per cent of all new housing put up

in Bristol in those years. The first homes built at Sea Mills were much closer to the ideal of the garden city movement than those on later estates, where detail and space had to be cut back as the budgets were squeezed.

Bristol's Sea Mills estate in 1949. First built in 1920, houses were located near green open spaces.

Bristol's municipal enterprise was impressive, but could not compare with that of Liverpool. In 1919 an investigation of existing housing found eleven thousand families living in single-room accommodation. It was suggested eight thousand houses would be needed to provide for those in the worst conditions plus another thousand a year to cope with a rising population. With an almost messianic fervour the newly appointed Director of Housing, F. E. Badger, began to acquire land, forty-two acres here, twenty-four acres there, and to earmark for new estates land already owned by the council. By the end of 1920 the council owned 1,076 acres reserved for new estates.

The building industry was just gearing up after four years of war and skilled labour was in short supply, as were timber and other materials. Nevertheless Liverpool managed to put up 5,809 houses by the end of 1923 and for those moving in they were, at first, a dream come true. Set out in blocks of two or four, they all had gardens at the front and the back. The style of those built on Larkhill and the other early estates was described as 'box-with-a-lid' neo-Georgian. They were, in their way, charming, set in a landscape of quiet roads with mature and newly planted trees. They were relentlessly uniform in appearance and not as picturesque as Bristol's Sea Mills, but they were built to a very high standard. Each house had three bedrooms, with gas fires in two of them, an upstairs bathroom, and a generously proportioned kitchen with a gas cooker, a gas wash boiler, and clothes rails.

Many of these very early council estates followed a government manual on the design of homes prepared in meticulous detail by the Tudor Walters Committee. It was perhaps a surprise to this committee to learn that 'the desire for a parlour or third room is remarkably widespread among both urban and rural workers.' The term parlour has the same root as the French *parler* to talk, and it was regarded as a room away from the kitchen and other communal rooms set aside for special occasions. According to Tudor Walters: 'Witnesses state that the parlour is needed to enable the older members of the family to hold social intercourse with their friends without interruption from the children, that it is required in cases of sickness in the house, as a quiet room for convalescent members of the family . . . that it is needed for the youth of the family in order that they might meet their friends.'

Not all houses built under the Addison Act had parlours: there was a variety of accommodation, which was supposed to ensure there was a social-class mix on these new estates. In reality it was the so-called 'respectable' working classes who could afford the rents and who occupied most of the newly built homes. The first of the London County Council estates built at Roehampton was opposed by those living locally who thought such modest housing would bring down the tone of the area. They were relieved to discover the first tenants were bus drivers, teachers, civil servants, and their families, as only those with permanent jobs qualified.

A great many of these thoughtfully designed estates, reflecting the tastes of the Arts and Crafts movement with its Romantic view of rural life and the ideals of the garden city movement, have survived to this day. They represent the first chapter in what was to become an extraordinary saga of council estate-building. But in 1921 the dream ended as abruptly as it had begun. An economic crisis led to cuts in public spending, and the generous subsidies for council housing that had alarmed the Treasury were withdrawn.

While subsidies for council house building were cut, the Conservative government elected in 1922 revived the belief that, with some help in the shape of grants, private builders could put up houses for sale to compensate. In 1923 subsidies to builders were made more generous in the belief that this would bring down the price of houses. But this attempt to stimulate the market for houses-for-sale was premature: it did nothing to address the problem of housing shortages.

This brief hiatus in the council building programme came to an end with new legislation that enabled councils to resume ambitious programmes of estate building. What become known as the Wheatley Act, after the Minister of Health John Wheatley in the Labour Government of 1924, again offered generous subsidies for house-building. As the land closest to the Victorian cities became built over, the newer council estates were established further and further away from the familiar social world of working-class life. At the same time the standards of house-building were falling. Fewer and fewer parlour houses were built. On Liverpool's council estates nearly half of the homes built between 1924 and 1930 had a parlour; this fell to a fifth between 1931 and 1934. Houses got smaller while estates became more extensive. Norris Green in Liverpool ended up with a population of about 56,000, the same size as Shrewsbury. In place of semi-detached houses, more and more terraces were built, some of ten or twelve houses, in a landscape with fewer trees. After 1934 Liverpool started building blocks of suburban flats to accommodate tenants with very low incomes.

If the style and size of homes offered on the largest cottage estates no longer expressed the aspirations of the garden city movement, for the tenants that was the least of the disappointments. Liverpool built houses and nothing much else, as was the case with schemes in other large towns, including those of the London County Council. This had not been the original intention: a 'garden city', particularly one in which many of the tenants had young families, would need schools and shops, and perhaps a public house or two.

There were three new schools planned for Liverpool's Larkhill Estate. They were not opened until several years after families moved in, but Larkhill was near enough to the limits of the Victorian town for parents to walk their children to schools there. In fact these new council estates, wherever they were built, nearly all lacked schools and shops in the early years after their completion. There were no churches, libraries, or public houses. Whereas it took time, and usually the efforts of a tenants' association, to get a church or a library, there was no prospect of any of Liverpool's inter-war estates getting a pub: in 1926 the city council had banned the building or setting up of any licensed premises on its land. This was in the spirit, as it were, of the garden city movement. Letchworth, the pioneer garden city had one establishment called the Skittles Inn, which was opened in 1907, serving hot chocolate and soft drinks but no beer nor anything with a whiff of alcohol. In the publess estates built by Liverpool Council getting a pint might mean a walk of two miles or more and men complained that by the time they got home they would be sober again. Their needs were met by deliveries of alcoholic drinks and a few pubs built on the periphery of the estates.

There was nothing unusual about the experience of the tenants on Liverpool's inter-war council estates: it was the same in all the towns which had made such an effort to provide better housing for their working population. Becontree, the largest council estate built by the London County Council, housed a hundred and twenty thousand people and had just six pubs. That was one for every twenty thousand tenants whereas in the London they had left there was on average a pub for every five hundred people. On the Downham Estate in south-east London there was just one pub for a population of thirty-five thousand. And the Downham Tavern did not fit the image Londoners had of a public house. There were no bars and waiter service only. The council called it a 'Refreshment House'. The people of Downham found it absurdly inconvenient.

Exactly how many of the tenants of council estates decided they would rather return to the more basic housing conditions they had left than live in soulless luxury is not recorded, but surveys of tenant satisfaction suggest it was quite high, maybe 10 to 15 per cent. Nearly all tenants lamented the loss of a close community feeling, even if they got on well enough with their new neighbours on the estates. Perhaps the majority, however, valued their first proper bathroom, a garden in which to grow vegetables, separate bedrooms, and electric light, and decided that these luxuries more than compensated for the loss of the richer social life they had left behind.

* * *

In 1924 an Electrical Association for Women (EAW) was formed to promote the use of new gadgetry, particularly among the working classes, who were thought to be suspicious or frightened of it. It was the experience of women working in munitions factories in the 1914–18 war which had persuaded the founders of the association that women were capable of handling electrical equipment. However, it seemed that the take-up of electricity was not as enthusiastic as they had hoped or thought it should have been. Hardly anyone had a vacuum cleaner.

Electricity companies demonstrated the use of various gadgets, here the electric iron c. 1913–14.

In the inter-war years the gas and electricity industries fought each other for the favour of housewives with propaganda films and advertisements. The companies were either privately or council-owned and run: although work had begun on creating the national electricity grid in 1926 it was not anywhere near completed until after the war. Some local authority electricity companies with their own generating stations had showrooms in which they demonstrated the wonders of the all-electric home. Many made equipment such as electric irons available for rent. Six London boroughs had on offer cookers, kettles, fires, water heaters, and washing machines. The take-up disappointed the EAW.

The association's members toured the country preaching and demonstrating electric appliances in towns and villages. They identified two types of potential customer: Mrs A, a country woman relying on coal for all her cooking and heating, and Mrs B, a working-class woman in town who had gas for cooking and heating and a coal fire to heat her water. What would their priorities be if offered electric power? The answer was that their order of preference was almost identical: lighting, iron, vacuum cleaner, cooker, water heater, kettle, washing machine, water boiler, and radiator. In the country Mrs A specified a pump between cooker and water heater. This was for the most part pie-in-the-sky: electricity was expensive, gas much more familiar and cheaper. And the EAW estimated that in 1934 around five million working-class homes did not have an electricity supply anyway.

Those moving out to council estates were more likely than those left behind in the crumbling tenements and run-down terraces of the Victorian towns to have an electricity supply, which at least gave them electric light. But, it was not the promise of new gadgetry and labour-saving devices which was most prized in the new council houses. It was the privacy of your own bathroom, an indoor toilet, and a garden in which to breathe fresh air which were the real luxuries. It was these that were denied those unable to leave the slums because the qualifications for tenancies for these 'palaces for the people' – steady incomes and a good record on rent payments – excluded the poorest.

In most towns the building of council cottage estates peaked in the late 1920s, by which time they were beginning to be eclipsed by a more opulent, privately owned, semi-detached suburbia, instantly recognizable as derived from the same garden city principles but more varied and eccentric in its layout and building styles. This was the suburbia built by private enterprise, with considerable help from governments, which by 1939 had dwarfed the council cottage estates. It is estimated that three-quarters of all housing built between the wars was privately funded. This was made possible and encouraged by an economic revolution, in which a large part of the nation's investments were poured into housing.

Before 1914, only about 10 per cent of houses in the country were owner-occupied. People rented their housing, whatever their social class: if they owned a house it was as an investment. The owners of even quite substantial Victorian and Edwardian houses did not live in them themselves. It was a reliable investment: 'safe as houses'. After the end of the war in 1918 new building for the private rental market collapsed. Munitions workers had persuaded the government to put a freeze on rents in poorer housing, taking away at the lower end of the market any incentive landlords may have had to provide rented accommodation for working people. Shortly after the war, this rent freeze was extended to higher income groups, as there was a severe shortage of private rented accommodation for the middle classes. Without constraint, landlords could have charged what they liked.

However, a new way of funding housing had been developing since the late Victorian period which would provide an alternative. Since the eighteenth century a building society movement had been developing in Britain with origins that can be traced back to friendly societies and freehold societies, relatively small groups of people who got together to acquire property and build houses. The freehold societies had originally been set up as a means to win the vote, which was only enjoyed by the owners of freehold property or land worth 40 shillings a year. Many of these societies were wound up after a few years, but others remained in existence after the founders had acquired their property, calling themselves *permanent* building societies. Established originally to encourage artisans and middle-class people to become property owners, they began to attract investors who wanted a safe investment. Overseas markets were not attractive immediately after the war, and the rented market was no longer 'safe as houses'.

Governments recognized that if houses were going to get built, the building societies were the most favourably positioned to put in the funds. Accordingly they were given some significant privileges. During the war, when income taxes had risen from 1 shilling to 5 shillings in the pound, building societies clinched a deal with the Inland Revenue whereby their investors paid these higher taxes at source, which worked out at a rate lower than that paid on income from other investments. This increased the attractiveness of investment in building societies, and funds began to flow into their reserves.

Just after the war, the largest building societies were still located in the north of England. However, a series of amalgamations, as well as the steady take-off of house-building in the south, induced half of the biggest societies to set up their headquarters in London and the south by 1930.

This reflected the extraordinary economic dominance London had in the inter-war years: it was a boom town when the great traditional industries in the north were closing down, causing untold hardship for workforces that had no alternative employment. Between 1918 and 1939 two-thirds of all new jobs in the country were based in London. The capital was a huge market, and on the newly built arterial roads leading out to the west brand-new factories appeared, many of them American.

Nine hundred new firms employing twenty-five people or more were established in just six years between 1932 and 1938. Inevitably London attracted ambitious people from all over the country. Privately funded semi-detached suburbia arose on the outskirts of many other towns, but there was nothing to compare with the square miles of London's inter-war suburbia. Together with the council cottage estates London's built-up area actually doubled.

The number of white-collar workers, clerks, and lower-grade professionals multiplied, creating in effect a middle class that was much larger, but rather poorer on average, than its Victorian counterpart. For this emerging social group, domestic servants were a luxury. The young girl who might have become a maid-of-all-work and cook found that there were many rival jobs in industry, catering, and hotels with better wages. Whereas the wealthier families of the West End were able to hang on to a living-in staff of maids and cooks, the suburban middle classes, the Mr Pooters of the mid twentieth century, in general rapidly gave up the employment of servants.

At the same time, the average age of marriage fell, so that the number of new households – that is, husband and wife wanting to set up a separate home from their parents – rose, while the number of children in the average family fell. The result was that there were more, but smaller, households, in search of smaller, more convenient, housing.

Those who wanted to escape from rented accommodation and to have a place that they owned would invest in a building society, increasing the pool of capital available to lend to homebuyers. When the idea of home ownership caught on, the building of private suburban houses increased rapidly. Land was relatively cheap on the outskirts of London because agriculture was depressed, and the large landowners agreed to sell plots to builders.

From very modest beginnings, building societies began to grow into large and powerful companies. The story of the Abbey Road Building Society's rapid expansion provides a colourful example. It was formed in 1874, and takes its name from its first address, Abbey Road, NW6. The founders were members of the Free Church and met in a schoolroom attached to the chapel. By the outbreak of war in 1914 the society had assets of £750,000. By 1925 assets had increased to £3.5 million, and it was developing rapidly into a modern-style building society, drawing funds from a wide range of investors and advertising itself extensively to both investors and borrowers. It had grown to such a size by 1927 that it moved out of Abbey Road and built a new headquarters in Upper Baker Street. Between 1929 and 1935 its assets rose dramatically from £19.1 million to £46.1 million, and outgrowing its headquarters yet again it moved in 1932 to another head office in the same street, the clock-tower of which was later converted into flats. It amalgamated with the National, to become Abbey National, in 1944.

The Woolwich had been founded earlier, in 1847, and was a substantial local society by the turn of the century, its strength founded on the contributions of working men from Woolwich Arsenal. It too took off after the First World War, its assets rising from £1.6 million to £27.1 million by 1934. It began to open branches all over London, in the City, in Ilford and Romford in Essex, in Finsbury Park, Ealing, and many other of the expanding semi-detached suburbs. Just as the building societies grew in size, so did a number of building firms, many of which moved from the north of England to cash in on the London market. Taylor Woodrow, Costain, Laing, and Wimpey were among those who expanded in the inter-war years during the house-building bonanza.

Working together, the largest building firms and building societies devised a way of bringing the amount needed for a deposit on a house to a level many could afford. A system of builders' 'pools' was agreed, whereby the developer of an estate would underwrite the initial cost of acquiring a house so that the first-time buyer – as most people were – had to put down only 5 per cent, instead of 20 per cent of the

HERE'S A WONDERFUL HOUSE FOR £395!

10 Different Types
Ready for Occupation

F
R
O
M

10/4

PER WEEK

£5 secures any house

● *"Never before such value at this popular price."*
Fine elevations—good square rooms, fitted with modern labour-saving devices planned for your convenience.
Two or Three Bedrooms, Lounge with Dining Recess and Service Hatch, or Two Reception Rooms, Modern Labour Saving Kitchen and Splendid Bathrooms, Large Gardens, Clean Finished Roads, Tree Lined, Delightful Country.

A few to be let
from 20s. per week.

NO ROAD CHARGES OR LEGAL COSTS
**WOOD BLOCK FLOORS
CENTRAL HEATING
FITTED WARDROBES
DECORATIONS FREE**

HOW TO GET THERE.—Book direct to RUISLIP by Metropolitan or Piccadilly Railway, or to RUISLIP GARDENS on the G.W.R. and L.N.E.R. Both Stations are facing the Estate Offices. Alight at RUISLIP or RUISLIP GARDENS (not Ruislip Manor). Weekly fares from Marylebone or Baker St. 5/1½. Telephone : Ruislip 378 for our private car to take you to Estate.
Please send for Brochure to :—

RUISLIP Gardens Estate

WEST END ROAD, RUISLIP
Please send me your brochure of Ruislip Gardens Estate, post free.   *Telephone: Ruislip 378*
NAME ....
ADDRESS... P.O.M.Oct.

Ruislip Gardens, Metroland, offered comfortable houses, labour-saving devices, and an idyllic picture of suburban life.

price. One builder, Laing, estimated that the pooling system tripled the rate of house sales. At the same time building-society propaganda emphasized the financial folly of paying rent.

A further boost to this building boom was the fall in price of raw materials during and after the slump, and a lowering of the wages of building workers who – despite all this activity – were in constant supply as industry outside London declined. This pool of unemployed or underemployed labourers enabled employers to demand a long working week of forty-seven hours, and to keep wage rates down to a meagre 1s 8d an hour. When building activity slowed during the winter months, some of these men who helped to build the new London suburbs – navvies, brickies, painters, and plasterers – found themselves on the breadline.

All sorts of people moved into the building business, and estate agents' clerks frequently set up on their own in an effort to make a fortune in the boom. Scouts scoured the countryside in search of new sites. House prices were driven down by fierce competition between builders. In the end there was an oversupply, with average prices of £500 for a house and in some areas as low as £395 – the average house price through the 1930s was three times the national average wage. Builders began a massive campaign to sell estates, and houses came to be sold in almost the same way as other mass-produced consumer goods that were coming on the market.

New developments were advertised with firework displays, concerts, and in one case, in Surbiton, a free car in the garage for the purchaser of a diminutive detached house. Film and radio stars promoted quite modest estates, while newspaper advertisements in the popular dailies were used to lure the middle classes into the suburbs. Among the free gifts on offer were railway season tickets, fridges, and furniture. Modern Homes Ltd tried to entice buyers to its relatively expensive estate at Joel Park in Pinner, where houses were on sale from £850 to £1500, with an electric refrigerator, washing machine, cooker, and seven fires in each one.

Inevitably, the London County Council (LCC) found it more and more difficult to find land for new estates. Adjoining boroughs on its county boundaries did not want the county council's estates, preferring to have housing schemes of their own. When the LCC began to expand the Downham Estate, near Bromley, local residents objected at an enquiry, saying: 'Such a scheme will reduce the respectability of the . . . streets by inundating the neighbourhood with working classes.'

On the borders between a council estate and a newly developing private estate there could be outright conflict. In 1926 the sensitive residents of a private estate in south-east London which abutted the southern edge of the Downham Estate took the law into their own hands, building a brick wall across a road that led straight from the private part of the street to the council houses. This meant that mothers with children and men heading for work had to take a long way round so as not to offend the fine sensibilities of the home-owners. Bromley Council refused to cooperate with LCC demands for its demolition, and it was not pulled down until the early years of the Second World War, when it impeded emergency services.

The story of the Downham wall is a small but graphic illustration of the kind of opposition the LCC and its tenants faced in territory regarded – not only by private residents and local authorities, but by many Conservative politicians as well – as the preserve of the middle classes. In fact the LCC, dominated politically by the Conservative Municipal Reform Party until 1934, had incorporated this notion in its original plans for cottage estates: one of the four basic principles it adopted was to take into account the possible detrimental effects on middle-class areas of large-scale working-class developments.

Partly as a result of these sorts of difficulties, by the late 1920s the LCC planners had a change of heart, and began to think again in terms of rehousing the poor in the centre of town, not in 'cottages' but in grand blocks of flats. However, finding sites on which to build in central areas was difficult. So when, in 1929, a Labour Government came to power at Westminster and put money back into the system, the LCC valuers set out again on a land hunt on the suburban fringes of the capital. But there was not much land left for sale.

The speed at which semi-detached suburbia expanded in London was in part due to the extension of London Underground lines into the countryside beyond the limits of the Victorian city. The Metropolitan line from Baker Street was already running out as far as Harrow before the turn of the century, giving the name Metroland to a large swathe of former countryside to the north-west of London. Metroland was accompanied by a clever marketing campaign by its developers and was later made famous by the poet and architectural observer Sir John Betjeman, in his 1973 documentary *Metro-Land*. The Piccadilly, Bakerloo, and Northern lines were also extended in the 1920s into open country. In south London, where geology meant the underground could not run, it was not uncommon for a builder to contribute to the construction of a railway station that would open up land for development.

To the untutored eye this huge expanse of speculatively built suburbia was delightful in its idiosyncratic mishmash of architectural styles. In London and in semi-detached suburbia wherever it was extensively built the smartest estates would boast 'Mock Tudor' homes with a fake half-timbered appearance and other imitative details: timbered gables, elaborate porches with red tiled roofs, lattice and coloured-glass windows, oak doors with Gothic panels, plus the inevitable bay windows. The period styling might penetrate indoors with oak-panelled halls and dining rooms.

Of all the retrospective stylistic references in inter-war suburbia it is the neo-Tudor which has been most reviled by architectural historians. Their critical rage goes back to the period the suburbs were built. In 2005 the late Gavin Stamp gave the annual lecture to the Society of Architectural Historians of Great Britain, with the title 'Neo-Tudor

and its enemies', addressing the question 'Has any architecture . . . received such consistent abuse as the neo-Tudor of the first half of the twentieth century?' He mentioned a few contemporary cutting remarks, 'The worst bogus Tudor housing estates' and 'Those repellent jerry built sham-Tudor houses that disfigure England', then quoted a 1935 book by the art historian Anthony

Osbert Lancaster's cartoon ridicules the building of 'Stockbroker Tudor' houses, complete with all the mod-cons.

Bertram, *The House: A Machine for Living In*, in which the creators of Tudor suburbia are cultural criminals: 'The man who builds a bogus Tudoresque villa or castellates his suburban home is committing a crime against truth and tradition: he is denying the history of progress, denying his own age and insulting the very thing he pretends to imitate by misusing it.'

In his *Pillar to Post* of 1938 Osbert Lancaster, the cartoonist and witty architectural historian, did his best to identify the absurdity of what was often dubbed 'Stockbroker Tudor': 'when the passer-by is a little unnerved at being suddenly confronted with a hundred and fifty accurate reproductions of Anne Hathaway's cottage, each complete with central-heating and garage, he should pause to reflect on the extraordinary fact that all over the country the latest and most scientific methods of mass-production are being utilized to turn out a stream of old oak beams, leaded window-panes and small discs of bottle-glass, all structural devices which our ancestors lost no time in abandoning as soon as an increase in wealth and knowledge enabled them to do so.' Tongue in cheek, Lancaster identified a number of suburban building styles: Wimbledon Transitional, Aldwych Farcical, and By-pass Variegated.

Gavin Stamp defended in his lecture the builders of suburbia against the snobbish commentators, as did others who regarded suburbia not as a visual and social disaster but as a huge success, and one that was immensely popular with home buyers. It was never intended as a showcase for British modernist architecture and the Tudor revival can be regarded as the discovery of the true English vernacular passed down through the centuries.

Osbert Lancaster referred to imitations of Anne Hathaway's cottage as having central heating and a garage. To make space to park a motor car was something quite novel in the 1930s as motoring had been a pleasure confined to the wealthy. As car ownership increased, traffic on the roads out of the main towns became jammed with a tangle of horse-drawn and petrol-driven vehicles. The solution was the building of new, wider, arterial roads which, at first, ran through countryside once they had left the Victorian limits of the city.

Speculative builders did not take long to spot the opportunity for a new kind of development. Semi-detached suburbia became elongated as houses went up all along these new roads, mostly noticeably around London, promising for the new generation of car owners easy access into the towns. The Kingston Bypass, opened in 1927 in Surrey, was soon lined with rows of speculatively built houses, as well as shops, pubs, and factories. Neo-Tudor 'roadhouses' appeared at regular intervals on the new roads: some of these had restaurants which were open for twenty-four hours a day, dance halls, and swimming pools, catering more for through traffic than the suburban residents along the route.

This kind of ribbon development became a public nuisance, blocking through-roads with local traffic and pedestrians. A Ribbon Development Act of 1935 gave local councils the power to restrict frontage developments along main roads – shutting the garage door after the car had accelerated off.

In the years just before the outbreak of the Second World War the price of cars fell significantly and they came within the range of the newly affluent middle classes of the outer suburbs. In the 1920s car showrooms were all in the West End of London, close to their aristocratic market.

In the 1930s they appeared along the Great West Road and motoring became part of the luxury of upmarket suburbia.

For a few years these arterial roads became race tracks, with bloody consequences. The motorist thrilled to the sensation of speed. In her memoir *Modern England: as Seen by an Englishwoman* (1938) Cicely Hamilton captured the mood: 'speed in itself produces an indifference alike to beauty and its lack. The suburbs we drive through are pretentious, unimaginative, but we pass them, at so many miles an hour – as we pass a cornfield bowing to the wind or a park that has not yet fallen to the bid of the speculative builder.'

Driving tests were first introduced in 1935 as the death toll on the arterial roads rose alarmingly. The year before, 7,343 people had been killed in road accidents, and a study of fatalities revealed that the victims were most commonly pensioners and young children, many of them killed riding their bikes. The motorists and motorcyclists involved in fatal accidents were mostly young men in their twenties or thirties. Night-time was especially deadly with little or no street lighting, no road markings, and cars capable of hitting 70 mph screeching to a halt with inefficient brakes. Drivers and passengers had no seat belts. It is hardly surprising that there were an estimated seventy-five thousand road-accident fatalities between the wars with a further two million people injured.

With the threat of war looming in the late 1930s, suburban expansion ceased, but concern about vulnerability to air attack provided useful propaganda for builders selling suburban houses. They took to advertising properties in so-called 'safety zones' with concrete shelters provided in back gardens. One enterprising builder in West London supplied windows with seventeen hinges that could be tightened to form a seal in the event of a gas attack. It was the last gasp of the private building boom which had won the inter-war battle of the suburbs, and had covered the countryside around London with wave after wave of bricks and mortar.

In the same period, there remained huge potential demand for more 'down-market' properties. New Ideal Homesteads offered houses for as little as a £5 deposit with repayments of 8 shillings a week. Home ownership became a real possibility for a substantial minority of working-class families. By 1939 about 14 per cent had a house and a mortgage.

But even the very low mortgage repayments on the cheapest of houses were often too much for those earning the average wage of £3 10s a week. Travel expenses and rates, in addition to the mortgage repayment, might amount to nearly half of that sum. Even at rock-bottom prices, the suburbs remained therefore the home of better-off Londoners.

There were a few, however, among the poorest who became home-owners, or, at least the owners of small plots of land on which they put together a kind of shanty-town shack. These were the 'plotlanders', suburban frontiersmen and women who built their dream homes in the country with their own hands. They might live in London during the week, in miserable privately rented accommodation, but at weekends they could set out for the countryside, usually beyond even the most far-flung of the railway suburbs and council estates, to a plot of their own.

The first moves had been made as far back as the 1870s when there was a steep decline in the value of agricultural land, especially to the east of London in the county of Essex. It was heavy clay soil, difficult to work with plough horses, and when cheap grain was imported from Canada many farms were abandoned. Small plots put up for sale attracted some working-class families from London in search of country air. The exodus grew after 1918 and whole plotland 'towns' arose, which caused much greater shocks to the idealistic planners of the day than the sprouting suburbs proper.

To places in Essex like Pitsea, Laindon, and Canvey Island they carted out bits of timber and building materials, often on bicycles, and created shanty towns. Anything might serve as a holiday and weekend home: disused railway carriages, garden sheds, ex-army huts, and bus bodies. In time, a more elegant edifice might take shape and the family would settle there. Some of these shanty towns became quite large, attracting a rather unusual social mix of bohemians, back-to-the-landers, and working-class families with the homeowner's pride but without the resources for a 'proper home'. In the end the post-1945 planners cleared most plotlands away: Basildon New Town in Essex was built on the site of one of the largest of the settlements. However, a few remain as a reminder of the many suburban endeavours that gave character to the inter-war years.

CHAPTER NINE

THE WAR IS OVER

The Age of Austerity to the Renovation Boom

In the summer of 1946, backed by the swell of an orchestra string section, Movietone News presented to the nation 'without prejudice or comment' the story of the Scunthorpe Squatters. The camera panned across an abandoned army camp on which there were a number of Nissen huts that had been transformed into family homes. The squatter who had first occupied the camp, which now housed twenty families, introduced himself as James Fielding, 'a married man with four children who came to Scunthorpe on a job of work.' Fielding had been appointed projectionist in a local cinema and had had to live there with his family as he could find no accommodation. 'At last,' he told the camera, 'having seen a disused army camp . . . on the outskirts of Scunthorpe, I decided to take over one of these huts . . . we take the view that any right-minded men would agree with the actions our desperation forced us to take.'

The Movietone newsreel showed some of the families who had followed him hanging out their washing. One woman was asked why she had chosen to live in a former army camp. She and her husband had been living in two rooms: the hut was luxury. A local councillor said what Fielding had done was illegal but in the circumstances they would help the squatters, laying on electricity and water.

The Scunthorpe Squatters' story went 'viral' and within a few weeks local newspapers all over the country were reporting the occupation of abandoned military camps by families desperate for better housing. Those interviewed did not generally claim to be homeless: they were just escaping confined spaces and in search of some privacy and dignity. Squatting became socially acceptable, often applauded by the Conservative newspapers, who thought it evoked the 'Blitz spirit' and, of course, embarrassed the newly elected Labour Government.

'Coventry Squatters Work Hard to Achieve Comfort' was the *Coventry Evening Telegraph*'s headline for a story of the transformation of 'merely desolate huts into happy little homesteads' in September 1946. A reporter who went to investigate found 'snow-white washing blowing against a blue sky in the best Monday morning tradition.' There seemed to be a pram at nearly every door, and 'a dozen lusty infants' frolicked in the country air. They had no hot water but the milkman and the butcher called regularly and a Mrs Ganley, who with her husband and baby had left two rooms, was very happy with her converted army hut.

It was all very genteel. A local vicar summed it up in a letter to the *Bristol Evening Post* in August: 'Their action was unusual, unconstitutional, but let no one think they are ruffians. They are ordinary people, they shave every day, eat at tables, go off to earn their living.' He might have added that these clean-shaven breadwinners had wives and children.

All that summer of 1946 the newspapers tracked the rapid and increasingly frantic squatter occupation of any available army camps. Desperate not to miss out, squatters soon came into conflict with other occupiers of this makeshift post-war accommodation. The *Birmingham Daily Gazette* reported squatters forcing their way into camps when they were refused permission, moving from one camp to another in a marauding mass.

> The party then went to a German P.o.W. camp in the Tupsley area where they were met at the closed gates by a British corporal on guard. About 20 men and women, some carrying babies, rushed the gates, pushing the sentry aside. German prisoners came out of their huts and were interested onlookers as the party went to one end of the camp and discovered some empty huts which were promptly taken over. The names of families selected to occupy the huts was [sic] chalked on the doors.

Wartime miners' hostels were occupied before they had been abandoned by the miners, and everywhere were debates about the rights and wrongs of squatting. The law was lenient until a group of squatters in London, organized in part by the Communist Party, took over some empty buildings in the West End. It made the headlines and the newsreels but it was not in the spirit of the army base squats and marked the beginning of the end of this colourful episode in the history of post-war housing, which had arisen spontaneously after the brief euphoria at the end of the war had turned to anxiety about the future.

The VE-Day celebrations were over, the bunting had come down, and the war hero Winston Churchill had been voted out of office in the general election on 24 July in which Labour won a huge majority. In August the atomic bomb had put an end to the war in the Far East. Now Labour, with Clement Attlee as Prime Minister, was in power, promising to cure all the ills of an exhausted and virtually bankrupt country. Of these ills the most urgent and intractable was the housing problem: a chronic shortfall of decent homes and hundreds of thousands forced to live in cramped and insanitary conditions.

Looking back it is extraordinary what some considered luxury in the post-war years of austerity and rationing. By today's standards the home John Quayle found in 62 Falkner Street when he returned from service overseas would be regarded as shockingly sub-standard. The story told by his son Bill in *A House Through Time* is as surprising as it is touching. John had spent the last years of the war in Sri Lanka as a mechanic repairing fighter planes for the Fleet Air Arm. He came to Liverpool to take a job as a mechanic, met his future wife Beryl at a dance, and they married and moved into the top floor of 62 Falkner Street. For Beryl the two rooms were paradise as she had had to share a room with four sisters when she lived at home. This was despite the fact that there was no running water and she and John had to bring it up in buckets, the only toilet was on the ground floor, and they had one primus stove for cooking.

The Quayles lived in this post-war 'paradise' for seven years, both still working, Beryl as a fitter in a dressmaker's and John promoted from mechanic to bus driver. Each day he would drive out to the new housing estates, dreaming of moving there when they saved enough money. Then they could have a child. They fulfilled their dream in 1954 when they bought their own house, furnishing it no doubt with the government issue 'Utility' range. Nothing luxurious, but they would have considered themselves lucky given the terrible conditions so many lived in at that time among the ruins of the bomb sites.

Whereas the housing stock had increased by two million between the wars, from 1939 it had inevitably shrunk. There were around a hundred and ninety thousand homes built during the war, but it has been estimated that the number of useable houses fell by four hundred thousand as air raids turned mostly working-class districts to rubble. An official wartime publication, *Front Line: 1940–1941*, divided the air raids into 'the onslaught on London' and 'the ordeal of the provinces'. London, with its huge port, manufacturing districts, historic buildings, and still then the heart of the Empire, was the main target: as Churchill, put it, 'the fat valuable cow'. Such was the ferocity and intensity of the London Blitz that it has tended to overshadow the German onslaught on industrial towns and major ports.

In *The Blitz Companion*, Mark Clapson looked at the extent of the air raids in 1940–41. The Germans had done their homework and identified key industrial centres. In the Midlands, Coventry was singled out, bombed more than once before the night raid of 14–15 November when 450 bombers came in waves lasting eleven hours which destroyed the entire centre of the city. Birmingham was also attacked on more than one occasion.

> Liverpool and Mersey-side. . . . was the second most-bombed conurbation after London. The city had taken small air raids during August 1940 but on the night of 28–9 November over 350 tons of HE (High Explosive) bombs smashed into the city. In common with East London the docks were a primary target, and the warren of small, often dilapidated terraced streets was heavily bombed. Liverpool was attacked for three nights at the end of August 1940, and many other raids followed. During December 1940 and May 1941 further raids took a terrible toll on Liverpool. The May raids alone killed 1,900 people and injured or seriously wounded 1,450 others. Extensive damage to the housing stock resulted in widespread homelessness in a city that already possessed large tracts of impoverished housing and some of the worst slums in Britain.

Death and destruction were visited on many other towns: Bristol, Plymouth, Portsmouth, Southampton, Hull, and Newcastle-upon-Tyne were all in the firing line. The Labour government in its election manifesto had promised 'a separate dwelling for everyone who wishes to have one', but the war had disrupted so many lives in so many ways: children evacuated and women working in factories and the auxiliary services far away from home, bombed-out families camping with relatives, often in the suburbs which were not heavily targeted. Men overseas for years who returned to join their wives found all domestic arrangements they had remembered were disrupted.

As the reporter who visited the Coventry squatters noted, 'there was a pram at nearly every door.' Immediately after the end of the war there was a baby boom which lasted for two years, 1946 and 1947. Many with newborn babies were sharing, crammed into old, overcrowded buildings. It was every couple and family's dream to have their own place, one the Scunthorpe Squatters turned into a short-lived reality.

It wasn't that the wartime government had failed to anticipate there would be a housing crisis when the war was over. Winston Churchill, as wartime Prime Minister, announced in a radio broadcast in March 1944 a Ministry of Works emergency project to build half a million 'new technology' prefabricated temporary houses directly at the end of the war. 'The emergency programme is to be treated as a military evolution handled by the government with private industry harnessed in its service', said Churchill. 'As much thought will go into the prefabricated housing programme as went to the invasion of Africa'.

The immediate post-war housing policy fell to Aneurin Bevan, who became Minister for Health in the victorious Labour government. Born in 1897 in Tredegar, a mining town in south Wales, Nye, as he was called, was one of ten children, two of whom died in infancy. He joined his father and brothers in the pit when he was fourteen. When coal mining went into decline he had a variety of jobs before he became a local councillor and began his long and controversial political career. As Professor Peter Hennessey says of him in his account *Never Again: Britain 1945–1951*, Bevan had the attitude that 'nothing is too good for the working classes.' His views on housing were, in the circumstances, overly ambitious. In Hennessey's view: 'Bevan was a sucker for the magic of the village in which all sorts of people lived alongside each other in harmony.' In his biography of Bevan, Michael Foot quotes him as saying: 'We should try to introduce in our modern villages and towns what was always the lovely feature of English and Welsh villages, where the doctor, the grocer, the butcher and the farm labourer all lived in the same street. I believe that is essential for the full life of a citizen . . . to see the living tapestry of a mixed community.'

The spontaneous squatter invasion of the former army bases which appealed to the Communists was not approved of or appreciated by Bevan, who saw it as an attempt to jump the housing queue: it was an offence against his idea of a paternalistic bureaucracy. *Picture Post* magazine published an article entitled 'The Squatters – and the Squatted Against' arguing that it was not landlords who were the losers but others on the council waiting lists.

Bevan hated the semi-detached suburbia created in the 1920s and 1930s, which he dismissed as 'the fretful fronts stretching along the great roads out of London.' He was opposed, generally, to private house-building and wanted local authority housing to be more generously apportioned than those built after 1914. However he had to accept that the prefabricated houses Churchill had promised were necessary in the dire circumstances.

The idea for prefabs was developed as early as 1942 when the Blitz had destroyed thousands of homes which the Coalition Government realized would have to be replaced somehow before more permanent building could begin again. A committee considered the alternatives and concluded that factory-made units were the answer. There was plenty of evidence from America, where prefabricated homes were common, some even sold through the Sears Roebuck catalogue. What were known originally as EFMs – emergency factory homes – were included as a provision in the Housing (Provisional Accommodation) Act 1944.

A prefab was as novel an idea for the public as the decent, clean-shaven squatter, and efforts were made to introduce people to the idea that they were not being fobbed off with what Bevan called 'rabbit hutches'. Several different designs of prefab were exhibited at the Tate Gallery and behind Selfridges. They went into production in 1945. All of the designs were for two-room units which would have a theoretical lifespan of ten years. Prefabs could be put down almost anywhere. They did not need foundations, though some were set on a low brick wall or

concrete slabs. The government owned them, while local authorities could buy land to put them on and arrange for roads and all the necessary amenities.

A mother and daughter leave a prefab house, one of thousands erected in the 1940s as an emergency measure to combat housing shortages.

Of the eleven approved designs one of the most popular was made by the aircraft industry with aluminium no longer needed for fighter planes. It had been on the drawing board from as early as 1942 and was the work of the AIROH – Aircraft Industry Research on Housing. Its prefabs came in units which could be carried to a site on lorries. They could be turned out at speed and were, by the standards of the day, dreamlike inside. A central service unit provided water and heating to both kitchen and bathroom from a central coal boiler. Astonishingly, the kitchens had a gas refrigerator, common enough then in America, but rare in England in even middle-class homes.

Prefabs appeared everywhere, not just on the bomb sites of the big cities, but in country areas where there had been some deliberate bombing of picturesque towns by the Luftwaffe in what were known as the 'Baedeker' raids, where the targets were chosen from the popular German guidebook to Britain.

Wherever they were placed, in parks or on derelict land, prefabs

Above: In the 1700s classic Georgian terraces graced the streets of fashionable Bath.

Below: The home of author Elizabeth Gaskell in Plymouth Grove, part of the then-exclusive suburb of Victoria Park, Manchester.

Above: Suffrage campaigner Emily Pankhurst's Victorian terraced house in Nelson Street, Manchester, now home to the Pankhurst Centre.

Left: H. G. Wells moved to this newly-built semi-detached house in 1895, escaping to the country air of Woking in Surrey. Looking more 1920s than Victorian, it was a foretaste of semi-detached suburbia.

Above: The houses of Letchworth Garden City in Hertfordshire combined the best of town and country living. This image is dated 1912.

Below: Wavertree Garden Suburb in Liverpool, here in 1911, was a privately-owned estate but it was a model for some council estates built in the 1920s.

Above: The first houses of the Old Oak Estate in West London were built before 1914 with the aim to provide working-class families with a garden city environment.

Below: The interior of a prefab. With more 'mod cons' than most Victorian flats and houses, they were regarded by many occupants as luxurious.

In May 1968 an explosion at Ronan Point, Newham in London caused part of the building to collapse. The block was later demolished like so many high-rise buildings in London and other cities.

Above: Famed marine biologist Joshua Alder was one of 5 Ravensworth Terrace's occupants.

Right: In the 1960s and 1970s 5 Ravensworth Terrace was a Salvation Army Goodwill Centre.

Below: 5 Ravensworth Terrace in Newcastle today.

Left: Rosina Curley and baby, almost certainly her son William, residents of 10 Guinea Street from 1911.

Above: 1 and 2 Guinea Street still showing signs of bomb damage and disrepair in 1952.

Below: 10 Guinea Street today with the flats of Underdown House next door.

Left: A young girl and child in Falkner Street, 1969, with appalling damp conditions behind.

Below: 62 Falkner Street in Liverpool today.

proved to be immensely popular and many had a much longer life than ten years. In the end around one hundred and fifty-six thousand prefabs were manufactured, the AIROH the most popular with a total of fifty-four thousand. The second most popular was the Arcon MkV, designed by the famous engineer Ove Arup. Nine of these Arcon detached prefabs were delivered to the outskirts of Tredegar in South Wales and one provided a dream home for Neil Kinnock, the future leader of the Labour Party.

He recalled living in cockroach- and rat-infested homes before his mother, a district nurse, became eligible for a prefab under a 'key workers' scheme. In the neighbouring prefabs were the families of two police constables, an ambulance driver, a dental technician, two council electricians, and a supervisor in a local engineering plant who came from Wolverhampton. The Arcon was a wonder of modernity for the Kinnocks. 'Hot-air central heating from the smokeless-coal grate in the living room warmed the house in winter and in summer hot water came from the immersion heater'. Visitors thought it a palace, except for an aunt who objected to the colour scheme applied to all prefabs: magnolia walls and green woodwork. She thought it looked like a railway station. His parents stayed for fourteen years before being allocated a proper house, built in the 1920s under the Wheatley scheme, with a parlour and in a proper road.

That would have been more Bevan's approved style. He was not opposed to prefabricated construction of houses but he wanted those with a more assured future. There were steel-framed houses he approved of and some were built, and he encouraged the use of local materials if they were available, such as Cotswold stone. Bevan-era houses were, as he wanted, roomier than those of the 1920s and 1930s. But they were a minor addition to the housing stock. He was preoccupied anyway in persuading the medical profession to accept a nationalization of the hospitals, and family doctors to give up the buying and selling of private practice. Notoriously he said that by allowing doctors to continue with private practice while raising their pay as contractors to the NHS he had 'stuffed their mouths with gold'.

While Bevan was otherwise engaged, the most ambitious post-war housing programme was in the hands of a remarkable politician and former solicitor who, like Bevan, had broken away from a life of poverty to become an ambitious member of the Labour Party. Lewis Silkin was born in Poplar in London's East End in 1889 into a Jewish family of refugees from Lithuania. His father, Abraham Silkin, was a wholesale grocer who also taught Hebrew. Lewis, his seventh child, was a precocious student who won a scholarship to a good school before going on to the East London College.

Silkin was awarded a mathematical exhibition at Worcester College, Oxford, but his parents could not afford to fund him and he ended up working for a while in the East India Docks. He answered an advertisement for a bright young lad to work as an articled clerk in a firm of solicitors, got the job, qualified as a solicitor, and set himself up in a firm which still thrives today. He became a Romantic lover of the countryside which he often visited, allegedly singing as he walked. Like Bevan he hankered after a return to an England of villages and rural life.

He failed to get elected to Parliament twice before he won a seat on the powerful London County Council and soon became leader of the opposition. He was a champion of the 'Green Belt' to prevent the encroachment of London suburbs on the countryside. He became an MP in 1936 and his views chimed with those of the planners in the Labour Party, so that in 1945 Attlee made him Minister of Town and Country Planning. He was responsible for the New Towns Act of 1946 and the Town and Country Planning Act of 1947.

There had been nothing in the Labour manifesto of 1945 about the building of new towns. The idea of creating satellite urban centres away from London and the other big cities to alleviate pressure in the Victorian inner city and offer a healthier lifestyle had first taken root when the London County Council commissioned Sir Patrick Abercrombie to propose a plan for the future development of the capital. His drawing board idealism had housing and industry segregated and a green belt to prevent further encroachment on the countryside. Encompassing some of the garden city philosophy, this was a blueprint for Silkin, who embarked on the designation of New Towns with the enthusiasm of a visionary. He told the House of Commons:

> The towns will be divided into neighbourhood units, each unit
> with its own shops, schools, open spaces, community halls and
> other amenities. I am most anxious that the planning should be

such that the different income groups living in the new towns will not be segregated. No doubt they may enjoy common recreational facilities, and take part in amateur theatricals, or each play their part in a health centre or a community centre. But when they leave to go home I do not want the better-off people to go to the right, and the less-well-off to go to the left. I want them to ask each other 'are you going my way?'

The answer to that question was, sadly: 'No.' It was the same dream of the classless suburb that had proved to be illusionary with the cottage estates and the early garden cities. New Towns had few houses for sale, nearly everything was owned by the development corporations which ran them and they were attractive chiefly to skilled workers who could afford the rents.

The first wave of building was ambitious. A ring of ten new satellite towns would be built twenty to thirty miles away from the capital, each housing between thirty and sixty thousand people. The prototype for the first generation of New Towns was the small, thriving agricultural town of Stevenage. It was particularly attractive to planners because it had good transport links, situated as it was on the Great North Road and on the main London to Newcastle railway line.

Early in 1946 word got around in Stevenage that it would be chosen as the first New Town. In April letters were sent to 178 residents telling them that their property was to be compulsorily purchased by the Ministry of Town and Country Planning. This began what soon became known as 'the Battle for Stevenage'. Angry locals, including many farmers who wanted to keep Stevenage as it was, formed a militant Residents' Protection Association.

On 6 May 1946 Lewis Silkin arrived in a chauffeur-driven Wolseley to explain to the local people why Stevenage had been chosen for what he called 'a daring exercise in town planning'. To his surprise, he found the town was festooned with posters saying HANDS OFF OUR HOUSES! and NO! NO! MR MINISTER! At the meeting he responded to barracking by replying, 'It's no good your jeering! It is going to be done!' Saboteurs put sand in the petrol tank of his Wolseley and let the tyres down. But Silkin could not afford to retreat and risk his whole New Town programme.

The protestors took the government to court and won an early round but were defeated by the passing of the New Towns Act. On 11 November 1946, Stevenage New Town was officially designated and the Stevenage Development Corporation, a government-appointed body, took over building and running it. In a despairing last gesture of defiance one night a prankster changed the name of the station to SILKINGRAD.

Now any towns in the home counties or close to large cities such as Liverpool and Newcastle-upon-Tyne waited to see if the planners would pick them out for development. Some breathed a sigh of relief when they learned that they were judged unsuitable. This was the case with Redbourn and Stapleford in Hertfordshire, Ongar and Margaretting in Essex, Meopham in Kent, Crowhurst and Holmwood in Surrey, and White Waltham in Berkshire.

London's new satellite towns were, in order of designation, Crawley, Hemel Hempstead, Harlow, Hatfield, Welwyn Garden City, Basildon, and Bracknell. Some places applied for New Town designation, notably Easington in County Durham, which became Peterlee in 1948. A year earlier another Durham town, Newton Aycliffe, had become Aycliffe New Town. The last of this first phase of designations was the steel town of Corby in Northamptonshire.

A second phase of designation in the 1960s created Skelmersdale in Lancashire, Dawley New Town in Shropshire, Redditch in Worcestershire, Runcorn in Cheshire, and Washington in Tyne and Wear. In a third and final phase from 1967, Dawley New Town in Shropshire was extended to become Telford New Town, Milton Keynes in Buckinghamshire and Peterborough in Cambridgeshire were designated as New Towns, as were Northampton in Northamptonshire and Warrington in Cheshire. Designated in 1970, the largest of all the New Towns was Central Lancashire incorporating Preston and several other local authority districts.

Since the war thirty-two New Towns of one kind or another have been created and they have housed two million people. Some have been more successful than others in fulfilling the dreams of Lewis Silkin and the garden city Romantics, but all have had their problems. A House of Commons committee report on some of the more serious problems New Towns had experienced was published in 2002. The low density of housing developments regarded as such a desirable feature of estates proved to be problematic for public transport, which needs high densities of population to be viable, so there was great dependency in the New Towns on cars. Not all the housing had stood the test of time: New Town corporations often chose to go for innovative construction which proved to be structurally unsound and had to be demolished. And the town centres were often unattractive.

The development corporations which created and managed the New Towns have been wound up, many of their assets sold off, and a series of interim administrations have been handing them over to local authorities. New Towns today have had to cope with the vicissitudes of political change which has made it hard for them to sustain anything of the dreams of the founders and those who were the first to enjoy their brand-new form of town life.

The fate of Stevenage is a case in point. Its population grew to eighty-four thousand, far higher than Silkin had imagined. As in most other New Towns, homes were rented from the development corporation and later the council. But the sale of council houses has reduced their number from thirty thousand to just over eight thousand. There are more privately rented houses now, a great many bought as buy-to-let. The council has over two thousand people on its waiting list. Properties in its once admired pioneer pedestrianized shopping centre have been sold off. 'Silkingrad' was put up for grabs.

Whatever judgement is made of the success or otherwise of the New Towns, the decanting of the populations of London and Liverpool, Newcastle-upon-Tyne, Birmingham, and other large towns did not solve the ever-present problem of families living in sub-standard housing. In the 1930s programmes of slum clearance saw whole communities moved into newly built blocks of flats. This continued under the Labour government from 1945 with 'walk up' blocks of flats no more than five storeys high. Precast concrete slabs were used in various forms of prefabricated construction. A shortage of bricks and timber encouraged the use of modernist designs, and despite all the economic difficulties Labour managed to create a million new homes between 1945 and 1950. Nevertheless, despite this achievement and the creation of a Health Service 'free at the point of demand', the electorate were not convinced socialism was the way forward.

At the 1950 General Election, Labour just scraped in with a majority of five seats in Parliament although it had won a clear majority of votes. Unable to function effectively, the government called a second election in 1951 and lost by a narrow majority. Churchill, at the age of seventy-seven, was back in 10 Downing Street with an instruction from his party conference to continue building houses, but in quantities which would far outstrip Labour's best efforts. A Conservative MP appeared to pluck a figure out of nowhere: they must build three hundred thousand homes a year.

The Conservative Research Department was asked to put meat on the bones of this proposal and suggested three hundred thousand units *might* be feasible if they diverted some shipping and foreign currency to buy timber, persuaded the cement industry to increase its output, and ordered a million tons of coal and two thousand million bricks. Accordingly the Conservative manifesto for the 1951 election proclaimed: 'Housing is the first of the social services. It is also one of the keys to increased productivity. Work, family life, health and education are all undermined by crowded houses. Therefore, a Conservative and Unionist Government will give housing a priority second only to national defence.'

There was no Bevan or Silkin available to Churchill to carry out the ambitious plan to build three hundred thousand council homes a year, and for want of anyone more suitable he summoned Harold Macmillan, an old Etonian, wounded hero of the First World War and partner in the family publishing firm. Macmillan did not feel he was the right man for the job and recorded in his diary:

> He asked me to 'build the houses for the people.' What an assignment! I know nothing whatever about these matters, having spent 6 years now either on defence or foreign affairs. I had of course hoped to be Minister of Defence and said this frankly to Churchill. But he is determined to keep it in his own hands . . . Churchill says it is a gamble – make or mar my political career. But every humble home will bless my name, if I succeed. On the whole it seems impossible to refuse – but, oh dear, it is not my cup of tea . . . I really haven't a clue how to set about the job.

Nonetheless, Macmillan got a team around him and set to work. It seems that he did not have the slightest interest in the appearance of the blocks of flats being thrown up or the quality of the building. It was all about numbers. When the next general election was held in 1955 Macmillan was able to boast that the Conservatives had beaten Labour at their own game, building three hundred and fifty thousand houses in the previous year. And in 1957 he became Prime Minister, though it is unlikely 'every humble home' blessed his name.

Not long after he succeeded Anthony Eden, who had resigned over the Suez affair, Macmillan visited Bedford to speak at a Tory rally held in the local football ground, where he made the speech for which he was ever after associated. He told an enthusiastic gathering: 'Indeed let us be frank about it, most of our people have never had it so good. Go around the country, go to the industrial towns, go to the farms and you will see a state of prosperity such as we have never had in my lifetime, nor indeed in the history of this country.'

These were early days for what became known as the 'consumer society' when goods of all kinds filled the once spartan homes of families on low incomes. Hire purchase, or the 'never never', made it misleadingly painless to acquire all the luxurious essentials of the time. Mass Observation, the social-survey company which had monitored the public mood during the war years, found in a 1952 survey that nearly half of all households had used hire-purchase schemes for household furnishings and television sets. By 1963 nearly three-quarters of all households had a vacuum cleaner; by the mid-1960s six out of ten homes had a refrigerator and just under half a washing machine.

While new houses and flats might have a bath, toilet, cooker, hot and cold running water, and heating, to cut costs rooms were made smaller and ceiling heights lowered. The layout of rooms had also changed: there was no longer a separate scullery as all cooking and washing was done in the kitchen. The front parlour 'for best' was gone and instead a living and dining room became the standard. The improving access to gas and electricity also meant changes in heating and a gradual move away from open fires to small gas, electric, or paraffin heaters.

As the home was being transformed, the choking atmosphere of the big cities was transformed within a few years with the banning of domestic coal fires. It was not a nationally imposed ban but one that could be adopted by local authorities under the Clean Air Act of 1956. Smokeless zones were designated in which burning fossil fuels, other

than smokeless ones, was illegal. In the old fireplace there would be a gas or electric heater. The last of the great smogs in London was in the cold winter of 1962–63, and all the major cities had cleaner air from this time onwards, the evidence of their sooty past the blackened Victorian buildings, many of which have since been cleaned up to reveal their true colours.

Prime Minister Harold Macmillan visits the householders of Stevenage New Town in 1959.

The banishing of one of the evils of the Victorian city also coincided with a kind of craze for 'modernization' which condemned anything dating from the nineteenth century as unattractive. Whole streets of terraced houses were dismissed as 'slums' even though they were cared for by house-proud tenants. Slum clearance had been going on since the Victorian age but now, in the 1960s, it took on a new urgency. How did it come about that in cities across the nation slums were replaced by tower blocks, often standing in what seemed like no-man's-land with the inhabitants cut off from life at street level?

There is no definitive explanation, but there were incentives for local authorities to prefer high-rise housing over more conventional low-level blocks or terraces. Continuing its drive for more and more vote-winning council homes, in 1956 the Conservative government offered an extra subsidy for every storey added to a building. This was at a time when prefabricated building techniques were being developed which made it possible to put up hundreds of flats very quickly. And for the architects there was the prospect of getting some modernist ideas off the drawing board. The Swiss architect Charles-Édouard Jeanneret-Gris had gained an international reputation for his architectural concepts and designs that emphasized light and clean lines. In 1920 he adopted the name Le Corbusier as a byline for his articles on architecture and that would become the name by which he was known.

Le Corbusier regarded a tower block as a 'machine for living', using all the latest technology to create a world full of light in contrast to the dark streets of traditionally built towns. He did design some himself, including the twelve-storey Unité d'habitation in Marseilles, built in 1952, which provided flats for 1,600 people. Originally called La Cité Radieuse, the block includes floors for shopping, social clubs, child care, a gym, and a hotel. There is a rooftop garden and a swimming pool. Just a few details missing from England's tower blocks of the 1950s and 1960s.

It was all about numbers and speed rather than architecture. The Greater London Council (created in 1965 and since abolished) built 384 high-rise blocks in ten years, while the outer boroughs added their own. It has been suggested that the tower block was a status symbol for a council and there was a form of competition to see which could build the tallest and the most.

The flats in high-rise blocks were mostly roomy and the views from the upper storeys, known as streets in the sky, often spectacular. But it was not long before their unsuitability was revealed. Many of those rehoused were families with babies and young children. If the lift broke down – which happened frequently in poorly maintained blocks – a young mother might face the prospect of hauling a pram up eighteen storeys. There was no place for toddlers to play. As there was no security at the entrances, the lower floors became a hangout for teenagers. A familiar pattern of decline would set in quickly, with those families who could find somewhere else to live moving away.

The Labour government scrapped the high-rise subsidy in 1964 and encouraged a return to low-level building. Architectural fashion was beginning to shift in that direction and the social problems of the high rise could no longer be ignored. The end of the high-rise era came dramatically and quite unexpectedly on the morning of 16 May 1968. In one of a number of 1960s tower blocks built in Newham there was a loud bang. Tenants still in bed woke to see the side wall of their flats fall away. When the rubble was cleared it was announced four people had died and eleven had been injured, an astonishingly low casualty rate for such a densely populated building. The collapse had been caused by an explosion of some kind. But what could it have been?

Local rumour insisted that it had been caused by either an accident with a store of 'gelly' kept by a bank robber and safe blower or that a stored IRA bomb had exploded prematurely. However, a forensic examination of the flat where it had occurred found no trace of explosives. The blast had been caused by fifty-six-year-old cake decorator Ivy Hodge, who had put the kettle on her gas stove and lit a match to make herself a cup of tea. Somehow the gas built up and then exploded with just enough force to blow out a wall.

As soon as the cause was known, all gas supplies were removed from slab blocks and all the joins in them were strengthened at great expense, but it was a final blow for the high-rise. Ivy Hodge brought to an end the programme in London and other towns. She had to move on to new accommodation, reportedly taking her old gas cooker with her. Although Ronan Point was refurbished and reoccupied a few years later, in 1986 it was demolished along with other Newham tower blocks. Many of Le Corbusier's 'machines for living' were demolished one after another.

The experience of Liverpool encapsulates the whole sorry story. Just after the war the need for new housing in the city was urgent: thirty thousand people were still living in buildings that had been condemned. Slum clearance began in the 1950s and the first tower block, hopefully named Coronation Court, was built seven miles from the city centre in 1956. The flats were regarded as luxurious, with central heating (still uncommon in private houses then) and indoor bathrooms. By the late 1960s there were more than seventy tower blocks in Liverpool with disillusioned tenants desperate for the council to do something about their maintenance.

In 1968 a mass meeting of two and a half thousand tenants voted to refuse to pay an increase in rents. Within five months they had forced

St Cuthbert's Village, Gateshead, home to David Olusoga as a child. Poor design and social problems led to it being demolished after just 25 years.

Liverpool council to accept lower rents from thirty thousand tenants. Liverpool's economy was in decline and conditions in the tower blocks got worse as they were left with no maintenance or security. It was a long time before the tenants were offered a way out of their plight. The Housing Act of 1988 made it possible for management of the blocks to be transferred from the council to a Housing Action Trust. The tenants voted overwhelmingly to put their faith in a Trust to care for the 5,332 properties in sixty-seven tower blocks. £260 million was offered by the government over twelve years with the possibility of bringing in private finance.

A decision was made to demolish fifty-four of the blocks and replace them with low-rise housing, while refurbishing the remaining thirteen. It has taken a long time to redress the mistakes made by the city planners and many of the tenants are now over the age of seventy. In Liverpool, as elsewhere, slum clearance had created more slums which were demolished at huge expense.

Across the country, the inescapable problems of poverty and deprivation had not gone away. In 1975, it was estimated that around one million homes were still considered below standard and categorized as slums, while a further 1.8 million were unfit for habitation, without such facilities as running water, baths, and toilets. In *A House Through Time* we saw the reality of these conditions for the residents of 62 Falkner Street, Liverpool, where many of the houses, if not demolished, had fallen into serious disrepair.

At the same time as the tower blocks were tumbling down, Mrs Thatcher's government introduced its plan to create what was called a 'property owning democracy'. Early Conservative policy had greatly increased the proportion of people living in council tenancies. Now they were to be sold off. There had never been a ban on the sale of council houses, but under the Housing Act 1980 if a tenant wanted to buy, the council had to sell at a price well below the market value. The discount was graded according to the length of a tenant's occupation.

Introducing the bill, the Secretary of State for the Environment Michael Heseltine said: 'There is in this country a deeply ingrained desire for home ownership. The Government believe that this spirit should be fostered. It reflects the wishes of the people, ensures the wide spread of wealth through society, encourages a personal desire to improve and modernize one's own home, enables parents to accrue wealth for their children and stimulates the attitudes of independence and self-reliance that are the bedrock of a free society.'

The fact that one million council homes were sold in ten years might be taken as support for Heseltine's claim. But it was the better houses and flats that were sold: detached preferred to terrace, low-rise flat to high-rise, fashionable areas over out-of-the-way properties. Sales slowed after a while but picked up again after 2012 with even more generous discounts. It became clear that the 'deeply ingrained desire' of one in four of those buying council flats was to let them on the private rental market.

The Conservatives' promotion of a homeowning democracy did not, however, attract the middle classes in any numbers, except perhaps as buy-to-let landlords. What was attractive now that so much of it had been destroyed in the slum-clearance programmes was the surviving Victorian and Georgian housing in the inner suburbs of the cities. The buildings were often in poor repair and many had been given a kind of plastic surgery to 'modernize' them, with the staircase enclosed with hardboard to make it streamlined, polystyrene tiles on the ceiling, and decorative plasterwork removed. In 1969 the Labour government attempted to encourage the renovation of older buildings as an alternative to demolition and offered some generous grants to refurbish older housing. A tenant with small savings could not afford to take up these grants, but for someone with a good income they could be a bargain.

The housing grants were an incentive to those people who did not want to live in suburbia with a long commute to work in town. By the mid-1960s, the Clean Air Act had made inner-city areas which had dedicated smokeless zones much more attractive. Steam trains which had belched soot and steam over houses and gardens were replaced by diesel engines. In *London: Aspects of Change* published in 1964 the sociologist Ruth Glass registered in observations of Notting Hill and Islington in London the first signs of a process she called 'gentrification': 'One by one, many of the working class quarters have been invaded by the middle class – upper and lower . . . Once this process of "gentrification" starts in a district it goes on rapidly until all or most of the working class occupiers are displaced and the whole social character of the district is changed.'

The pattern became familiar: a few pioneers braved the last days of working-class occupation and moved into 'an old wreck' which they would renovate over time. Unscrupulous property developers would try to winkle out sitting tenants from the more desirable old properties, in some instances smashing doors down and harassing them until they accepted a small compensation to quit. As working-class industries declined, professional jobs tended to increase and a second wave of wealthier 'gentrifiers' would move in.

Each of the Georgian properties featured in *A House Through Time* survived years of multiple-occupation and neglect to become beautifully renovated homes bought by the professional middle classes, the equivalent of the moneyed merchants who first lived in them in the 1800s. Their stories are not identical and the process of gentrification started later in Liverpool, Newcastle, and Bristol than in London, but all survived and then rose, phoenix-like, from the rubble and ashes of the slum clearances that left them isolated and vulnerable.

In the 1970s, 62 Falkner Street in Liverpool retained much of its Georgian facade but had become very run-down. It was sold in 1971 for £620, much less than it was worth in the 1840s. For seven years up to 1977 it was left empty, no names appearing on the electoral rolls

for those years. With similar houses judged to be out-of-date and unsalvageable 62 Falkner Street was earmarked for demolition. However, these fine old terraced houses were still of interest architecturally and in 1981 a planning officer gave it a reprieve by awarding it a Grade II listing.

By 1969, many houses in Falkner Street, Liverpool had been swept away in slum clearances. 62 Falkner Street was lucky to survive.

At the same time as the preservation order kept the wrecking ball at bay, a change in policy in the provision of decent subsidized housing recognized the failure of so much of the modernist tower blocks and estates and encouraged the refurbishing of the surviving older buildings. 62 Falkner Street was bought by Liverpool Housing Trust for a mere £400 and converted into three flats, one on each floor, all with proper kitchens and bathrooms. It was one of a hundred and fifty similar old properties which in a ten-year programme created four hundred brand-new flats.

However, the renovated Falkner Street house existed in a Liverpool that was suffering chronic industrial decline. Unemployment stood at 40 per cent and young people, especially black men and women, felt abandoned while the police constantly harried them on the streets. In

1981 tensions rose and disturbances between young people, black and white, and the police turned into what became known as the Toxteth Riots. Falkner Street was in the middle of them.

In the aftermath new investment in Liverpool created a thriving city centre and a familiar pattern of gentrification followed. Falkner Street went 'bohemian', attracting artists of various kinds, sculptors, poets, musicians. These are the people the sociologist Ruth Glass called the 'pioneers'. As a result the potential value of the houses rose, and the Housing Association which had converted 62 Falkner Street put it on the market. It is now owner-occupied, part of Liverpool's now celebrated Georgian Quarter.

5 Ravensworth Terrace in Newcastle-upon-Tyne had stood empty after the Salvation Army had closed it down as a Goodwill Centre. It had had the insides ripped out and it was more like a public building than a private house. However, it caught the eye of a legal-aid lawyer, then living opposite who bought it in 1982, paying £15,000 for what was essentially a wreck. He spent years restoring it before he moved away from Newcastle and sold it still with work to be done. It was now in an increasingly fashionable area, close to the centre of town which was undergoing a renaissance very like that in Liverpool. It has been bought and sold as a single-family house several times since.

10 Guinea Street near the centre of Bristol had lost its value over the years and in 1969 was bought by the council for £750. It was cheap but, like Falkner Street, it was listed and safe from demolition. The council did some basic repairs and gave it a lick of paint and then sold it on to owner-occupiers who began to renovate it in 1970. Ten years later it was sold again to a family who continued the restoration. Then it was bought by an owner who rented it out for a while and then sold it on again in 2006 as a very desirable home.

This account of the reoccupation by present-day professional people brings the history of housing full circle, as it were, the vicissitudes of history played out in the same structures of bricks and mortar that were inhabited in the time of Queen Victoria or King George I. That is the fascination of *A House Through Time* as it captures not just the biographies of some venerable buildings but the fate and fortunes of those who have spent part of their lives there.

CONCLUSION

Changing Fortunes

Looking back from the vantage point of the early twenty-first century it is difficult to believe that within living memory elegant Georgian and Victorian houses, like 62 Falkner Street, 5 Ravensworth Terrace and 10 Guinea Street, came to be regarded as virtually worthless. Yet during the post-war decades thousands of such houses from the eighteenth and nineteenth centuries, homes that we today so value and that had been symbols of fashionable respectability for their original inhabitants, were dismissed as defunct relics of a moribund past. In parts of Britain's cities they were regarded as obstacles standing in the way of an exciting, car-centred and thrillingly modernist future. Although many British architects had a greater affinity for Georgian architecture (with its classical roots) than they did for the homes built by the Victorians, they and the planners with whom they worked were often unsentimental when such properties occupied portions of the valuable urban land that was required for the realization of their schemes of 'comprehensive redevelopment' or road construction. It is shocking to think how many Georgian and Victorian properties were demolished in the decades after 1945, as it is to imagine what those houses would cumulatively be worth today.

Even before the end of Second World War, 10 Guinea Street had been ear-marked for demolition. The shadow of the wrecking ball later came to loom over 62 Falkner Street and 5 Ravensworth Terrace. Both were spared and while 10 Guinea Street also survived, the rest of that street did not; today only five of the original properties remain standing. The fact that so many terraced Georgian townhouses had fallen into terrible states of decay and disrepair made it easier for planners and their supporters in local government to rationalize and justify large-scale demolitions. In an age in which restoration was so often considered the poor relation of redevelopment, whole terraces were erased from the map in towns and cities across the country.

There are multiple reasons, economic, cultural and political, that explain why this bizarre act of urban vandalism was permitted to take place, yet just as curious is the fact that from some time in the late 1960s onwards, increasing numbers of people began to look afresh at the houses of the eighteenth and nineteenth centuries as a passion for refurbishing and restoring them developed. All three of the houses featured in *A House Through Time* were beneficiaries of that great cultural shift. This revived appreciation of ordinary homes from the eighteenth and nineteenth centuries has become firmly established as feature of contemporary British culture. The great centres of Georgian architecture – Bath, Bristol, Cheltenham, Harrogate, Edinburgh, Liverpool, Newcastle and parts of London – have undergone waves of restoration. People who had previously harboured no great interest in antiques or 'heritage' came to fixate over 'original features' and 'period details'. A sizable industry has risen up to assist the home-owner in their private quest to preserve or restore their tiny corner of the domestic past. With such assistance, acres of once barely noticed wood-work have been covered with heritage paints, all of verifiably authentic hues. Ornate covings, classical mouldings, and window shutters have been all been returned to their former glory.

Another lost feature of Britain's older houses that many residents have sought to rediscover is their histories. Increasingly a home's past is coming to be seen as part of what gives it character and authenticity, part of what makes it, in estate-agent speak, a 'desirable residence'. House historians, like Melanie, are commissioned by proud home-owners, eager sellers, and astute agents to uncover the lives of past residents and decipher lost meanings contained within physical clues. When the lives of former residents are made manifest, such as when English Heritage fix one of their blue plaques on a London home, the property in question can, on occasion, become more marketable. The official imprimatur of history is said to be particularly alluring to overseas buyers. In the same spirit the Sunday newspapers run special features on homes for sale that come adorned with heritage plaques, with the link between prospective buyer and famous past resident stamped onto the facade.

This passion for the past lives of our homes seems to be growing stronger yet the history I learnt at school had nothing to say about the little histories of ordinary houses and the lives of the people who lived within them. The vogue then was for great men and great deeds, along with lists of 'days that shook the world'. The very idea that what had taken place within the walls of millions of anonymous homes in centuries past represented a valid form of history, or that our homes themselves were valuable historical relics, rich in telling details, was never suggested to me and my classmates. In the mid-1990s I did a degree in urban history. I learnt how to read houses and how to understand how our cities had developed. In the years since, every drive and every taxi ride though unfamiliar city streets has been shaped by that learning. On my journey from Manchester Piccadilly station to the University of Manchester I marvel at the fact that for much of the way the only Victorian buildings I see in the great industrial metropolis of the nineteenth century are red-brick pubs, the terraces in which their customers once lived replaced with glass towers and apartment blocks. When driving around parts of Bristol I note how the cityscape is laid out like the rings of a tree, the ancient centre surrounded by later Georgian streets and exclusive suburbs, which were themselves later enveloped by acres of Victorian homes, which in turn came to be framed by an outer ring of inter-war homes. What all this, and working on *A House Through Time*, has taught me is that within each home lies the history of Britain in microcosm.

Yet our new-found appreciation for the histories of our homes and their former residents is perhaps stronger than our appreciation of the fact that throughout much of our history access to housing, its affordability, the standards to which homes were built, and the capacity of the poorest members of society to afford domestic shelter were very often among the great political and social issues. During the decades in which we collectively learnt to appreciate and value the nation's Georgian and Victorian homes many of the social and economic forces that shaped their development began to slowly re-emerge. The housing crisis of the early twenty-first century is about spiralling costs and increasing unaffordability, rather than sanitary standards or cellar-dwelling. Yet it is rightfully regarded as a crisis. The pressure on urban land, especially in London, is again encouraging large houses in expensive districts to be subdivided. They are carved up, creating warrens of corridors that lead to tiny rooms in layouts that are akin to some degree to those of the tenements and the lodging houses of Victorian London. Even newly built homes in England are now smaller than they are anywhere else in Europe, with an average of just 71.9 square metres. While the living standards and the conditions within most British homes are a far cry from those experienced by our Victorian ancestors, 28 per cent of privately rented homes in Britain in 2016 did not meet the government's own Decent Homes Standards. Tellingly, the living conditions that can be found within the worst apartments and bleakest bedsits, into which so many of the poorest and most vulnerable are deposited, are often described by journalists and politicians as 'Victorian'. At the same time gentrification, which has been the salvation of the three houses explored in *A House Through Time*, is not an unalloyed force for good. It has downsides as well as upsides and generates losers as well as winners. When a city district goes from being demonized as 'inner city' and is transformed into a 'heritage quarter', homes are renovated and house prices rise but poorer communities, who have often put down deep roots, are displaced. Gentrification, like the coming of the railways in the nineteenth century, presents new opportunities for the wealthy but scatters poorer people to other parts of the urban landscape or even to other cities in a process that today is often called 'social cleansing'. Our national passion for our homes and their histories exists side by side with a new housing crisis and a new age of inequality. Perhaps what we might also take from the past are the lessons learned by previous generations of reformers and social campaigners who took on the ills of earlier housing crisis and championed the rights of all people to have a home of their own.

David Olusoga, March 2020

ACKNOWLEDGEMENTS

The authors would like to thank Gavin Weightman for his invaluable contribution to this book. Thanks also go to Georgina Morley, Emma Marriott, Nicholas Blake and Dan Newman at Picador. Additional historical research for this book was carried out by Susie Painter.

As this book has been written to accompany the television series of the same name we would like to thank the remarkable production team at Twenty Twenty Television and in particular Mary Crisp. We are grateful to BBC Commissioners Tom McDonald and Simon Young who have championed *A House Through Time* through three series.

Finally we would like to express our thanks to the many historians and scholars whose primary research and ground-breaking scholarship underpins this book and whose papers and books are listed in the bibliography.

RESOURCES AND BIBLIOGRAPHY

Resources
Online

General and genealogy

The homepage of Historic England: **https://historicengland.org.uk**

An ever-increasing number of personal documentary sources, including census returns, is becoming available through genealogical sites, including **https://www.ancestry.co.uk/**, **https://www.findmypast.co.uk/** and **https://www.thegenealogist.co.uk/** They can be viewed for free at most County Record Offices and local archives.

A guide to the British census records from 1841 to 1911, where to find them and how to search them, is provided by the National Archives: **https://www.nationalarchives.gov.uk/help-with-your-research/research-guides/census-records/**

Additional London sources can be searched through London Lives, **https://www.londonlives.org/** This is a searchable database made up of a range of primary sources related to eighteenth-century London. It is also linked to another combined database for Britain in 1500–1900, Connected Histories, **https://www.connectedhistories.org/**

https://www.oldbaileyonline.org/ A 'fully searchable edition of the largest body of texts detailing the lives of non-elite people ever published, containing 197,745 criminal trials held at London's central criminal court', provided by the Open University, University of Hertfordshire and University of Sheffield.

Local history

A comprehensive list of local history and related societies, arranged by county, is available at **https://www.local-history.co.uk/Groups/**. There is also the British Association for Local History, **https://www.balh.org.uk/**

A guide to the Victoria Country Histories, with downloadable content, provided by the Institute of Historical Research: **https://www.history.ac.uk/ research/victoria-county-history**

Victoria County History, Survey of London and other local history sources can also be viewed and searched at British History Online, **https://www. british-history.ac.uk/**

A guide to tithe apportionments can be found at **https://www. nationalarchives.gov.uk/help-with-your-research/research-guides/tithes/** but each county will have guides to its specific records.

Information about the National Farm Survey can be found through The National Archives, **https://www.nationalarchives.gov.uk/help-with-your-research/research-guides/national-farm-survey-england-wales-1941-1943/** This guide outlines the extent of the survey and the type of material you are likely to find.

Manorial records and title registers

Details of manorial records can be found at **http://www.nationalarchives. gov.uk/help-with-your-research/research-guides/manorial-documents-lordships-how-to-use-manorial-document-register/** and **http://discovery. nationalarchives.gov.uk/manor-search**

Details of title registers can be found by visiting The Land Registry, **https:// www.gov.uk/search-property-information-land-registry**

Maps

Ordnance Survey maps: there is a free online index provided by the Charles Close Society **https://sheetfinder.charlesclosesociety.org/** which provides maps for Great Britain, Northern Ireland, the Republic of Ireland, the Isle of Man and Guernsey, with many historical OS maps, geological and public transport maps, and many others.

The National Library of Scotland has an easy map search for Ordnance Survey maps covering all of the United Kingdom, **https://www.maps.nls.uk/**

Insurance maps, images, and manuscript collections can also be found at the British Library, **https://www.bl.uk/**

The National Archives' Valuation Office map finder is 'a simple way to identify and order a map without having to visit The National Archives'. **http://www.nationalarchives.gov.uk/labs/valuation-office-map-finder/**

Details of the Valuation Survey can be found here: **https://www. nationalarchives.gov.uk/help-with-your-research/research-guides/ valuation-office-survey-land-value-ownership-1910-1915/**

Details of parish boundaries and options for documents in your area can be found on Genuki (UK and Ireland Genealogy): **https://www.genuki.org.uk/** and Vision of Britain **http://www.visionofbritain.org.uk/**

Additional maps can be found at Know Your Place: West of England – **http://www.kypwest.org.uk** This covers Somerset, Devon, Wiltshire, Gloucestershire, and Bristol and Bath.

A growing number of London maps (from the Romans to today) can also be searched at Layers of London, **https://www.layersoflondon.org**

The Bomb Sight project 'is mapping the London WW2 bomb census between 7/10/1940 and 06/06/1941 . . . The project has scanned original 1940s bomb census maps, geo-referenced the maps and digitally captured the geographical locations of all the falling bombs recorded on the original map'. **http://bombsight.org/bombs/26786/**

A guide to the bomb census maps at the National Archives is provided at: **https://www.nationalarchives.gov.uk/help-with-your-research/research- guides/bomb-census-survey-records-1940–1945/**

A blog and a downloadable A2 map of Southampton that 'pinpoints where 712 of the bombs fell based on records from the time', provided by the Ordnance Survey, is here: **https://www.ordnancesurvey.co.uk/blog/2010/11/ mapping-the-southampton-blitz-70-years-on/**

The website for Charles Booth's London poverty maps and police notebooks, provided by the London School of Economics & Political Science, is here: **https://booth.lse.ac.uk/**

Domesday Book

The National Archives have a guide to Domesday Book, with a search field that allows you to use 'name, modern place name, Domesday place name or folio number', and order a colour facsimile of the folio on which your entry appears. **https://www.nationalarchives.gov.uk/domesday/**

A free online copy of Domesday Book with a searchable map is at **https:// opendomesday.org/** The Domesday Book Online 'has been set up to enable visitors to discover the history of the Domesday Book, to give an insight into life at the time of its compilation, and provide information and links on related topics': **http://www.domesdaybook.co.uk/index.html**

Newspapers and trade directories

A growing number of newspapers can be searched on the British Newspaper Archive, **https://www.britishnewspaperarchive.co.uk/** and on **https://www. findmypast.co.uk/**

The *Gazette* is available to search at **https://www.thegazette.co.uk/**

A collection of 689 trade directories, 'with at least one directory for every English and Welsh county for the 1850s, 1890s and 1910s. Searchable by name, place and occupation'. Provided by the University of Leicester. **http://specialcollections.le.ac.uk/digital/collection/p16445coll4**

A more comprehensive collection of directories can be viewed on subscription websites, particularly **Ancestry.co.uk**

Homes and architecture

Architectural prints and sources can be found at the Royal Institute of British Architects (RIBA), **https://www.architecture.com/about/riba-library-and-collections**

Bricks & Brass 'provide free, impartial and practical advice so you can buy and care for houses.' **http://www.bricksandbrass.co.uk**

Buildinghistory.org has many useful resources for researching the history of your house. **http://www.buildinghistory.org/**

The history of bricks and brickmaking: **https://brickarchitecture.com/aboutbrick/why-brick/the-history-of-bricks-brickmaking**

Details of house interiors can be found at The Museum of the Home, **https://www.museumofthehome.org.uk/** and the Museum of Domestic Design and Architecture, **www.moda.mdx.ac.uk**

'Domestic Architecture from 1700 to 1960', a well-illustrated guide provided by the University of the West of England: **https://fet.uwe.ac.uk/conweb/house_ages/flypast/print.htm**

Miscellaneous

Scunthorpe Squatters on Movietone News, 5 August 1946 **http://www.aparchive.com/metadata/youtube/bee89d2ca53e498da3de86b99b1baa3e**

Military records can be found at **https://www.forces-war-records.co.uk** plus material viewed at The National Archives, the Imperial War Museum and regional military museums.

Resources
Books

Backe-Hansen, Melanie, *House Histories: The Secrets Behind Your Front Door* (The History Press, 2019)

Barratt, Nick, *Tracing the History of Your House* (The National Archives, 2006)

Bede (editor D. Farmer, translator Leo Sherley-Price), *Ecclesiastical History of the English People* (Penguin Classics, 1990)

Beech, Geraldine, and Rose Mitchell, *Maps for Family and Local History: the records of the Tithe, Valuation Office and National Farm surveys of England and Wales, 1836–1943* (National Archives, 2004)

Blanchard, Gill, *Tracing Your House History* (Pen & Sword, 2017)

Cornwall, Julian, *An Introduction to Reading Old Title Deeds* (2nd Edition, Federation of Family History Societies: Birmingham, 1997)

Fletcher, Valentine, *Chimney Pots and Stacks: An introduction to their history, variety and identification* (Centaur, 1968)

Hey, David (ed.), *The Oxford Companion to Local and Family History* (Oxford University Press, Oxford, 1998)

Hollowell, Steven, *Enclosure Records for Historians* (Phillimore, Chichester, 2000)

Kain, Roger, *The enclosure maps of England and Wales, 1595–1918: a cartographic analysis and electronic catalogue* (Cambridge University Press, 2004)

Kain, Roger J. P. and Hugh C. Prince, *Tithe Surveys for Historians* (Phillimore, Chichester, 2000)

Morgan, Mary, *Charles Booth's London Poverty Maps* (Thames & Hudson, 2019)

Oates, Jonathan, *Tracing Your Ancestors from 1066 to 1837* (Pen & Sword, Barnsley, 2019)

Short, Brian et al., *The National Farm Survey 1941–43: State Surveillance and the Countryside in England and Wales in the Second World War* (Oxford: Oxford University Press, 2000)

Thom, Colin, *Researching London's Houses* (Phillimore, 2005)

Tiller, Kate, *English Local History: An Introduction* (Alan Sutton: Stroud, 1992)

Ward, Laurence, *London County Council Bomb Damage Maps 1939–1945* (Thames & Hudson, 2015)

Weightman, Gavin, *Restoration Home: the Essential Guide to Tracing the History of Your House* (BBC Books, 2011)

Yorke, Trevor, *The Georgian and Regency House Explained* (Countryside books, 2007)

—, *The Victorian House Explained* (Countryside books, 2005)

—, *The Edwardian House Explained* (Countryside books, 2006)

—, *The 1930s House Explained* (Countryside books, 2006)

—, *Timber Framed Buildings Explained* (Countryside books, 2010)

—, *Tudor Houses Explained* (Countryside books, 2009)

Bibliography

Contemporary sources

Anonymous, *Papers relating to the Noxious Effects of the Fetid Irrigations around the City of Edinburgh. Published by authority of a Committee of the Commissioners of Police* (1839)

Baines, Thomas, *History of the Commerce and Town of Liverpool* (1852)

—, *Liverpool in 1859* (1859)

Beames, Thomas, *The Rookeries of London: Past, Present, and Prospective* (1850; 2nd edn., 1852)

Bertram, Anthony, *The House: A Machine for Living In* (1935)

Blackburne, E. L. (ed.), *Suburban & rural architecture, English & foreign* (1867)

Booth, Charles, *Life and Labour of the People in London* (1892–97)

Booth, William, *In Darkest England and the Way Out* (1890)

Buccleuch, Duke of, et al., *First Report of the Commissioners for Inquiring into the State of Large Towns and Populous Districts: Presented to Both Houses of Parliament by Command of Her Majesty* (1844)

Bunting, T. P., *Prospectus of the Victoria Park Tontine* (1836)

Chadwick, Edwin, *Report from the Poor Law Commissioners on the sanitary conditions of the labouring population of Great Britain* (1842)

Chadwick, Ellis H., *In the Footsteps of the Brontës* (1914)

Clarke, William Spencer, *The suburban homes of London: a residential guide to favourite London localities, their society, celebrities, and associations, with notes on their rental, rates and house accommodation* (1881)

Collins, Wilkie, *Basil: A Story of Modern Life* (1852)

Crosland, T. W. H., *The Suburbans* (1905)

de Tocqueville, Alexis, *Journeys to England and Ireland* (trans. George Lawrence and K. P. Mayer; ed. J. P. Mayer, 1958)

Defoe, Daniel, *A tour thro' the whole island of Great Britain, divided into circuits or journies* (1724)

Disraeli, Benjamin, *The Novels & Tales of the Right Hon. B. Disraeli* (1866)

Eagle, William, et al. (eds), *Justice of the Peace and County, Borough, Poor Law Union and Parish Law Recorder*, Vol. 5 (1841)

Elmes, James, *Metropolitan Improvements; Or London in the Nineteenth Century* (1827)

Engels, Friedrich, *The Condition of the Working Class in England* (1844)

Gaskell, Elizabeth Cleghorn, *The Letters of Mrs. Gaskell* (ed. John Chapple and Alan Shelston, 2003)

Gaskell, Peter, *The Manufacturing Population of England, Its Moral, Social and Physical Conditions* (1833)

Gavin, Hector, *Sanitary Ramblings: Being Sketches and Illustrations of Bethnal Green* (1848)

Ginswick, J. (ed.), *Labour and the Poor in England and Wales – The Letters to The Morning Chronicle from the Correspondents in the Manufacturing and Mining Districts, the Towns of Liverpool and Birmingham, and the Rural Districts: Volume I: Lancashire, Cheshire, Yorkshire* (1983)

Godwin, George, *London Shadows: A Glance at the 'Homes' of the Thousands* (1854)

—, *Town Swamps and Social Bridges* (1859)

Grosley, Pierre-Jean, *A Tour to London, Or, New Observations on England and Its Inhabitants, Volume 1* (trans. T. Nugent, 1772)

Grossmith, George and Weedon, *The Diary of a Nobody* (1892)

Hamilton, Cicely, *Modern England: as Seen by an Englishwoman* (1938)

Hollingshead, John, *Ragged London in 1861* (1861)

Howard, Ebenezer, *Garden Cities of To-morrow* (1898)

Hunter, Dr Julian, *Report of Dr Julian Hunter on the Housing of the Poorer Parts of the Population in Towns, particularly in regards to the Existence of Dangerous Degrees of Overcrowding . . . 1866* (repr. in Simon's *Eighth Annual Report . . . to the Privy Council*, 1865)

Kay, James, *The Moral and Physical Condition of the Working Classes Employed in the Cotton Manufacture in Manchester* (2nd edn, 1832)

Knox, John, *The masses without! A pamphlet for the times, on the sanatory, social, moral and heathen condition of the masses* (1857)

Lancaster, Osbert, *Pillar to Post* (1938)

Liepmann, Kate, *The Journey to Work: Its Significance for Industrial and Community Life* (1944)

Loudon, John Claudius, *The Suburban Gardener and Villa Companion* (1838)

Low, Sampson, *The Charities of London. Comprising an Account of the Operations, Resources, and General Condition of the Charitable, Educational, and Religious Institutions of London* (3rd edn., 1867)

Malcolm, James Peller, *Anecdotes of the manners and customs of London, during the eighteenth century* (2nd edn., 1810)

Manchester Corporation Transport Dept., *A Hundred Years of Road Passenger Transport in Manchester* (1935)

Masterman, C. F. G., *The Condition of England* (1909)

Mayhew, Henry, *London Labour and the London Poor* (1850

Mearns, Andrew, and W. C. Preston, *The Bitter Cry of Outcast London: An Inquiry into the Condition of the Abject Poor* (1883)

Miller, William Haig, et al., *The Leisure Hour*, volume 2 (1853)

Ministry of Information, *Front Line, 1940–1941: the official story of the civil defence of Britain* (1942)

Muthesius, Hermann, *The English House* (1904)

Niven, James, 'On back-to-back houses', *The Journal of The Sanitary Institute*, Vol. XVI, part II (1895)

Plummer, B. (Jr.), *Newcastle-upon-Tyne: Its Trade and Manufactures* (1874)

Panton, Jane Frith, *From Kitchen to Garret: Hints For Young Householders* (1888)

Rawlinson, Robert, *On House Accommodation: Its Social Bearing, Individually and Nationally* (1858)

—, *On the Drainage of Towns* (1842)

—, *Report to the General Board of Health on a preliminary inquiry into the sewerage, drainage, and supply of water, and the sanitary condition of the inhabitants of the borough of Gateshead* (1850)

Richards, James, *The Castles on the Ground* (1946)

Robinson, P. F., *Designs for Ornamental Villas, In Ninety-six Plates* (3rd edn., 1836)

Ruskin, John, *Of Queen's Gardens* (1865)

—, *Praeterita* (1885)

—, *The Seven Lamps of Architecture* (1849)

Schlesinger, Max, *Saunterings In and About London* (1852)

Shimmin, Hugh, *Low Life and Moral Improvement in Mid-Victorian England: Liverpool Through the Journalism of Hugh Shimmin* (ed. John K. Walton and Alastair Wilcox, 1991)

Simond, Louis, *Journal of a Tour and Residence in Great Britain, During the Years 1810 and 1811, Volume 1* (1815)

Sims, George R., *How the Poor Live* (1883)

Smith, Charles Manby, *The Little World of London, or Pictures in Little of London Life* (1857)

Smith, Hubert Llewellyn, *The New Survey of London Life and Labour* (P.S. King & Son, 1930–35)

Smith, James, *Report to the Health of Towns Commission. Report on the State of the City of York and other Towns* (1845)

Southey, Robert, *Letters from England by Don Manuel Alvarez Espriella* (1807)

Stonestreet, G. G., *Domestic Union, or London as it Should Be!!* (1800)

Stuart, James, *Critical Observations on the Buildings and Improvements of London* (1771)

Taine, Hippolyte, *Notes on England* (trans. W. F. Rae, 1872)

Unwin, Raymond, *Cottage Plans and Common Sense* (1905)

Walford, Edward, *Old and New London: a narrative of its history, its people, and its places. Illustrated with numerous engravings from the most authentic sources. Volume 5. The Western and Northern suburbs* ('popular edition', 1897)

Weir, W., 'St Giles, Past and Present', in *London* (ed. Charles Knight, vol. 2, 1842)

Modern sources: online

A14 Cambridge to Huntingdon, the improvement scheme: https://headlandarchaeology.com/the-a14-cambridge-to-huntingdonheadlandspart-in-the-uks-largest-archaeological-project/

Basildon Plotlands: the plotlands of Basildon New Town are described here: http://www.essexrecordofficeblog.co.uk/tag/plotlands/

Council housing: its history: https://fet.uwe.ac.uk/conweb/house_ages/council_housing/

'Gentrification': its history and an explanation: https://sites.google.com/site/gg2wpdermotmitchell/history-and-explanation-of-gentrification

Government's Response to the Transport, Local Government and the Regions Committee Report: 'The New Towns: Their Problems and Future': https://publications.parliament.uk/pa/cm200102/cmselect/cmtlgr/newtowns.pdf

Laindon Plotlands: 'The four-roomed bungalow built by the Mills family in 1934 is the last remaining home of the Laindon Plotlands phenomenon of the turn of the last century': https://www.laindonhistory.org.uk/content/areas_and_places/dunton/the-haven-and-plotlands

'Peasant houses in Midland England': https://www.archaeology.co.uk/articles/peasant-houses-in-midland-england.htm

Prefabs: a short history of prefabs – building the post-war world, The Prefab Museum: https://www.prefabmuseum.uk/

* * *

Clapson, Mark, 'The English new towns since 1946: What are the Lessons of their History for their Future?', Société française d'histoire urbaine | « Histoire urbaine » 2017/3 n° 50 https://www.cairn.info/revue-histoireurbaine-2017-3-page-93.htm

Department for Communities and Local Government, '50 Years of the English Housing Survey: 1967 and 2017' (2017), https://assets.publishing.service.gov.uk/government/uploads/system/uploads/attachment_data/file/658923/EHS_50th_Anniversary_Report.pdf

Glendinning, Miles and Stefan Muthesius, *Tower Block: Modern public housing in England, Scotland, Wales and Northern Ireland* (published for The

Paul Mellon Centre for Studies in British Art by Yale University Press, New Haven, 1994) http://towerblock.org/TowerBlock.pdf

HATC Limited, 'Housing Space Standards, A report by for the Greater London Authority' (2006) https://www.hatc.co.uk/wp-content/uploads/ GLA_Space_Standards_Report.pdf

Park, Julia, 'One Hundred Years of Housing Space Standards. What now?' (2017) http://housingspacestandards.co.uk/

Nevell, M. D., 'Living in the industrial city: Housing quality, land ownership and the archaeological evidence from industrial Manchester', University of Salford (2011) https://usir.salford.ac.uk/id/eprint/19367/1/Poverty_article_ MN_peer_review_edited_version_Sept_2011.pdf

Stilwell, Martin, 'Housing the returning soldiers: "Homes Fit for Heroes" ' (2017) http://www.socialhousinghistory.uk/wp/wp-content/ uploads/2017/04/Homes_Fit_For_Heroes.pdf

Turner, Clive, NHBC Foundation, and Richards Partington Architects, 'Homes through the decades: The making of modern housing' (2015) https:// www.nhbcfoundation.org/publication/homes-throughthe-decades-the- making-of-modern-housing/

Modern sources: books and articles

The place of publication is London unless noted.

Ackroyd, Peter, *London: The Biography* (Vintage, 2000)

Alcock, Nat, and Dan Miles, *The Medieval Peasant House in Midland England* (Oxbow Books, 2012)

Allen, Rick, *The Moving Pageant: A Literary Sourcebook on London Street Life, 1700–1914* (Routledge, 1998)

Aslet, Clive, *The English House: The Story of a Nation at Home* (Bloomsbury, 2008)

Ayres, James, *Building the Georgian City* (Yale University Press, 1998)

Backe-Hansen, Melanie, *Historic Streets and Squares: The Secrets on Your Doorstep* (The History Press, 2013)

Baer, William C., 'The house-building sector of London's economy, 1550– 1650', *Urban History* Vol. 39, No. 3 (August 2012), pp. 409–30

—, 'Is speculative building underappreciated in urban history?', *Urban History*, Vol. 34, No. 2 (August 2007), pp. 296–316

Barke, Michael, 'The development of public transport in Newcastle upon Tyne and Tyneside, 1850–1914', *Journal of Local and Regional Studies* 12 (1992), pp. 29–52

—, 'The Middle-Class Journey to Work in Newcastle upon Tyne, 1850–1913', *Journal of Transport History* 12 (1991), pp. 107–34

Bell, Yvonne, *The Edwardian Home* (Shire Publications, Oxford, 2010)

Berbiers, J. L., 'Back-to-Back Housing, Halifax', *Official Architecture and Planning*, Vol. 31, No. 12 (December 1968), pp. 1595–6, 1599

Binney, Marcus, *Town Houses: Evolution and Innovation in 800 years of urban domestic architecture* (Mitchell Beazley, 1998)

Blanchet, Elizabeth and Sonia Zhuravlyova, *Prefabs: A social and architectural history* (Swindon: Historic England, 2015)

Blount, Trevor, 'Dickens's Slum Satire in "Bleak House" ', *Modern Language Review*, Vol. 60, No. 3 (July 1965), pp. 340–51

Borsay, Peter (ed.), *The 18th century town. A reader in English Urban History 1688–1820* (Longman, 1990)

Broughton, John, *Municipal Dreams: The Rise and Fall of Council Housing* (Verso, 2019)

Brunskill, Ronald, *Illustrated Handbook of Vernacular Architecture* (Faber, 2000)

Bryson, Bill, *At Home: A Short History of Private Life* (Black Swan, 2011)

Burnett, John, *A Social History of Housing 1815–1970* (Newton Abbot: David and Charles, 1978)

—, *A Social History of Housing, 1815–1985* (2nd edn.: Methuen, 1986)

Caffyn, Lucy, 'Housing in an Industrial Landscape: A Study of Workers' Housing in West Yorkshire', *World Archaeology*, Vol. 15, No. 2, *Industrial Archaeology* (October 1983), pp. 173–83

Cave, Lyndon F., *The Smaller English House: Its History and Development* (Robert Hale, 1985)

Chalkin, Christopher W., *The Provincial Towns of Georgian England. A Study of the Building Process 1740–1820* (Edward Arnold, 1974)

Clapson, Mark, *The Blitz Companion* (University of Westminster, 2019)

Clark, Peter and Paul Slack, *English Towns in Transition 1500–1700* (Oxford: Oxford University Press, 1976)

Cockayne, Emily, *Hubbub: Filth, Noise and Stench in England, 1760–1770* (Yale University Press, 2008)

Corton, Christine L., *London Fog: The Biography* (Cambridge, Massachusetts: The Belknap Press of Harvard University Press, 2015)

Crossick, Geoffrey, 'The Emergence of the Lower Middle Class in Britain: A Discussion', in *The Lower Middle Class in Britain 1870–1914*, ed. Geoffrey Crossick (Croom Helm, 1977)

Cruickshank, Dan, and Neil Burton, *Life in the Georgian City* (Viking, 1990)

Cruickshank, Dan, and Peter Wyld, *Georgian Town Houses and Their Details* (Butterworth Architecture, Oxford, 1990)

Curtis, M., and M. Walker, *Bristol Omnibus Services: The Green Years* (Bath: Millstream Books, 2007)

Cunnington, Pamela, *How Old is Your House?* (Yeovil: Marston House, 2002)

Daunton, Martin J., *House and home in the Victorian city: working-class housing 1850–1914* (Edward Arnold, 1983)

Dennis, Richard, *Cities in Modernity: Representations and Productions of Metropolitan Space 1840–1930* (Cambridge: Cambridge University Press, 2008)

Denison, Edward and Guang Yu Ren, *The Life of the British Home: An Architectural History* (John Wiley & Sons, 2012)

Drew, John, and Michael Slater, *Dickens' Journalism* (Vol. 4, Dent, 2000)

Dyos, H. J., *Exploring the Urban Past: Essays in Urban History* (ed. David Cannadine and David Reeder, Cambridge: Cambridge University Press, 1982)

Eveleigh, David, *Privies and water-closets* (Shire Publications, 2008)

Ferry, Kathryn, *The Victorian Home* (Shire Publications, Oxford, 2011)

Foot, Michael, *Aneurin Bevan* (Macgibbon & Kee, 1962)

Flanders, Judith, *The Making of Home: The 500-year story of how our houses became homes* (Atlantic Books, 2014)

—, *The Victorian City: Everyday life in Dickens' London* (Atlantic Books, 2013)

—, *The Victorian House: Domestic Life from Childbirth to Deathbed* (Harper Collins, 2004)

Fraser, Derek, *Urban Politics in Victorian England: the Structure of Politics in Victorian Cities* (Leicester: Leicester University Press, 1976)

Gauldie, Enid, *Cruel Habitations: a history of working-class housing 1780–1918* (Allen and Unwin, 1974)

George, Susan, *Liverpool Park Estates: Their Legal Basis, Creation and Early Management* (Liverpool: Liverpool University Press, 2000)

Glass, D. V., 'The Population Controversy in Eighteenth-Century England. Part I. The Background', *Population Studies*, Vol. 6, No. 1 (July 1952), pp. 69–91

Glass, Ruth, et al., *London: Aspects of Change* (Macgibbon & Kee, 1964)

Guillery, Peter, *The small house in eighteenth-century London: a social and architectural history* (Yale University Press, 2004)

Harper, Roger Henley, 'The Evolution of the English Building Regulations 1840–1911', Volume one, PhD thesis, University of Sheffield, June 1978

Harrison, Joanne, 'The Origin, Development and Decline of Back-to-Back Houses in Leeds, 1787–1937', *Industrial Archaeology Review*, Vol. 39, No.2 (November 2017), pp. 101–16

Hemming, T. D., E. Freeman, Ted Freeman, David Meakin, *The Secular City: Studies in the Enlightenment: Presented to Haydn Mason* (Exeter: University of Exeter Press, 1994)

Hennessey, Peter, *Never Again: Britain 1945–1951* (Jonathan Cape, 1992)

Hibbert, Christopher, and Ben Weinreb, *The London Encyclopaedia* (1983; 3rd edn., Macmillan, 2010)

Highmore, Ben, *The Great Indoors: At Home in the Modern British House* (Profile Books, 2014)

Hilton, Timothy, *John Ruskin* (Yale University Press, 1985–2000)

Hinton, James, 'Self-Help and Socialism: the Squatters' Movement of 1946', *History Workshop*, No. 25 (Spring, 1988), pp. 100–126

Hole, Christina, *English Home Life, 1500 to 1800* (B.T. Batsford, 1947)

Hopkins, Eric, 'Working-class Housing in Birmingham during the Industrial Revolution', *International Review of Social History*, Vol. 31, No. 1 (1986), pp. 80–94

Humphries, Steve and John Taylor, *The Making of Modern London 1945–1985* (Sidgwick & Jackson, 1985)

Jackson, Alan A., *Semi-detached London: suburban development, life and transport, 1900–39* (Allen and Unwin, 1973)

Jekyll, Gertrude and Sydney Jones, *Old English Household Life* (B.T. Batsford, 1945)

Johnson, Malcolm, *Bustling Intermeddler?: The Life and Work of Charles James Blomfield* (Leominster: Gracewing, 2001)

Johnson, Matthew, *English houses, 1300–1800: vernacular architecture, social life* (Routledge, 2010)

Johnson, Steven, *The Ghost Map: The Story of London's Most Terrifying Epidemic – and How it Changed Science, Cities and the Modern World* (New York, N.Y.: Penguin Group, 2006)

Kellett, J. R., *The Impact of Railways on Victorian Cities* (Routledge and Kegan Paul, 1969)

Lambert, Carolyn, *The Meanings of Home in Elizabeth Gaskell's Fiction* (Brighton: Victorian Secrets, 2013)

Law, Michael John, 'Speed and blood on the bypass: the new automobilities of inter-war London', *Urban History*, Vol. 39, No. 3 (August 2012), pp. 490–509

Lawrence, Richard, *The Book of the Edwardian and Interwar House* (Aurum Press, 2009)

Leckie, Barbara, *Open Houses: Poverty, the Novel, and the Architectural Idea in Nineteenth-Century Britain* (Philadelphia: University of Pennsylvania Press, 2018)

Leighton, Sophie, *The 1950s Home* (Shire Publications, 2009)

Lewis, Philippa, *Everyman's Castle: the story of our cottages, country houses, terraces, flats, semis and bungalows* (Frances Lincoln, 2014)

Long, Helen, *Victorian Houses and their Details: the role of publications in their building and decoration* (Oxford: Architectural Press, 2002)

Mack, Joanna and Steve Humphries, *London at War 1939–1945* (Sidgwick & Jackson, 1985)

McKenna, Madeline, 'Municipal Suburbia in Liverpool, 1919–1939', *The Town Planning Review*, Vol. 60, No. 3 (July 1989), pp. 287–318

Malpass, Peter, *The Making of Victorian Bristol* (Suffolk: Boydell & Brewer, 2019)

Miller, Mervyn, *English Garden Cities. An Introduction* (Swindon: Historic England, 2010)

—, *Letchworth. The First Garden City* (Chichester: Phillimore, 2002)

Mount, Harry, *A Lust for Window Sills* (Abacus, 2011)

Muñoz, Iván, and José Márquez, 'The rise and fall of concrete tower blocks in Britain: a Love–Hate relationship with the material', *International Conference on construction research*, AEC 2018

Muthesius, Stefan, *The English Terraced House* (Yale University Press, 1982)

Myerson, Julie, *Home: The Story of Everyone Who Ever Lived in Our House* (Flamingo, 2004)

Platt, Colin, *The English Medieval Town* (Secker & Warburg, 1976)

—, *The Great Rebuildings of Tudor and Stuart England: Revolutions in Architectural Taste* (Routledge, 1994)

Priestley, Harold, *The English Home* (Frederick Muller, 1971)

Pope, Ged, *Reading London's Suburbs: From Charles Dickens to Zadie Smith* (Houndmills: Palgrove Macmillan, 2015)

Porter, Roy, *London: A Social History* (Hamish Hamilton, 1994)

Porter, Stephen, *The Great Fire of London* (new edn., Stroud: History, 2016)

Pugh, Martin, *The Pankhursts: The History of One Radical Family* (Vintage, 2008)

Quiney, Anthony, *House and Home: A History of the Small English House* (BBC, 1986)

—, *Town Houses of Medieval Britain* (Yale University Press, New Haven, 2003)

Rackham, Oliver, *The History of the Countryside* (Weidenfeld and Nicolson, 1995)

—, *Trees and Woodland in the British Landscape* (J. M. Dent, 1983)

Rodger, Richard, 'Political Economy, Ideology and the Persistence of Working-class Housing Problems in Britain, 1850–1914', *International Review of Social History*, Vol. 32, No. 2 (1987), pp. 109–43

Rosen, George, *A History of Public Health* (New York: MS Publications, 1958)

Sheldon, R. D., 'Nicholas Barbon', *Oxford Dictionary of National Biography*, 2008

Spooner, Sarah, *Regions and Designed Landscapes in Georgian England* (Routledge, 2016)

Stamp, Gavin, 'Neo-Tudor and its Enemies', *Architectural History*, Vol. 49 (2006), pp. 1–33

Stedman Jones, Gareth, *Outcast London* (Oxford: Clarendon Press, 1971)

Stevenson, John, *Social Conditions in Britain Between the Wars* (Harmondsworth: Penguin, 1977)

Sugg Ryan, Deborah, *Ideal Homes, 1918–39: Domestic Design and Suburban Modernism* (Manchester: Manchester University Press, 2018)

Sutherland, John, *The Longman Companion to Victorian Fiction* (Longman, 1988)

Swenarton, Mark, *Homes Fit for Heroes: The Politics and Architecture of Early State Housing in Britain* (Heinemann Educational Books, 1981)

Taylor, I. C., *The court and cellar dwelling: the eighteenth-century origin of the Liverpool slum* (Liverpool: Historic Society of Lancashire and Cheshire, 1970)

Uglow, Jenny, *Elizabeth Gaskell: A Habit of Stories* (Faber and Faber, 1993)

Upton, Chris, *Living Back-to-Back* (2nd Revised edition, The History Press, 2010)

Vickers, Tom, Borders, *Migration and Class in an Age of Crisis: ucing Immigrants and Workers* (Bristol: Bristol University Press, 2019)

Vickery, Amanda, *Behind Closed Doors: At Home in Georgian England* (Yale University Press, 2009)

Ward, Colin and Dennis Hardy, 'The Plotlanders', Oral History Society, *Oral History*, Vol. 13, No. 2, *City Space and Order* (Autumn, 1985), pp. 57–70

Weightman, Gavin, *Children of Light: How Electricity Changed Britain Forever* (Atlantic Books, 2011)

—, and Steve Humphries, *The Making of Modern London 1914–1939* (Sidgwick & Jackson, 1984)

Whelan, Lara Baker, *Class, Culture and Suburban Anxieties in the Victorian Era* (Routledge, 2010)

White, Jerry, *London in the Eighteenth Century: 'A Great and Monstrous Thing'* (Bodley Head, 2012)

—, *London in the Nineteenth Century: A Human Awful Wonder of God* (Vintage, 2008)

Whitehand, J. W. R., and Christine M. H. Carr, 'The creators of England's inter-war suburbs', *Urban History*, Vol. 28, No. 2 (August 2001), pp. 218–34

Wild, Jonathan, *The Rise of the Office Clerk in Literary Culture, 1880–1939* (Houndmills: Palgrave Macmillan, 2006)

Wohl, Anthony S., *The Eternal Slum: Housing and Social Policy in Victorian London* (Routledge, 2017)

Wolff, Michael, H. J. Dyos (eds), *The Victorian City: Images and Realities* (Routledge and Kegan Paul, 1973)

Wood, Margaret, *The English Medieval House* (Ferndale, 1981)

Woodforde, John, *Georgian Houses for All* (Routledge and Kegan Paul, 1977)

Worsley, Lucy, *If Walls Could Talk: An Intimate History of the Home* (Faber and Faber, 2011)

INDEX

Note: page numbers in *italics* refer to information in captions.

For the houses featured in the series, see Falkner Street, Liverpool, No 62; Ravensworth Terrace, Newcastle-upon-Tyne, No 5; and Guinea Street, Bristol, No 10.

A

A14 road archaeological dig 41, 42
Abbey National 214
Abbey Road Building Society 214
Abercrombie, Sir Patrick 230
Act for the Rebuilding of the City of London 1667 57–8
Act of the Relief of the Poor 1601 51
Adam brothers, Adelphi scheme 68
Addison, Christopher 204
Addison, Joseph 75–6
Addison's Oak 204
Agar, William 130
Agar Town 129–31, 150–1
agricultural land 213, 221
    see also farmland
Aigburth, Liverpool 164–5, 178, 184
air pollution 73, 113, 159, 187–8, 189, 235
air raids 4–5, 21–4, *23*, 225–6, 227, 228
Aircraft Industry Research on Housing (AIROH) 228–9
Aire River 118
Albert, Prince 26, 148, *148*

Alder, Joshua (Ravensworth Terrace) 87
Alder, Mary (Ravensworth Terrace) 87
Aldwych 43
Alfred the Great 43, 45
Alma, battle of 192
Anderson shelters 5
Anglo-Saxons 42–5
animal husbandry 111–12
animal waste 111–12, 159
Antigua 162
Archibald Constable & Co. 32
architecture 3
Arcon MkV (prefab) 229
Arden-Close, Colonel Sir Charles 13
aristocracy 20, 48–9, 55, 83–4, 167
    see also gentry
Arkwright, Richard 64
Armistice 203
army camps, squatter invasion 222–3, 227
artisans 31, 55, 67, 72, 93, 95, 132, 133, 150, 151, 195, 197
Artisans' and Labourers' Dwellings act 1875 116–17
Arts and Crafts movement 207
Arup, Ove 229
Asser, Bishop 44
Athenaeum (magazine) 174, 176
atomic weapons 224
attic rooms 62, 78, 80, 97
Attlee, Clement 224, 230
austerity 224
Australia 86
Aycliffe New Town 232